Network Processor Design
Issues and Practices
Volume 1

D1733781

Network Processor Design

Issues and Practices

Volume 1

Edited by

Patrick Crowley

Mark A. Franklin

Haldun Hadimioglu

Peter Z. Onufryk

MORGAN KAUFMANN PUBLISHERS

AN IMPRINT OF ELSEVIER SCIENCE

AMSTERDAM   BOSTON   LONDON   NEW YORK
OXFORD   PARIS   SAN DIEGO   SAN FRANCISCO
SINGAPORE   SYDNEY   TOKYO

Senior Editor   Denise E. M. Penrose
Publishing Services Manager   Edward Wade
Senior Developmental Editor   Marilyn Uffner Alan
Cover Design   Ross Carron Design
Cover Image   Getty Images
Text Design, Composition   Windfall Software
Technical Illustration   LM Graphics
Copyeditor   Robert Fiske
Proofreader   Jennifer McClain
Indexer   Steve Rath
Printer   The Maple-Vail Book Manufacturing Group

Designations used by companies to distinguish their products are often claimed as trademarks or registered trademarks. In all instances in which Morgan Kaufmann Publishers is aware of a claim, the product names appear in initial capital or all capital letters. Readers, however, should contact the appropriate companies for more complete information regarding trademarks and registration.

Morgan Kaufmann Publishers
An imprint of Elsevier Science
340 Pine Street, Sixth Floor
San Francisco, CA 94104-3205
www.mkp.com

Library of Congress Control Number: 2002108919
ISBN: 1-55860-875-3

This book is printed on acid-free paper.

Contents

Preface   xiii

1   Network Processors: An Introduction to
Design Issues   1

*Patrick Crowley, Mark A. Franklin, Haldun Hadimioglu,
Peter F. Onufryk*

1.1   **Design Challenges**   3
1.2   **Design Techniques**   4
1.3   **Challenges and Conclusions**   7

PART I   **DESIGN PRINCIPLES**   9

2   Benchmarking Network Processors   11

*Prashant R. Chandra, Frank Hady, Raj Yavatkar, Tony Bock,
Mason Cabot, Philip Mathew*

2.1   **Benchmarking Framework Overview**   12
2.2   **Hardware-Level Benchmarks**   15
2.3   **Microlevel Benchmarks**   18

2.4 **Function-Level Benchmarks** 21

2.5 **Related Work** 23

References 24

3   A Methodology and Simulator for the Study of Network Processors   27

Deepak Suryanarayanan, John Marshall, Gregory T. Byrd

3.1 **Previous Work** 28

3.2 **Component Network Simulator (ComNetSim)** 30

3.3 **The Cisco Toaster2** 32

3.4 **Implementation of ComNetSim** 35

3.5 **Application Development** 44

3.6 **Organization and Configuration** 48

3.7 **Experiments and Results** 48

3.8 **Conclusion and Future Work** 52

References 53

4   Design Space Exploration of Network Processor Architectures   55

Lothar Thiele, Samarjit Chakraborty, Matthias Gries, Simon Künzli

4.1 **Models for Streams, Tasks, and Resources** 58

4.2 **Analysis Using a Scheduling Network** 63

4.3 **Multiobjective Design Space Exploration** 79

4.4 **Case Study** 81

Acknowledgments 86

References 87

5   Compiler Backend Optimizations for Network Processors with Bit Packet Addressing   91

Jens Wagner, Rainer Leupers

5.1 **Bit-Level Data Flow Analysis and Bit Value Inference** 95

5.2 **Code Selection** 99

5.3   **Register Allocation Considering Register Arrays**   106

5.4   **Dead Code Elimination**   109

5.5   **Implementation**   110

5.6   **Results**   112

Acknowledgments   113

References   113

6   A Network Processor Performance and Design
         Model with Benchmark Parameterization   **117**

Mark A. Franklin, Tilman Wolf

6.1   **The Performance Model**   119

6.2   **Workload and System Characteristics**   126

6.3   **Design Results**   130

6.4   **Conclusion**   138

References   138

7   A Benchmarking Methodology for Network
         Processors   **141**

*Mel Tsai, Chidamber Kulkarni, Niraj Shah, Kurt Keutzer,
Christian Sauer*

7.1   **Related Work**   143

7.2   **A Benchmarking Methodology**   146

7.3   **The Benchmark Suite**   158

7.4   **Preliminary Results**   160

7.5   **Conclusion and Future Work**   163

References   164

8   A Modeling Framework for Network
         Processor Systems   **167**

Patrick Crowley, Jean-Loup Baer

8.1   **Framework Description**   168

8.2   **System Modeling**   177

8.3   **IPSec VPN Decryption**   184

8.4   **Packet Size Distributions**   186
8.5   **Conclusion and Future Work**   187
         Acknowledgments   187
         References   187

PART II   PRACTICES   189

9   An Industry Analyst's Perspective on Network
           Processors   191
           John Freeman

9.1   **History of Packet Processing**   191
9.2   **The Need for Programmability**   199
9.3   **Network Processors**   203
9.4   **Where Do NPs Fit in a System?**   205
9.5   **Evaluating NP Solutions**   209
9.6   **Trends**   215

10   Agere Systems—Communications Optimized
           PayloadPlus Network Processor Architecture   219
           Bill Klein, Juan Garza

10.1   **Target Applications**   220
10.2   **PayloadPlus Optimized Pipeline-Based Hardware Architecture**   220
10.3   **3G/Media Gateway Application Example**   225
10.4   **FPP Details**   225
10.5   **RSP details**   228
10.6   **Software Architecture and Overview**   230
10.7   **Agere Performance Benefits at OC-48c**   232
          References   233

11   Cisco Systems—Toaster2   235

John Marshall

11.1   **Target Application(s)**   235
11.2   **Packet Flow Example for a Centralized System**   238
11.3   **Packet Flow Example for a Distributed System**   239
11.4   **Toaster2 Hardware Architecture**   240
11.5   **External Memory Controller**   241
11.6   **Internal Column Memory**   241
11.7   **Input and Output Header Buffers**   241
11.8   **Toaster MicroController**   242
11.9   **Tag Buffer**   245
11.10   **Route Processor interface**   245
11.11   **Lock Controller**   245
11.12   **Software Architecture**   246
11.13   **Toaster Development Methodology and Environment**   246
11.14   **Performance Claims**   247
11.15   **Family of Toaster Network Processors**   248
11.16   **Conclusion**   248

12   IBM—PowerNP Network Processor   249

Mohammad Peyravian, Jean Calvignac, Ravi Sabhikhi

12.1   **Hardware Architecture**   251
12.2   **Software**   255
12.3   **Performance**   257
12.4   **Conclusion**   258
     Acknowledgments   258
     References   258

13   Intel Corporation—Intel IXP2400 Network Processor: A Second-Generation Intel NPU   259

Prashant Chandra, Sridhar Lakshmanamurthy, Raj Yavatkar

13.1   **Target Applications**   259

13.2 **Hardware Architecture** 260

13.3 **Software Development Environment** 266

13.4 **IXP2400 System Configurations and Performance Analysis** 273

13.5 **CONCLUSION** 274

References 275

14 Motorola—C-5e Network Processor 277

Eran Cohen Strod, Patricia Johnson

14.1 **Target Applications** 278

14.2 **Hardware Architecture** 280

14.3 **Software Architecture** 287

14.4 **Conclusion** 290

References 290

15 PMC-Sierra, Inc.—ClassiPI 291

Vineet Dujari, Remby Taas, Ajit Shelat

15.1 **Target Applications** 291

15.2 **ClassiPI Architecture** 294

15.3 **System Interface (SI)** 295

15.4 **Field Extraction Engine (FEE)** 295

15.5 **Classification Engine (CE)** 295

15.6 **External RAM (ERAM) Interface** 297

15.7 **ClassiPI Control and Sequencer Block** 297

15.8 **Cascade Interface** 298

15.9 **ClassiPI Implementation** 299

15.10 **Software Architecture and Development Kit** 299

15.11 **Platforms** 299

15.12 **Modules** 300

15.13 **Software Development** 300

15.14 **Simulator** 301

15.15 **Debugger** 301

15.16 **ClassiPI Application Example: A Complex Security-Enabled Router** 302

15.17 **Performance**   304

15.18 **Conclusion**   304

References   305

16   TranSwitch—ASPEN: Flexible Network
Processing for Access Solutions   **307**

Subhash C. Roy

16.1 **Applications**   307

16.2 **ASPEN Operation and Architecture**   310

16.3 **Programming Environment**   316

16.4 **Conclusion**   317

References   318

Index   319

About the Editors   337

Preface

This book is an outgrowth of the first Workshop on Network Processors, which was held in conjunction with the Eighth International Symposium on High-Performance Computer Architecture (HPCA-8), in Cambridge, Massachusetts, on February 3, 2002. The concept of a book devoted to network processors emerged during the summer and fall of 2001 as we worked together on the workshop. Both the workshop and this book are based on the notion that future networks will require both the ability to execute complex applications at high line rates and the flexibility to respond to changing application and protocol demands. We believe that the network processor is an important component required to achieve this vision.

The workshop program committee consisted of the four editors of this book and three additional distinguished researchers and practitioners in the networking field: Nick McKeown (Stanford University), George Varghese (University of California, San Diego) and Raj Yavatkar (Intel). Extended and updated versions of seven of the nine workshop papers appear in this book.

The workshop program also included a keynote address by William J. Dally of Stanford University and an industry panel session moderated by one of the editors, Mark A. Franklin. The panel consisted of John Freeman (Industry Analyst), Larry Huston (Intel), Mike Lerer (Avici Systems), Keith Morris (AMCC), Dimitrios Stiliadis (Lucent/Bell Labs), and John F. Wakerly (Cisco Systems). The discussion included a range of network processor topics from an industry perspective, and, as it turned out, focused heavily on issues associated with developing network processor–based systems and on software for these systems.

The high attendance and favorable reception of the workshop, along with industry input, inspired us to add a practice component to the book consisting of commercial product descriptions. We hope to have produced a balanced and informative book representing both current research activities in this area and the pragmatics associated with delivering products. Our target audience includes scientists, engineers and students interested in network processors and related networking components.

The book begins with a chapter that introduces several key design issues associated with network processors. The remainder of the book is divided into two parts: the first presents a set of research papers that investigate a range of topics, including network processor modeling, simulation, architecture, and software, and the second contains a set of papers from industry that describe commercial network processor products.

We would like to extend our thanks to the workshop program committee members, the keynote speaker, the authors who presented papers at the workshop, the industry panelists and the HPCA-8 organizers. We also offer particular thanks to those authors whose contributions appear in this book; indeed, this edited volume would not exist without them.

Our special thanks go to those at Morgan Kaufmann Publishers who diligently walked us through the process of producing this book. These include Denise E. M. Penrose, Senior Editor, Marilyn Uffner Alan, Senior Developmental Editor, and Edward Wade, Publishing Services Manager.

Network Processors: An Introduction to Design Issues

Patrick Crowley
University of Washington

Mark A. Franklin
Washington University in St. Louis

Haldun Hadimioglu
Polytechnic University, Brooklyn

Peter Z. Onufryk
Integrated Device Technology, Inc.

The objective of this book is to survey current issues in the design of *network processors*: high-performance, programmable devices designed to efficiently execute communications workloads. A number of factors have contributed to the development of network processors (NPs) and the NP industry. Over the last 25 years, VLSI circuit performance and the number of transistors on a die have dramatically increased following Moore's law. This has enabled the cost-effective use of relatively high-performance embedded processors for communications functions. There has also been an equivalent increase in telecommunications bandwidth, which, in turn, has been driven by a rapidly growing demand for more functionality and intelligence within the communications network. The term *network processor* is used here in the most generic sense and is meant to encompass everything from task-specific processors, such as classification and encryption engines, to more general-purpose packet or communications processors.

Figure 1.1 shows an NP in a typical router line card application. In this application, the NP must examine packets at line speed (e.g., OC3 to OC768) and perform a set of operations ranging from basic packet forwarding to complex queuing and quality-of-service (QoS) processing. The real-time processing demands imposed on NPs lead to the use of advanced and novel computer architectures along with the latest VLSI and packaging technologies. Not only must NPs achieve high performance, they also must have the flexibility to deal with

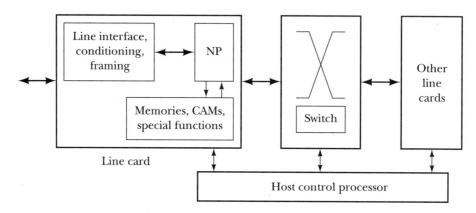

1.1

FIGURE

Network processor in a router application.

the large and ever-changing set of communications protocols and the increasing demands for new and more complex network services. For some functions, flexibility can be achieved by providing various levels of programmability. For other functions, the real-time demands on NPs dictate the use of dedicated hardware. Thus, the NP designer is forced to balance three key elements against one another:

+ Real-time processing constraints

+ Flexibility

+ Executing the preceding two elements in a cost-effective and competitive manner given physical constraints related to VLSI technologies, packaging, and power

This book considers various aspects of this difficult task. The first part presents a set of research papers devoted to questions related to analyzing, simulating, and designing network processors. The second part begins with an industry analyst's perspective of the NP field, and then continues with a set of papers contributed by companies that describe commercial network processors.

The remainder of this chapter introduces some of the design challenges and corresponding architectural approaches currently used in NP research and development. To this end, problems and solutions are merely sketched; greater detail can be found elsewhere in the book.

1.1   DESIGN CHALLENGES

There are many challenges associated with designing network processors. Many of these are common to general-purpose processor and VLSI design, including external memory bandwidth, power dissipation, pin limitations, packaging, and verification. However, the specific requirements of NPs exacerbate these problems. Although general-purpose processors typically have been designed to improve common-case performance with slight regard for certain design elements such as power efficiency, NPs, due to the dual concerns of real-time, link-rate processing and port density, must emphasize worst-case performance in an area- and power-efficient manner. Additionally, NP design involves a host of other systems challenges, including high levels of device integration (on-chip interfaces and controllers for external memories, switch fabrics, co-processors, network interfaces, etc.); management of critical shared resources in a chip-multiprocessor environment (e.g., shared program state, memory interfaces); compiler and software design for high-performance, real-time, parallel, and heterogeneous systems; and real-time system verification. As an example, we now consider two NP design challenges: line speed and application complexity.

As line rates have increased, the time associated with processing a minimum-sized packet has decreased. Consider, for example, a line rate of 10 Gbps along with the simplifying assumption of no interpacket gap. Under these conditions, a stream of minimum-sized packets of 64 bytes will result in the arrival of a packet approximately every 51 nanoseconds. While a stream of minimum-sized packets does not generally represent average traffic, it is under some circumstances the worst-case condition. Buffering and queuing will not help in this situation since, in order to process each packet and meet QoS guarantees, the processing rate must be at least slightly higher than the incoming packet rate. Otherwise, packets will be lost indiscriminately and queues will build up indefinitely.

Given a single-issue embedded RISC processor that executes a single instruction per clock cycle at a clock frequency of 500 MHz and assuming no hazards or memory delays, each instruction executes in 2 nanoseconds. The result is that for the minimum-sized packet and line rate described, only about 25 instructions can be executed in one packet time. Since it is difficult to accomplish much in 25 instructions with a "standard" RISC instruction set, high-performance NPs (i.e., those oriented toward the core of the network) resort to various design techniques to address this challenge. This is considered in the next section. As one moves away from the core of the network to the edge where flows are aggregated, line rates dramatically decrease. In these edge applications, it is possible to process packets purely in software on a standard RISC processor; however, cost and power constraints in these applications often drive designers to more innovative solutions.

One might expect that the increase in processor performance enabled by Moore's law would yield enough computing power to keep up with the increase in line speeds. However, that is not the case: over the past 10 years, line speeds and overall bandwidth have increased even faster than processing power. The increase in line speeds is due to the incorporation of fiber-optic links and associated high-speed electronics, whereas the increase in overall bandwidth is due to advances in fiber-optic technologies such as WDM (wavelength division multiplexing).

Added to these challenges is the increasing complexity of network applications that customers are requiring. A simple view of complexity partitions applications into the following three domains:

+ Applications that operate on individual packet headers (e.g., routing and forwarding).

+ Applications that operate principally on individual packet payloads (e.g., transcoding).

+ Applications that operate across multiple packets within a single flow (e.g., certain encryption algorithms) or across multiple flows (e.g., QoS and traffic shaping). A "flow" is considered to be a single source-destination session.

Early networking applications and associated functions focused primarily on the first item, that is, on dealing with packet headers with the principal application being that of determining the forwarding address associated with a given packet. More recently, applications have focused on applications in the second two categories. One aspect of the increasing complexity associated with these applications is the current need to perform packet classification on incoming packets. This requires matching selected fields in a packet with stored bit patterns and then appropriately processing the packet. Since the number of patterns, positions, and resulting actions can be very large, this can be a time-consuming process. Another example is the problem of encryption/decryption. Studies indicate that certain encryption/decryption algorithms are roughly two orders of magnitude more complex than typical header processing applications. When operating at high line rates, real-time solutions to these more complex applications represent challenging design problems.

1.2   DESIGN TECHNIQUES

A variety of architecture techniques have been employed to address the issues discussed in the previous section. These techniques can be broken down into three categories:

- ✦ Application-specific logic
  - Extending the RISC instruction set
  - Use of customized on-chip or off-chip hardware assists
- ✦ Advanced processor architectures
  - Multithreading
  - Instruction-level parallelism
- ✦ Macroparallelism
  - Multiple processors
  - Pipelined processors

For certain applications, selected time-consuming subtasks can be identified and implemented as new instructions in a standard RISC processor instruction set architecture (ISA). Examples of this include bit matching operations, pointer addressing calculations, tree and other data structure searching operations, and CRC polynomial calculations. Naturally, care must be taken that, in implementing these customized instructions, processor clock cycle times are not extended and instruction pipeline stalls are avoided. This approach is widely used since it preserves downward compatibility with existing code, operating systems, and tools. Furthermore, using modern development techniques, the process of adding instructions to an existing instruction set architecture and modifying the development tool chain (e.g., assemblers, compilers) is often a relatively straightforward task. A key area of research, however, is in identifying the optimal set of customized instructions to implement for a given application. Additionally, though compilers can be extended to recognize new instructions that have been explicitly included in a program, compiler methods for automatically generating these new instructions is still an area of research.

However, the use of customized instructions does not work well for all applications and functions. For more complex functions and applications, larger blocks of hardware/logic may be needed to meet real-time constraints. In these cases, depending on die area, speed, and cost constraints, the functions may be implemented as accelerators or hardware assists located either on-chip or off-chip. Examples of this include hardware accelerators for encryption/decryption and classification. In both of these cases, companies have developed and marketed specialized stand-alone chips implementing these applications while others have implemented these functions directly on their NP chip.

Another approach to meeting real-time application and bandwidth demands is to move toward more advanced processor designs. One common problem with NP applications is that they require access to large tables and data structures that are held in off-chip memory. With a nonmultithreaded processor, when an application program makes a reference to data that is not already in its cache, it will stall for a number of cycles waiting for the data to be fetched from off-chip memory. On a multithreaded processor, once such a stall is detected, the processor switches automatically to another application process or thread. This thread can then start executing, thereby utilizing otherwise wasted stall cycles. Thus, processors are used more efficiently and, as a consequence, more packets can be processed per second with a given set of resources. Numerous NP designs employ multithreading techniques. Although this does not alleviate the problem of meeting the given input line speed, it does enhance processor efficiency and throughput.

Another approach to improving processor performance is to exploit instruction level parallelism (ILP) in programs. This is a very broad topic encompassing a host of design variants. The main idea is to use either the compiler (static techniques) or a hardware instruction scheduler (dynamic techniques) to determine if a group of program instructions can be executed simultaneously on the given set of processor resources. If so, then the instructions are executed in parallel, and the application potentially runs faster. Examining alternative ILP implementation strategies is beyond the scope of this introduction. ILP techniques have not yet enjoyed widespread use in commercial network processors since macro-parallelism is generally considered a more efficient method of achieving speedup in packet processing applications.

Employing macroparallelism is very common in NP designs. One approach is based on the fact that at the flow level, different flows can be considered to be independent. Therefore, if a packet scheduler can, in a balanced manner, route flows to different processors that act independently and in parallel, the application processing associated with these flows can be executed in parallel. Thus, with n processors, we can theoretically achieve an n-fold speedup in processing. Parallelism can also be achieved at the individual packet level within a flow if mechanisms are employed to maintain packet ordering.

Further increases in processing power can be obtained if we consider the set of tasks associated with packet processing as a sequence that can be executed in a pipelined manner. Thus, a packet might go through a sequence of pipeline processing stages involving classification, packet processing (e.g., forwarding, encryption), and output processing (e.g., QoS, queuing). By doing this, packet throughput of the processor is improved (at the expense of an increase in packet latency). A research question of interest is just how we should allocate tasks and subtasks to pipeline stages in a manner that optimizes the cost performance. This is a difficult question since pipeline stages can be viewed as being programmable processors, customized logic, or some combination of the two. Given the addi-

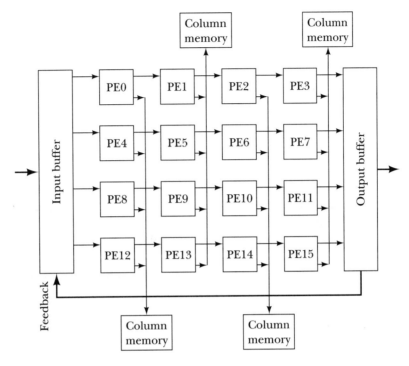

1.2   The Cisco Toaster2 NP (from Chapter 3).

FIGURE

tional options involving application algorithms and implementation, the number of choices is enormous.

Figure 1.2 exemplifies macroparallelism. It shows a simplified view of the Cisco Toaster2 NP architecture. The architecture consists of 16 processing elements divided into 4 pipelines, each having 4 stages. Details on the operation of this network processor can be found in Chapters 3 and 12.

1.3   CHALLENGES AND CONCLUSIONS

Designing cost-effective network processors is one of the most challenging of current computer architecture problems. In this introduction, we have touched on some of the central architecture themes that cut across a number of current NP designs. The general issue is that both the design space and the application space are very large. Additionally, both are changing as the underlying hardware technology continues to rapidly improve, and as protocol standards and driving applications continue to evolve. Naturally, there are key topics that, though important, we have not addressed here. Not the least of them is the issue of NP software and programmability. A key feature driving the use of NPs is the ability to change functionality in response to the changes cited earlier. Providing this flexibility is a difficult tradeoff since different locations in the network (e.g., the core versus the edge) can have significantly different flexibility and performance requirements. It is therefore unlikely that a single approach will work across the entire network.

Part I of this book presents research directed at issues associated with the NP design process. These include developing NP benchmarks, modeling performance, and using these models to aid in selecting designs and in generating code for them. Part II presents descriptions of commercial network processors that focus on the architecture, performance, and software aspects of these devices. As you read through Part II, you will find illustrations of most of the architecture elements discussed in this introduction. Industry has led the way in NP design, and it is only recently that academic research has begun to focus on the interesting and important problems associated with processor design in this environment.

PART
I

DESIGN PRINCIPLES

2 Benchmarking Network Processors

Prashant R. Chandra, Frank Hady, Raj Yavatkar, Tony Bock, Mason Cabot, Philip Mathew

3 A Methodology and Simulator for the Study of Network Processors

Deepak Suryanarayanan, John Marshall, Gregory T. Byrd

4 Design Space Exploration of Network Processor Architectures

Lothar Thiele, Samarjit Chakraborty, Matthias Gries, Simon Künzli

5 Compiler Backend Optimizations for Network Processors with Bit Packet Addressing

Jens Wagner, Rainer Leupers

6 A Network Processor Performance and Design Model with Benchmark Parameterization

Mark A. Franklin, Tilman Wolf

7 A Benchmarking Methodology for Network Processors

Mel Tsai, Chidamber Kulkarni, Niraj Shah, Kurt Keutzer, Christian Sauer

8 A Modeling Framework for Network Processor Systems

Patrick Crowley, Jean-Loup Baer

2 CHAPTER

Benchmarking Network Processors

Prashant R. Chandra, Frank Hady, Raj Yavatkar, Tony Bock, Mason Cabot, Philip Mathew

Intel Corporation

Network processors (NPs) are an emerging field of programmable processors that are optimized to implement data plane, packet processing networking functions. Unlike the general-purpose CPUs such as Pentium processors, NPs typically support some form of a distributed, parallel programming model. They are also optimized for fast packet processing and I/O. Standard benchmarks for network processors do not yet exist, and existing processor benchmarks designed to evaluate performance of compute-intensive applications are not applicable to them. This void makes measuring, communicating, and comparing NP performance difficult.

The definition of a standard set of benchmarks applicable to network processors is needed. The goals of such a set of benchmarks should be to (1) cover different NP architectures, (2) be applicable to different NP application domains, and (3) cater to audiences with different expectations. In this paper, we propose a four-layered approach for NP benchmark definition to meet these goals. We show the utility of this hierarchical approach by specifying and measuring one or more benchmark examples at each level. Our measurements are performed on the Intel IXP1200 network processor. We are currently contributing our work toward the definition of NP benchmarks in the Network Processing Forum.

2.1   BENCHMARKING FRAMEWORK OVERVIEW

Benchmarking NPs is complicated by a variety of factors. First, NPs from different
vendors employ widely varying hardware architectures and present different programming models and languages. Second, NPs are being used in a wide variety
of application domains all the way from edge application such as TCP offload, to
core network application domains such as switching and routing. Some NP application domains are still emerging and do not yet have standard definitions. This
makes even the simplified problem of specifying benchmarks for a single NP difficult. Finally, NP benchmarks have to cater to different audiences. NP application
developers are more interested in benchmarks that exercise particular pieces of
an NP, whereas other customers look for benchmarks that benchmark the entire
application.

To deal with this complexity, this paper proposes a hierarchical framework
that employs benchmarks at four different levels of abstraction: system, function,
micro, and hardware. The paper also proposes a benchmarking reference platform that enables an "apples-to-apples" comparison between different NPs. The
benchmark framework is described in greater detail in the following sections.

2.1.1   Benchmarking Hierarchy

In order to target different application domains and different audiences, we
propose a four-level hierarchical framework for defining benchmarks for NPs. We
call the four levels system, function, micro, and hardware. Each level benchmarks
the NP at a lower level of abstraction than the previous level and is targeted to a
different audience. The details of each level are as follows:

- ✦ *System level.* Benchmarks at this level are targeted at performance of complete
  systems such as routers. They include both control plane and data plane
  functionality and measure the performance of the entire system consisting
  of one or more NPs and other components. A set of system-level benchmarks
  has already been defined by the IETF and is targeted at end users (ISPs) who
  will use the systems in their networks. Examples of system-level benchmarks
  are benchmarks for IP routers, firewalls, Web switches, and the like.

- ✦ *Function level.* These benchmarks measure the performance of individual NP
  application functions. They only focus on data plane functionality implemented within the NP. Typically, most system-level benchmarks include multiple application functions. For example, a firewall includes IP forwarding, fil-

tering, and NAT applications. However, a system-level benchmark cannot pinpoint the performance of a particular application on a single NP. Function-level benchmarks are, therefore, useful for evaluating the performance of an NP for a single function such as IP forwarding. Function-level benchmarks are targeted toward NP customers who will use NP vendor-provided application functions out of the box.

✦ *Microlevel.* These benchmarks target significant, elementary operations that arc commonly put together to make up a function. The operations used must be separable from other operations to facilitate independent measurement. A microlevel benchmark is generally found in more than one function-level benchmark. Examples of microlevel benchmarks include longest prefix match (LPM) table lookups, 5-tuple table lookups, string searches, and CRC calculations. Microlevel benchmarks are targeted at NP developers who implement value-added data plane functionality and therefore need to measure and compare NP performance for a particular operation.

✦ *Hardware level.* These benchmarks measure the latencies and throughputs for accessing the various hardware resources within an NP. Latency/throughputs for accesses to the memories provided by an NP and other units (e.g., CAMs) make good hardware-level benchmarks. These benchmarks allow an NP programmer to make appropriate choices in data placement and hardware resources to achieve maximum performance. Each microlevel benchmark exercises a particular subset of hardware-level benchmarks.

Using the described hierarchy, we have defined and implemented a number of NP benchmarks on the IXP1200 processor. *However, our approach is general and is equally applicable to other network processors.* In this paper, we describe implementations of a function-level benchmark (IPv4 forwarding, a microlevel benchmark), LPM (longest prefix match), and a set of hardware-level benchmarks. Each benchmark presented will demonstrate the utility of the framework proposed here as it measures the performance of the IXP1200.

2.1.2 Benchmarking Reference Platform

Unlike general-purpose microprocessors, NPs employ a wide variety of architectures, programming models, and programming languages. Sometimes, an NP can consist of multiple chips performing different functions. Therefore, unlike microprocessor benchmarks (e.g., SPEC), benchmark specifications cannot be in the form of C (or other high-level language) code. Instead, benchmarks must

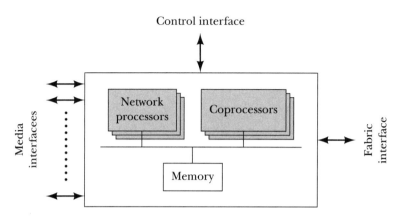

NP benchmarking reference platform.

be developed as functional specifications that characterize a given workload and measure external metrics such as throughput and latency.

In order to enable an apples-to-apples comparison to the extent possible, different network processors must be benchmarked under the same conditions. In the ideal case, this could be a reference platform with a well-defined socket that every network processor would plug into. However, given the differences in network processor architectures, this is not practical. Therefore, this paper proposes a loosely defined "reference platform" for benchmarking network processors.

Reference platforms are defined by their external data and control interfaces. A reference platform has one or more media interfaces through which network traffic is injected. A reference platform may also have one or more control interfaces and switch fabric interfaces. A control interface is used for control plane setup operations (e.g., route table updates). A typical reference platform is shown in Figure 2.1. The choice of the media, fabric, and control interfaces may be left to a network processor vendor benchmarking its part, or to customers comparing different network processors.

The internals of the reference platform are left undefined and may contain one or more NPs, one or more co-processors, and other additional hardware required for the benchmark. Every benchmark report is accompanied by a detailed inventory of what is on the reference platform. This enables comparisons between different network processors through the use of derived performance metrics such as throughput/sq-in, throughput/watt, and throughput/cost.

A reference platform may also be defined by a customer interested in selecting a network processor for his or her application. Each network processor vendor would then run the benchmark on that reference platform to enable more direct comparison with other network processors.

2.2   HARDWARE-LEVEL BENCHMARKS

Hardware-level benchmarks form the lowest level of the benchmark hierarchy. These benchmarks state the latencies and bandwidths encountered when accessing NP resources. Resource examples include memories, special-purpose accelerators, bus interfaces, and other computation elements. The metrics should include unloaded (otherwise free) and a loaded (busy) resource.

Hardware-level benchmarks are useful to a programmer trying to get the most out of a given NP. Knowing the latency to a given resource tells the programmer how many other operations can be completed while waiting for returning read data. Knowing the throughput of a memory lets the programmer calculate an upper-bound for a memory-intensive application. Hardware-level benchmarks are also useful for calculating rough performance upper bounds for algorithms the programmer is intimately familiar with. For example, the upper-bound performance for a memory-intensive function equals the bandwidth of the memory divided by the number of accesses per unit function. This assumes that there are a sufficient number of computational threads to amortize the latency of each memory read, a condition that hardware-level benchmarks enable a programmer to easily check.

Hardware-level benchmarks are architecture specific, meaning they can only be defined in terms of a given architecture. *For this reason, hardware-level benchmarks don't make good metrics for comparing the performance of two different network processors.*

This section presents a set of hardware-level benchmarks for the IXP1200. A similar set could be created for any NP. Figure 2.2 shows an architectural drawing of the IXP1200 with hardware-level benchmarks superimposed. Latencies are shown to/from DRAM, SRAM, Scratch, Hash Unit, TFIFO (Transmit FIFO), RFIFO (Receive FIFO), and to another microengine. For a description of the IXP1200 architecture, see [1]. Latency is the time between the execution of a reference-generating op-code and the clock cycle upon which the corresponding completion signal returns, as shown in the following example:

```
sdram[read,$xfer,address,0,1],sig_done
// Reference starts here
wait#: br_!signal[sdram,wait#]
next operation
// Reference is complete when this op-code executes
```

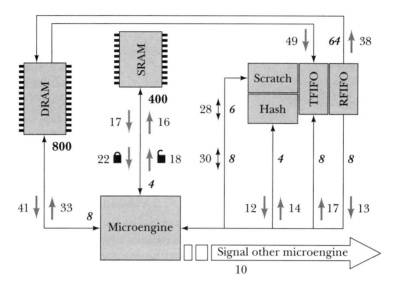

Regular font—clock counts (200 MHz clocks)
Bold—throughputs (MB/sec)
Italicized—transfer size

2.2   IXP1200 unloaded latencies.

FIGURE

Individual latency measurements were made by executing this set of transactions between two reads of a cycle counter on a 200 MHz IXP1200. It is important to note that on an IXP1200, a memory access is usually followed by a
context switch to another computational thread, not by polling for the completion
signal. For these benchmarks, polling enables direct measurement of memory
access latencies.

Throughputs for SRAM and DRAM are also listed in Figure 2.2. Since these
off-chip resources see requests from a number of different computational elements, likely saturating the resource and perhaps creating resource contention,
a throughput measurement makes more sense. Throughput measurements were
made by allocating a memory space to each microengine and then executing code
on each microengine to read from that memory space as rapidly as possible while
recording the number of successful reads.

The latencies presented so far are unloaded latencies, taken with the rest
of the NP idle. Most NPs feature multiple computational elements sharing a
single memory, and for most applications more than one of these elements access
memory at the same time. To properly plan for the latencies encountered in

such a program, developers also need to know the latency for requests made concurrent with requests from other computational elements. We call these *loaded latencies*.

To measure loaded latencies, the loading placed on memory must be variable and controllable, but will differ in definition depending on the NP architecture. For the IXP1200, we introduced contention for main memory by instructing five of the microengines to generate reads to main memory at known, programmable intervals. Each microengine ran a single thread. The first of these microengines issued a memory read command every x clocks, where x is a value assigned at compile time. After issuing a memory read, this first microengine signaled the second microengine. Upon receiving the signal, the second microengine issued a read and then signaled the third microengine. This continued through the set of five microengines. Interthread signaling is only used during the initialization phase to get all five microengines to start issuing memory reads. Thereafter, each microengine generated a memory read every x cycles. Each microengine walked across its own unique contiguous space in memory. The remaining microengine measured read latency just as already described for idle latency measurements.

Figure 2.3 shows the resulting measurements for both SRAM and DRAM on a 232 MHz IXP1200. Measured latency is on the y-axis, and the time between requests for the five loading microengines is on the x-axis. As expected, for a low concurrent load (large x-axis value), both SRAM and DRAM accesses return with near idle latencies. As the concurrent load increases, SRAM latency remains at idle levels until SRAM saturation is reached. Here SRAM latency increases rapidly with increases in load. Finally, the latency reaches a limit set by the total number of concurrent outstanding read requests allowed. At this point, SRAM is saturated—returning data at the maximum rate allowed by the memory. The loading microengines cannot further decrease the delay between requests.

DRAM is less bandwidth efficient (it must refresh memory and manage memory pages), so latency for reads to this memory begins to increase well before complete saturation is reached. The odd peak in the otherwise expected smooth DRAM latency curve is an artifact of the measurement technique we used. Programmers should consider the latency with a smoothed curve (dotted line). The artifact arises because of interactions between the algorithm used to generate the load and the algorithm used to measure latency. The loading microengines generate a block of five reads within a short interval. With some finite probability, a transaction from the latency measuring microengine will end up behind five transactions from the loading microengine, requiring it to wait until all five transactions are serviced. Since many such measurements make up each test run, all test runs will feature a number of these unlucky accesses. When such an access occurs for

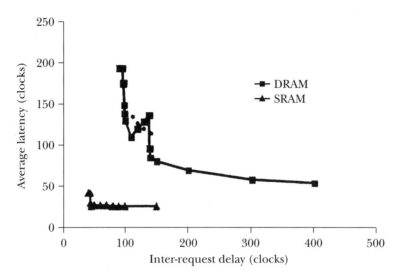

IXP1200 loaded latencies.

a test with just the right *x*-axis inter-request delay, the read will return to the measurement microengine just after the five loading microengines have generated a new batch of reads. Once lined up, accesses from the measurement microengine will always encounter five fresh reads from the loading microengines. This phenomenon accounts for the sharp rise in latency before the saturation point. As the inter-request delay is made smaller, this resonant frequency becomes correspondingly smaller since the request from the measuring microengine arrives later in the servicing of the sequence of the block of five loading reads. This accounts for the track back to the real latency curve along $x = y$. This continues until load inter-request delay becomes small enough that transactions back up in the DRAM request queue and latencies start to increase sharply. Since programmers will not encounter such regular opposing traffic (or at least not the exact opposing traffic generated here), they should ignore the peak when using this graph by following the dotted line instead. The lesson is that loaded hardware benchmarks require very careful construction of loads and/or very careful interpretation.

2.3   MICROLEVEL BENCHMARKS

Microlevel benchmarks seek to isolate and measure the performance of the basic networking operations that make up a networking function. A microlevel benchmark will exercise a number of hardware-level benchmarks. To make a useful microlevel benchmark, an operation must

+ *Require significant computation.* There is little value in creating a benchmark out of an operation whose runtime can easily be calculated by a programmer.

+ *Be separately measurable.* Enabling the benchmark to isolate the operation in a way that assures the benchmark score reflects the performance of that operation on that NP.

+ *Be found in more than one function-level benchmark.* Otherwise, it can be argued that performance of the operation is more accurately measured by the single function-level benchmark in which the operation is included.

Examples of microlevel benchmarks include longest prefix match, 5-tuple lookup, string search, and CRC calculation.

Microlevel benchmarks apply across different network processors. These benchmarks are likely to be useful both in picking a network processor and in programming the network processor. Microlevel benchmarks provide the developer selecting an NP with a measure of the ability of the network processor to complete specific operations that are required for the target applications. These operations are likely required on top of some base functionality that is covered by a function-level benchmark. In implementing an application, microlevel benchmarks show the programmer the top speed and resource utilization to expect for a particular operation.

Here we present longest prefix match (LPM) as an example of a microlevel benchmark. Before performance measurement begins, the benchmark loads the route table into memory. To provide a realistic routing table, we used a 2/7/01 Mae-West snapshot available at *www.merit.edu/ipma/routing_table/#snapshot*. This route table contains about 30,000 entries. Furthermore, the benchmark starts with a list of destination IP addresses stored in memory. To provide a realistic network traffic address stream, we downloaded an anonymized trace for Mae-West from MOAT (*moat.nlanr.net/PMA/*) and associated each incoming IP address with a randomly selected IP address from the route table. The IP address from the route table was then stored in memory as the traffic IP address and the association remembered for repeat IP addresses in the traffic stream. Such a scheme preserves the locality of reference in the incoming traffic's destination addresses. Both the list of IP addresses and the route table would need to be published to standardize the benchmark. It may be desirable to have multiple route tables and multiple IP address lists.

Description	Value
LPMs per second	3.6 million
Microengine zero execute time	78%
Microengine zero abort time	16%
Microengine zero stall time	0%
Microengine zero idle time	5.9%
DRAM bandwidth utilization	15%
DRAM footprint	960 Kbytes
SRAM bandwidth utilization	24%
SRAM footprint	1112 Kbytes

2.1

TABLE

LPM microlevel benchmark for a single IXP1200 microengine.

With the route table loaded into SRAM and the destination address stream loaded into DRAM, the benchmark executes LPM route lookups for each destination IP address. The time to run through the entire list of IP addresses was measured and converted into the benchmark metric, LPMs per second. The results for a single microengine (running four threads) are shown in Table 2.1.

To be of most use, microlevel benchmark reports should specify more than just the benchmark score—the utilization of important NP resources should also be included. Resource utilizations give the NP selector or code developer a deeper understanding of the resources required to implement a particular operation.

Table 2.1 shows the results of the benchmark example for a single 200 MHz IXP1200 microengine. A rate of 3.6 million LPMs per second was achieved—enough to satisfy a 1.8 Gbps stream of minimum-sized Ethernet packets. The microengine utilization statistics show that the single microengine used in the test was almost completely consumed with useful work, spending only 16% of its time going down the wrong code path due to branch prediction errors, and 6% of its time idle. The SRAM and DRAM utilization statistics indicate that there is substantial memory bandwidth and memory storage left to concurrently service the needs of the other five microengines. The other microengines could be employed to implement additional LPM lookups on the same table, increasing the benchmark score, or to perform other parts of an application. The results also show that the hardware-level benchmark most useful in estimating LPM performance is SRAM and DRAM latency. This is because the latencies determine the total elapsed time for a single thread executing an LPM and therefore determine the total number of LPMs per second that can be performed by the threads in a given microengine. SRAM and DRAM bandwidth hardware-level benchmarks are of secondary importance and are useful when more than one microengine is used to perform LPMs.

Variations on this benchmark are possible. One compelling variation acts on packets moving from input ports to output ports. This would add realism since destination IP addresses are not likely found in a list in main memory and since it includes standard packet movement on the NP. Unfortunately, this addition of realism also introduces a significant potential disadvantage. Line speed may limit benchmark performance masking the ability of the NP to perform the LPMs.

2.4   FUNCTION-LEVEL BENCHMARKS

Function-level benchmarks are intended to characterize the performance of well-defined application functions within the network processor domain. These functions typically implement data plane functionality for networking protocols like IPv4, MPLS, Diffserv, and NAT. Function-level benchmarks are one level higher in the benchmark hierarchy than microlevel benchmarks. A function-level benchmark can be related to one or more microlevel benchmarks based on the operations that compose a function. For example, the IPv4 forwarding function-level benchmark is related to the longest prefix match microlevel benchmark.

Function-level benchmarks are targeted at network box suppliers who will use NP vendor–provided application functions out of the box. Function-level benchmarks also serve as a likely starting point for developers implementing value-added data plane functionality. These developers may then use microlevel benchmarks to estimate performance of value-added code not present in the function-level benchmark.

In this section, we present the results of the IPv4 forwarding function-level benchmark. This benchmark was implemented on a 232MHz IXP1200 network processor. The benchmark measured the IPv4 forwarding performance of the IXP1200 with two gigabit Ethernet ports using the metrics and procedures described in IETF RFC2544.

Figure 2.4 shows the zero-loss throughput at various frame sizes. The x-axis represents the Ethernet frame size in bytes, and the y-axis represents the throughput as a percentage of the maximum possible throughput. The results show that the throughput is close to the theoretical maximum over the entire range of frame sizes. The slight dip at a frame size of 128 bytes is an artifact of the IXP1200 architecture that handles data internally in 64-byte chunks.

Figure 2.5 shows the frame loss rate at various frame sizes. The x-axis plots the input frame rate as a percentage of the maximum possible frame rate. The y-axis plots the loss rate as a percentage of the input frames dropped as a result of

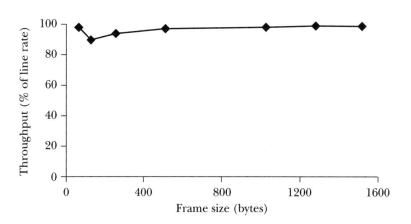

2.4   IPv4 forwarding throughput.

FIGURE

congestion. The frame loss rate decreases with increasing frame size. This is to be expected because the input frame rate decreases with increasing frame size and therefore the per-frame processing overhead also decreases.

Figure 2.6 shows the latency through the IXP1200 at various frame sizes. The x-axis plots the frame size in bytes, and the y-axis plots the measured end-to-end latency in microseconds. The end-to-end latency includes the latencies contributed by the gigabit Ethernet MAC, the framer chips, and the tester itself.

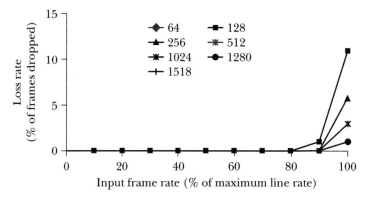

2.5   IPv4 forwarding loss rate.

FIGURE

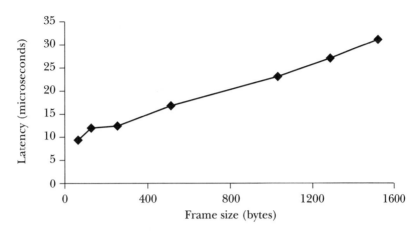

IPv4 forwarding latency.

Forwarding latency increases slightly with increasing frame size. This is because with increasing frame size, the per-byte processing overhead increases.

2.5   RELATED WORK

Two networking benchmark suites have been proposed in the literature. Both consist primarily of general-purpose (as opposed to NP) routines. NetBench [2] presents a suite of nine benchmarks that the authors split into three categories: low or microlevel (CRC calculation and table lookup), IP-level programs (IPv4 routing, deficit round robin scheduling, NAT, firewall), and application-level (URL-based switching, Diffie Helman public key encryption, MD5 signature generation). The authors measure the computational characteristics of these benchmarks on a general-purpose processor simulator and show that these characteristics differ from those of multimedia applications. The authors go on to test the CRC, MD5, and routing benchmarks on the IXP1200 network processor simulator finding the NP most suitable for routing. Commbench [3, 4] focuses on eight small program kernels fitting into the microlevel benchmark category presented in our paper. The benchmarks are split into two categories: header processing (radix tree search, IP packet fragmentation, deficit round robin scheduling, TCP traffic monitoring) and payload processing (block cipher, ZIP data compression, Reed-Solomon forward error correction, JPEG compression). The authors analyze the computational characteristics of the benchmarks in a general-purpose processor context for code size, computational complexity, instruction set characteristics, and memory hierarchy characteristics, and contrast these measures to the SPEC95 [5] benchmark suite. In contrast to these efforts, the focus of this paper is on developing a methodology for benchmarking and comparing different network processors.

Others have investigated the performance and architectural characteristics of network processor–based routers and network interfaces. Spalink et al. [6] describe their implementation of a router on the IXP1200 and find it to be an order of magnitude faster than a pure PC-based router. The authors also measure memory latencies to NP DRAM, SRAM, and scratch memories and use the measurements to explain the performance of the router. These measurements correspond directly to the hardware-level metrics presented in our hierarchy. Crowley [7] et al. list eight programmable network interface workloads and then use three of them—namely, IP forwarding, MD5 signature generation, and 3DES bulk encryption—to study the suitability of different processor architectures for such an interface. The authors find simultaneous multithreaded to perform better than chip multiprocessor, while both of these perform much better than fine-grain multithreaded and superscalar.

Several standards bodies have been involved in the creation of benchmarks. These include organizations such as SPEC for general-purpose processors, EEMBC for embedded processors, and the IETF for networking systems. EEMBC has defined a set of networking benchmarks [8], which contain two benchmarks that fall within the microlevel benchmarks defined here. "Patricia" corresponds to the LPM microlevel benchmark presented, and "Packet Flow" models the packet-level checks included in RFC1812. EEMBC also defines "Open shortest Path First/Dijkstra," which builds a route table; this would run on the control plane. IETF's Benchmarking Working Group has defined several system-level benchmarks for routers and switches [9]. The Network Processing Forum [10] is currently defining both function-level and microlevel benchmarks (called "application level" and "task level" in that forum). The authors of this paper are active contributors to the forum.

REFERENCES

[1]   Intel IXP1250 Network Processor—Datasheet, Intel Corporation, December 2001 *ftp://download.intel.com/design/network/datashts/27837106.pdf*.

[2]   G. Memik, W. Mangione-Smith, and W. Hu, "NetBench: A Benchmarking Suite for Network Processors," *International Conference on Computer Aided Design 2001*, pp. 39–42.

[3]   T. Wolf, and J. Turner, "Design Issues for High Performance Active Routers," *IEEE Journal on Selected Areas of Communications*, Vol. 19 No. 3, March 2001.

[4]   T. Wolf, and M. Franklin, "Commbench—A Telecommunications Benchmark for Network Processors," *IEEE International Symposium on Performance Analysis of Systems and Software*, Austin, Texas, 2000.

[5]   Standard Performance Evaluation Corporation [1995], *SPEC CPU95* Version 1.10, August 21, 1995, *www.specbench.org/osg/cpu95/*.

[6]   T. Spalink, S. Karlin, L. Peterson, and Y. Gottlieb, "Building a Robust Software-Based Router Using Network Processors," *18th ACM Symposium on Operating Systems Principles*, Chateau Lake Louise, Bantf, Alberta, Canada, October 2001.

[7]   P. Crowley, M. Fiuczynski, J.-L. Baer, and B. Bershad, "Characterizing Processor Architectures for Programmable Network Interfaces," *2000 International Conference on Supercomputing*, Santa Fe, New Mexico, May 2000.

[8]   "Networking Benchmark Datasheets," EEMBC, *www.eembc.org/Benchmark/datasheet /Networking/default.asp*

[9]   IETF Benchmarking Working Group, *www.ietf.org/html.charters/bmwg-charter.html*.

[10]   "Network Processing Forum Completes First Set of Milestones," Network Processing Forum Press Release, Sacha Arts, Slider and Associates, 408-356-3099.

3

CHAPTER

A Methodology and Simulator for the Study of Network Processors

Deepak Suryanarayanan, John Marshall
Cisco Systems

Gregory T. Byrd
North Carolina State University

Network processors (NPs) have recently emerged as a new class of processors that combine programmable ASICs and microprocessors to implement adaptive network services. NPs leverage the flexibility of software solutions with the high performance of custom hardware. With the development of such sophisticated hardware, there is a need for a holistic methodology that can facilitate the study of network processors and their performance with different networking applications and traffic conditions. This combination of study techniques is accomplished in the component network simulator (ComNetSim) developed by the authors. The simulator includes both a traffic-modeling component and a detailed architectural framework, allowing the study of complete networking applications under varying network traffic conditions.

The simulator is modeled on a generic line card from a distributed routing system. Packets flowing into the router arrive at its input ports, are aggregated into a single queue, and are then processed by different logic blocks. The simulator reproduces this scenario by using packet traces to simulate the arrival of packets belonging to different traffic flows in real time. Both actual captured traces [4] and analytical traffic models [13] may be used to generate the packet traces used for simulation.

At the core of the real-time simulator is a detailed framework for modeling an NP architecture. The first release includes a model of a Cisco Toaster network processor [12], a parallel-pipelined processor optimized for high-data throughput network applications. The Toaster is organized as a four-by-four matrix of VLIW cores. The cores in each row operate as a pipeline, processing packet segments as they pass from one to another. The corresponding cores in different rows run the same code and thus perform the same operations. In order to reduce contention for shared memory, the operation of the cores in each column are phase shifted in time. Packet segments entering the processor are passed to any one of the four rows in round robin fashion. The processor has a two-level shared memory system that trades off memory size against access speed.

The simulator includes a program template used to implement networking applications. For this paper, we implement a weighted round robin scheduling algorithm, adapted to the Toaster architecture and capable of scheduling up to 1024 flows in a deterministic manner. The implementation showcases the ability of the simulator to study the interactions among network traffic, applications, and hardware architecture. Analysis is facilitated by the data that can be gathered on a per-flow basis and also directly from the hardware. Preliminary work has shown the effects of implementation tradeoffs on the behavior of the traffic flowing through the system.

ComNetSim provides a unified tool that allows NP architectures to be studied in the context of realistic applications and traffic conditions. The environment supports architectural studies, application development, and traffic modeling under a common framework. Such analysis can undoubtedly influence architectural decisions that have a bearing on the performance, application, and cost of network processing systems.

The rest of the paper is organized as follows: Section 3.1 describes related work and justifies the motives for developing the simulator. Section 3.2 describes the high-level simulator design. Section 3.3 details the Toaster network processor. Section 3.4 describes the implementation of the simulator, including the cycle-accurate model of the Toaster architecture. Section 3.5 describes the implementation of the weighted round robin (WRR) algorithm within ComNetSim. Section 3.6 briefly presents the simulator organization. In Section 3.7, we present performance results and analysis. We summarize the paper and conclude with Section 3.8.

3.1   PREVIOUS WORK

With the advancement of network equipment, system-level modeling to explore design space and verify concepts has gained importance. Past research has covered different aspects of communication system design such as algorithms, protocols, and benchmark applications.

A methodology for studying performance of network hardware is Comm-Bench [20]. Its purpose is to develop benchmark applications that can be used in the design and evaluation of network processors. CommBench's focus is on implementing networking applications that provide a distribution of various instructions and their frequency. These can have a role in designing the ISA of a network processor. Independent of any particular architecture, it resembles the microarchitect's approach of design and evaluation using a standard set of benchmark applications.

Crowley et al. [5], combine a system of benchmarks with microprocessor simulators. This has the twin benefit of arriving at a system for evaluating network processors and using these to explore the network processor design space. The initial experiments in this body of work evaluated the benchmarks on several conventional microarchitecture paradigms.

A simulator that has a very broad development community is the network simulator (NS) [19]. This system is used to study behavior of algorithms and protocols at a network level with interaction between different nodes. NS incorporates code developed by its several users and contains a rich set of libraries for traffic generation and algorithm studies. While the researchers working with NS study various issues related to the operation of the Internet, the simulator is not built to address hardware architecture issues.

The packet lookup and classification (PALAC) [1] simulator developed at Stanford University provides a framework for studying the behavior of packet classifying algorithms. The system includes a traffic generator, packet classifier algorithms, and statistics collection mechanisms. The goal of this simulator is to assist in the design and implementation of efficient classification algorithms.

The design space explored by methods discussed so far can be organized into three segments: applications, hardware/software architecture, and traffic generation. None of preceding methods considers combining all three of these segments to study their interaction. The conventional microarchitect's approach has been to study hardware architectures using benchmarks. This technique neglects the role that network traffic can play in shaping the performance of a particular architecture [6]. The approach of researchers in the networking field has been to simulate a network and study the interaction between nodes implementing protocols and algorithms and passing simulated traffic through them.

There is a space that remains to be explored that combines the three different segments. This space, which would bridge the gap between design, implementation, and deployment from a network systems perspective, should address the interaction between traffic vectors, applications, and the platforms used to implement these applications. The purpose of the component network simulator

(ComNetSim) is to address this space and implement a methodology that demonstrates the benefit of such a multipronged initiative.

3.2   COMPONENT NETWORK SIMULATOR (ComNetSim)

The simulator is modeled from the perspective of a line card on a distributed router. The entire simulator can be construed as a simplex path on a line card, as illustrated in Figure 3.1. The traffic generator creates a stream of packets, which are received, buffered, and multiplexed to form an input queue to the network processing component (NPC). The direct memory access (DMA) component handles the packet buffering function. A network processor processes the packet headers and returns them to the DMA component. The headers are reattached to their respective payloads and stored in the packet memory. Packets are allowed to exit the packet memory at an appropriate time, determined by the NP. In the case of the simulator, the packets are discarded once they exit the NPC, but in a realistic scenario, these would be bound for an output port or a switch fabric.

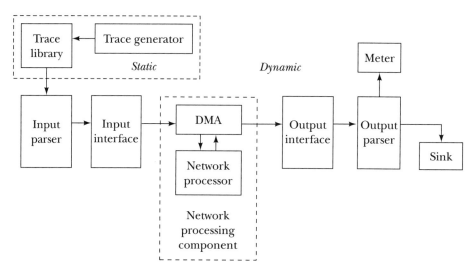

3.1   Component network simulator.

FIGURE

Each of the components in the packet flow pipeline is configurable and allows scope for study. The NPC is a model of a real network processor, complete with its memory system, that permits implementation of applications.

3.2.1 Trace Generator

A critical requirement for network simulation is the availability of realistic traffic traces. Network traffic traces can be obtained by several methods. A popular scheme is to collect real traces from routers for extended periods of time [4]. These traces represent the mix of traffic flowing through a router and are collected on one of the input or output links. While providing a picture of aggregate traffic, these traces may not be flexible for simulation studies. They contain a mix of traffic from different sources that is very generic and have a preset arrival pattern that cannot be changed. These traces can instead be used to derive characteristics such as packet sizes and packet types to produce packet traces. These traces can be generated based on statistical models that can be parameterized for rate, type, length, average packet size, and so forth.

The prevalent idea in the networking research community is that self-similar processes best model network traffic [16]. The basis for this theory is that network traffic has been observed to be bursty across different time scales. The trace generator uses a self-similar traffic generator (SSTG) available in the public domain [13]. The traffic generator generates traffic trace files. The fields in each line of the trace files correspond to packet arrival time and packet size. The parameters for the traffic generator are rate (megabits per second), minimum packet size (bytes), maximum packet size (bytes), number of packets, and number of sources. The trace generator parses the packet traces produced by the SSTG and generates formatted packet traces. The traces are stored in the trace library along with a descriptor file. The descriptor file contains information about each trace in the library. The trace library and the trace generator form the static components in the simulator and are set up prior to running simulations.

3.2.2 Input Parser

The Input Parser selects the traces to read and present as input to the input interface unit. Packet streams are selected from the trace library and are linked with specific interfaces dynamically based on their configuration. Entries are read from the trace file and are buffered. Each entry or line in the trace file corresponds to a packet. The arrival of each packet is simulated at the input interface based on the arrival time recorded in the trace file.

3.2.3   Network Processing Component

The network processing component (NPC) implements the packet processing functions of the system. For our Toaster-based model, the NPC has two parts: the DMA component and the network processor.

The DMA component receives packets from the input interface and holds them in a temporary memory. The packet headers are separated from the packet body and directed to a network processor. The packet headers when returned are attached to their respective payloads and are queued in an external memory unit until they are ready to exit.

The NPC receives packet headers from the DMA component and buffers them for processing. The packet headers are processed based on the applications configured on the NPC. On completion, they are returned to the DMA component.

The NP in the simulator is modeled based on the Toaster network processor [12] architecture. The presence of an external DMA component is peculiar to the choice of NP. The Intel or IBM NPs would not need an additional DMA component [9, 10]. Theoretically, any NP can be modeled within the simulator, but Toaster offers itself as a flexible, robust, and independent platform. In addition, Toaster's shared memory system offers an interesting opportunity for study.

3.2.4   Output Interface and Meter

The output interface models the reverse functionality of the input interface. Packets are received from the DMA and are parsed to measure characteristics such as latency and jitter. The packets are then sent to the sink, where they are discarded.

3.3   THE CISCO TOASTER2

The Toaster2 network processor, developed at Cisco Systems, Inc., is an example of a parallel, pipelined multiprocessor system, shown in Figure 3.2. The processor is a 4×4 matrix of custom-designed processing elements (PEs). The PEs are laid out to form four parallel data flow pipelines. Each pipeline has four stages and corresponds to a row in the PE matrix. Buffers on either side of the pipeline provide a high-bandwidth exterior interface. The PEs in each column share a hierarchical memory system.

A Toaster processor works in conjunction with a DMA device. Packets are received at the DMA device and are translated into contexts, the Toaster unit of

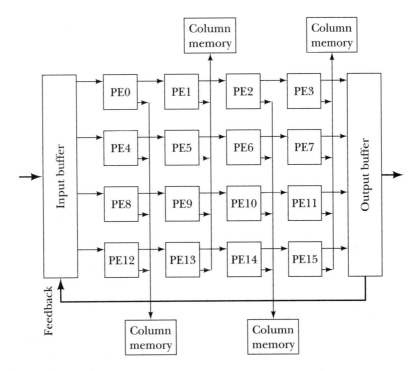

3.2   Toaster2 network processor.

FIGURE

data. A context is 128 bytes long and may contain the packet header and additional fields for control information transfer. The portion of the packet that is not a part of the context is buffered at the DMA device while the context is processed.

Once generated, contexts enter the Toaster processor and are queued in a buffer on the entry side of the data flow pipelines. At periodic intervals, each pipeline accepts a data unit for processing. As a context traverses the data flow pipeline, it is operated on by every PE in its path. In order to provide uniform context processing, each data flow pipeline executes the same processing code. To illustrate, an application may be divided into four sequential segments with each part residing on a Toaster PE in its relative position. The code is reproduced on each of the pipelines, and the treatment of a context is independent of the pipeline that it enters.

The time allowed for processing in a context in each PE is constrained and is called a *phase*. The length of a phase is programmable but is applied uniformly to all the PEs on the processor. In order to reduce contention for memory among the PEs in a column, the code being executed on each of them is skewed by an amount called a *phaselet*. The minimum length of the phaselet is guided by the number of cycles taken to transfer a context from an upstream stage to a downstream stage. In case a particular context requires more processing than can be accomplished by a single phase in each PE, Toaster provides a feedback path from the output buffer to the input buffer. This path can be used to pass contexts through the pipeline for additional processing.

Contexts leave the Toaster processor through an independent high-speed interface and re-enter the DMA device. Processed contexts are stripped off the control segment to leave just the packet headers that are reattached to their respective payloads.

The Toaster PE is a very long instruction word (VLIW) core with independent cache, 12 KB instruction RAM (IRAM), and two 4-stage instruction pipelines. The instruction set architecture (ISA) is native to Toaster and is optimized for network processing. This includes fast lookups, atomic memory operations, preset masks, and bit-level operations. A Toaster PE's instruction is 64 bits in length and is segmented, with each part being tied to a pipeline.

The memory system in Toaster is a multilevel hierarchy with data memory devices shared by each column. Local memory on each core is in the form of a register file, a 64-byte data cache, and space for context storage. Large data structures are stored in the column memory devices that are present on-chip and off-chip. The on-chip (internal) column memory (ICM) is typically a 16 KB SRAM device. The off-chip (external) column memory (XCM) is typically a 32 MB SDRAM device. A memory controller for each of these devices manages its accesses. The memory controller for the XCM is partitioned into two parts, each of which can support up to eight banks.

Memory accesses take the form of requests that travel from each core to independent FIFO queues in the memory controllers. Requests are processed based on bus and device availability; deadlocks are broken based on the row number of the originating core. Data is returned to the originating cores on 32-bit result buses available to each memory controller. The external memory controller splits the result bus equally between its two sections.

There are three basic memory operations: read, write, and prefetch. The selection of the memory device is determined by the address. Memory requests operate on 32 or 64 bits of data. The prefetch operation is essentially a nonblocking load. It is used to fetch data from the column memory and place it in the local cache, helping to hide the long latency of a load. Read operations never spawn a request to memory as long as data is available in the local cache.

Given the constraints imposed by the skewed execution of code, the best processing throughput is achieved by deterministically executing memory operations. They are hence carefully laid out in application code to minimize interference between the requests from the cores in each column. A lock controller is used to maintain data coherence.

The control point for the Toaster NP is located off-chip and could be any off-the-shelf microprocessor. It is connected to Toaster on a dedicated interface.

The Toaster NP operates with a 125 MHz clock. A phase length of 64 cycles would allow a context to enter the pipeline every 16 cycles (phaselet). This translates to a throughput of 7.8 million contexts per second.

3.4 IMPLEMENTATION OF ComNetSim

The design and implementation of the simulator have had a focus on modularity and scalability. Hence, the simulator is partitioned into separate components by way of an object-oriented approach such that they can be modified individually. The source code for the simulator comprises C++, PERL, and shell scripts. The simulator has been compiled on SunOS 5.6 using gcc version 2.9.

The following sections elaborate on the implementation details. The input parser and input interface are combined to form a single unit that is called the *input interface*. The output interface has the sink and meter built in. The NPC is treated as two separate components: DMA and NP. Each component is sufficiently complex to be treated as a separate structure within the simulator. Hence the dynamic portion of the simulator is reduced to four components: the input interface, DMA, network processor, and output interface.

3.4.1 Input Interface

The input interface brings to the simulator the functionality of link buffers. At startup, the physical interface's data processing rates and the size of the various link buffers are configured. The data processing rates correspond to the speeds of the incoming links. Based on this configuration, the trace data file is parsed to associate different trace files with each of the physical interfaces. The number of traces associated with each interface depends on the sum of the rates of all the traces associated with the interface. As packets in the trace files are exhausted, new files are associated to the interface to maintain the configured rate. This functionality is achieved by maintaining a linked list of streams for each physical interface. Whenever the aggregate rate of the physical interface drops below a configured rate, a *file_agent* function is called to make new trace file associations.

A *get_packet* function is used to simulate the packet arrival process at the ports. In this function, the trace file corresponding to each port is parsed to find all eligible packets. Eligible packets are those with an arrival time that is past the simulator's system time. The arrival time for a packet is computed as the sum of the arrival time obtained from the trace file and the start time for the trace. Once an eligible packet is found, a packet element is created and added to the corresponding buffer. Its fields are set based on the trace file data.

Once the packets enter the individual port buffers, they have to be funneled into a single link buffer that is hooked up to the DMA component. A simple round robin (RR) approach is inappropriate for ports operating at different speeds since it does not allow more packets from the higher speed link to be delivered. Applying, a weighted round robin (WRR) solves this problem. The weights for each of the port buffer queues are set in proportion to their rates. Bus constraints are in operation throughout the simulator. When packets are funneled into the multiplexed link queue, the number of bytes transferred per cycle is limited by bus width parameters.

3.4.2   The DMA Component

The DMA interface rids the network processor of the complex task of memory management. The DMA in the case of the simulator resembles a traffic light where data is directed from one section to another. It is the composite of many different queues with associated functions operating on them to effect movement of data.

The link input queue (LIQ) is the buffer for packets entering the DMA system. Packets are queued here until they can be transferred to the internal packet memory (IPM). As packets enter the IPM, their header is stripped off and used to form a Toaster context, consisting of control and data segments. The control segment contains fields that are used for communicating information between the DMA and Toaster. The data segment contains the entire packet header.

Every packet entering the DMA system causes a Toaster context to be generated. These contexts are queued in the to toaster context (TTC) buffer until they are ready to be transferred to the Toaster NP's input buffer. Since packet payloads are not handled by the simulator, the IPM and TTC queues are abstracted to form a composite queue that is referred to as the *IPM*.

Contexts are returned from the Toaster NP after processing. The control segments contain information that is used for enqueue and dequeue purposes. The control segment contains the queue number of the packet in the current context. Based on this information, that packet is stored in the external packet memory (XPM). In a conventional line card, the packet header would be attached to its payload residing in the IPM before being enqueued. The control segment also contains the queue number that has to receive outbound service. A packet is read from the corresponding XPM queue and placed in the fabric output queue (FOQ).

Bus constraints are applicable between the DMA and the simulator components to which it interfaces. This limits the number of bytes that can be transmitted per clock cycle. The limits are configurable from a common parameter file.

3.4.3   The Network Processor

The network processor is the heart of the simulator and is based on the Cisco Toaster network processor, described in Section 3.3.

Toaster Components

The basic structures within the Toaster framework are the input buffer, the core matrix, and the output buffer. The input buffer collects Toaster contexts from the DMA. The queued contexts are directed to one of the free Toaster rows when it becomes available. The rows form a context pipeline, and the columns share control memory. The output buffer collects contexts that exit from any of the rows. The queued contexts are sent to the DMA component.

Generic buffer   The functionality of the input and output buffers are similar to one another. A single buffer class is used of which the input and output buffers are instantiations. The buffer is primarily a queue structure. It has no intelligence built in. Contexts are added or deleted based on external commands.

Toaster core   The Toaster core is specified as an abstract base class with a virtual pipeline function. The specification of the pipeline function within a derived class determines the application running on top of the core. If the pipeline function is not defined, a context will pass through the core unaffected. This function is defined to simulate cycle accurate behavior of the Toaster core.

On a real system, each core in the Toaster framework executes applications in the form of microcode. The applications are time constrained and consume cycles for each instruction that is executed. In order to incorporate this in the simulator, the pipeline function is made to resemble a sequence of instructions, each of which is executed in finite time. (Figure 3.3 shows the pipeline function for a PE executing the scheduler code described in Section 3.5.) This is accomplished by organizing the source code within a *case* statement whose switch parameter is a cycle number. As a core steps through the same code in every phase, the cycle number corresponds to the temporal position within a phase. The code selected for execution is based only on the cycle number passed to the pipeline function as a parameter. A stall results when the code corresponding to a particular cycle fails to complete. This is modeled by not updating the cycle number for that core. Doing so results in code belonging to the stall cycle being re-executed until it becomes successful—that is, until the condition causing the stall is resolved.

The Toaster core class contains several control variables and the local cache. In addition, several functions operate as part of the toaster memory hierarchy. A virtual function is included that can be used to perform data checks.

Toaster column   The major components within this structure are the Toaster cores and the column-level memory system. The toaster cores are objects of the base abstract class (tmc). The number of cores in a column is a configurable parameter. The column memory system consists of the internal and external memory structures. Many functions perform the role of processing memory requests and play a support role in the memory state machine. The memory system is discussed later in this section. Other simulator-related functions perform time updates, print statistics, and make function calls to the Toaster cores.

The Toaster column structure also contains a lock mechanism for use by the cores. There are four column-level lock elements. Each element has two fields: lock identifier and lock busy fields. A Toaster core can request a lock for a specific identifier. This identifier could be a memory address or any value computed, such as a queue number. A lock is granted if the specified identifier is not already locked by another core and the lock tied to the requesting core is free.

Toaster   This is the top-level Toaster structure. The Toaster columns, the input and output buffers, are instantiated as objects in this structure. The configuration of the applications being executed on the framework takes place at this level. As mentioned previously, each application class is derived from the Toaster core class. The specification of the pipeline function within the derived class determines the functionality of the core—for example, a scheduling application would be coded within the pipeline virtual function of a derived class called *scheduler* (see Figure 3.3). Objects of this class would be instantiated within the Toaster structure. A pointer to each such application object would be instantiated and passed as a parameter to the column of that type. The pointers to the generic core declared at the column level can be associated with the derived class cores instantiated at the framework level. The Toaster structure contains functions that configure the internal and external memories for each column.

Function calls that are made to the column level execute functions every cycle. The parameters for this call include two important array structures: the cycle map and the context map.

Cycle map   This is a two-dimensional array that contains the current cycle number for each of the cores in the Toaster framework. The cycle map overlaps

```
// pipeline() method gives cycle-by-cycle work for PE's in a column

bool scheduler::pipeline(t2_context *context, unsigned int cycle)
{
  ...
  update_tmc_timer();      // update the TMC timer
  tmc_memory_pipeline();   // update the memory pipeline

  // cycle-specific processing
  switch (cycle) {

    case 0:
      // Set pdone to false to indicate a context in the core.
      // Flush tag buffer and set the context ptr.
      pdone = false;
      tb_flush();

      break;

    ...
    // an example showing a prefetch and a subsequent read

    case 31:  // prefetch the queue-specific info

      if (lock_q != 0)
        prefetch(_64BIT, 4, loc_q_var(WEIGHT, (q_tag_num*32 + qid)), pending);
      break;

    case 48:  // read the weight
      if (lock_q != 0) {
        result = read(_64BIT, 4, 0xdeadbeef, weight, q_prev_config);
        if (!result) break;
        weight_ctr = (weight & 0xFFF);
        ...
      }
    ...
    }
  }
  return(complete);  // return TRUE if cycle finished, FALSE if stall
}
```

3.3 Excerpts from the pipeline method for the WRR scheduler described in
Section 3.5.

FIGURE

the Toaster framework. Within the simulator, only a segment of the cycle map is passed to each column. This segment is a single-dimensional structure that contains the current cycle number for each of the cores in that column.

Context map   This is a two-dimensional array of pointers to Toaster contexts. This structure, like the cycle map, overlaps the Toaster framework. By maintaining a context map, movement of contexts between cores is facilitated since a "context switch" is merely a transitioning of pointer variables. This is accomplished at the Toaster framework level, and the cores do not have any role to play except for informing the top level when they are finished with a context. Information flow for this purpose begins at the core as a flag (pdone—processor done) that is set at the end of a phase. At the end of each cycle, the flag within each core is sampled. If the logical AND of all the pdone flags in a row is detected to be TRUE, a context switch is carried out, although an extra condition applies. This condition accounts for the phase difference that needs to be maintained between the processor rows.

Toaster Memory Hierarchy

The Toaster memory hierarchy is composed of three sections: tag buffer, internal column memory (ICM), and external column memory (XCM).

Tag buffer   The tag buffer is local to the Toaster cores and is akin to a software-managed register file with eight 64-bit wide entries. The tag buffer is the only memory unit to which the core has direct access. All memory requests pass through the tag buffer. Memory reads to the tag buffer are zero latency operations and are similar to reading local registers. Write and prefetch operations cause requests to be spawned to the column-level memory structures. The tag buffer is maintained as a structure within the Toaster core class (tmc). The tag buffer element has the following fields:

✦ *Address.* Memory address of the data stored in the tag element.

✦ *Valid bits 1 and 2.* Indicates validity of the two 32-bit data segments.

✦ *Pending.* Indicates if the tag element is waiting on a request that has been spawned to column-level memory.

✦ *Pending timer.* A simulator variable to compute latencies.

✦ *Data 1 and 2.* Data is stored as two 32-bit elements.

Internal column memory (ICM)   The ICM is a column-level memory structure that is physically located on-chip as an SRAM device. The ICM size is limited to 16 KB and is organized as 32-bit elements. Memory requests are received from each core in a column and serviced in the order of arrival. The ICM exists as a column-level structure in the t_column class.

External column memory (XCM)   The XCM is also a column-level memory but is located off-chip as an SDRAM device. The XCM size is upwards of 32 MB and is composed of eight banks, each line being 16 bits in length. A set of four banks shares a 32-bit request bus, and all eight banks share a 32-bit result bus. There are two possible addressing schemes for the banks: block and stream modes. In block mode, the address map is split into eight segments, and each segment corresponds to a bank. In stream mode, addresses stride banks continuously. While stream mode is preferred for storing and reading datagram structures, the bank mode would be preferred when operated as a control memory. Memory requests to the XCM experience a higher latency. The service order of the requests is the same as in the case of the ICM. The XCM exists as a column-level structure in the t_column class.

With respect to the simulator, memory operations start out as requests within the application code. Requests are for data of 4 or 8 bytes in length. Requests are of three different types:

1. *READ*. This is a request to read data from memory. The request can be for either 32 bits or 64 bits of data. The request contains the tag buffer element to be used and the location of the data in memory. Data is read from the tag buffer from the specified memory element if the element is marked as valid and the pending flag is not set. Thus, the management of data is up to the application code. If a read request is not fulfilled, the processor stalls until the situation is remedied. A read operation in the simulator does not spawn a request to main memory under any circumstance.

2. *PREFETCH*. A prefetch request fetches data from column memory and writes the data to the specified tag buffer element. These are nonspeculative requests for data and can be viewed as a nonblocking load. A prefetch request is spawned as a memory request to the column memory. The traversal of the request within the Toaster framework is modeled as a state machine. This is described in the next section.

3. *WRITE*. A write operation is spawned as a request to column memory. The request contains new data, the target address, and data width. A request has to include a reference to a tag buffer element. It is accepted only if the tag buffer element is not already in a pending state. WRITE and PREFETCH requests have access to separate buses to the column-level memory controllers.

Memory Request Handling

The software design of the Toaster framework realizes its shared memory design. By handling all the memory requests outside the cores from which they originate, they can be pooled and serviced at the column level. This brings to the fore the shared memory characteristic.

In a physical system, a memory request would pass between the originator and the memory in either or both directions depending on its type. During this passage, the request travels on several buses from one location to another and is decoded and serviced by a sequence of state machines. The software design models both of these aspects. Each memory request transitions through a sequence of states until its objective is met. These transitions are guided by

1. *Type and length.* The request can be a PREFETCH or a WRITE operation. The latency of the operation is also affected by the length of the request—32/64 bits.

2. *Tag buffer availability.* All requests have to target a tag buffer element. They are accepted by the tag buffer only if the target element is not already in a pending state. A pending state indicates that a previous request using the same element is incomplete.

3. *Memory location.* The request may be to the internal or external column memories. The latency of the request and the operations that need to be performed vary.

4. *Bank availability.* If the request is the external memory, the target bank needs to accept the request.

5. *Bus availability.* As requests have to pass from one device to another, they compete for usage of the buses.

6. *Resource prioritization.* Requests are prioritized based on the originating core and on an FCFS basis.

Requests to memory are made using explicit function calls. The WRITE and PREFETCH requests cause a memory request element to be generated. The fields of the memory request structure are set based on the parameters of the function call. The structure is then added to a request queue at the core.

The following are the states that a memory request encounters:

1. *ISSUE.* This state corresponds to a request that has been issued and is awaiting transmission to the tag buffer.

2. *LOCAL_BUS1.* Once an instruction references a memory location, a request is issued that traverses the local bus to the tag buffer. The WRITE and PREFETCH requests have a dedicated bus on the Toaster core, and requests travel on this bus. In the case of the simulator, the memory request is placed in this state before being added to the request queue.

3. *LOCAL_BUS2*. This state corresponds to the second cycle spent by the write or prefetch request on the channel to the tag buffer.

4. *TAG_BUFFER*. This state corresponds to a request that has been accepted by the tag buffer and is being communicated to the column memory controllers. The request is directed to the XCRAM or ICRAM controller based on the target address. Within the simulator, once a request transitions to this state, it is popped from the core-level queue and added to the ICM composite column-level queue or the XCM composite column-level queue, depending upon the target device. Requests are popped by calling the req_to_column() function.

5. *XCRAM_REQ*. A request enters this state if it has been issued to the XCM. A request to access the XCM is made if the bus to the XCM is found free. Once a request enters this state, the bus is locked as long as it takes to communicate the request.

6. *XCRAM_ACC*. A request to XCM transitions to this state while the XCM is being accessed. The time spent in this state is dependent on the SDRAM's configuration (CAS latency and the time between the active and read/write commands and the width of the request).

7. *XCRAM_RES*. Only prefetch requests transition to this state. This state accounts for the cycles consumed in communicating the data to the originating core.

8. *XCRAM_COMPLETE*. This is an artificial state to extract statistical data and is of relevance only within the simulator. The actual transfer of data takes place when the request is in this state. The target address is used to determine the index of the element and the bank in which it resides. A prefetch request results in data being read and written to the data elements in the memory request structure. A write request causes contents of the data elements in the request to be written to the XCM.

9. *ICRAM_REQ*. This is analogous to the XCRAM_REQ state.

10. *ICRAM_ACC*. This is analogous to the XCRAM_ACC state, though the latency of the operation is different because the ICM is an SRAM device.

11. *ICRAM_RES*. This is analogous to the XCRAM_RES state.

12. *ICRAM_COMPLETE*. This is analogous to the XCRAM_COMPLETE state.

When a request transitions to any of the memory states, a timer is set that corresponds to the number of cycles the request is supposed to spend in that state on a real device. On expiration of this timer, the request is ready to transition to its next state. Similar timers exist for the various communications buses and XCM banks. These resources are marked as free in the cycle that the corresponding timers expire. The structures corresponding to this functionality are bus_status and bank_status. Several "update" functions operate on these structures.

3.4.4   Output Interface

The output interface drains packets from the FOQ in the DMA module and processes them for information. The information recorded corresponds to the latency that the packet experienced within the system. The information is recorded on a per-queue basis. The queue information is the same as that used by the XPM. The latency metric also allows the jitter to be computed. Other statistics collected are maximum and minimum delay and delay jitter in the system. Once the statistics are updated, the packet is destroyed and the count of the number of packets passed through the system is updated.

3.5   APPLICATION DEVELOPMENT

One of the goals of the simulator is to implement a networking application on the Toaster platform. ComNetSim implements diffserv [2] components for the purpose of study. The basis for diffserv has found acceptance in the industry, and the components that form the framework are widely used in routing systems manufactured by different vendors [3]. In looking for a sample set of network applications that can be used for the purpose of study, diffserv components offer themselves as generic applications that will find use in any routing system independent of its position in a network.

Narasimhan [14] describes a baseline implementation of diffserv router components on a Linux system. The basic components in the system implemented in ComNetSim are classifier, conditioner, and scheduler [18].

3.5.1   Classifier

A packet entering a system needs to be classified to determine the policy used to service it. The classification can be based on two different techniques. A behavioral aggregate (BA) classifier uses the diffserv field [15] alone to establish the classification. The diffserv field is defined as the type-of-service (TOS) byte of an Internet protocol version 4 packet. It has two segments, one of which is currently unused. The useful segment of the field is 6 bits in length and starts from bit 7 of the TOS byte. This is called the *diffserv code point* (DSCP). A multifield (MF) [2] classifier uses a number of different characteristics of a packet to determine the flow to which the packet belongs. This can include the source address, destination address, DS field, protocol identifier, source port, and destination port. A large number of fields allow greater flexibility in configuration and provisioning of service.

A multifield classifier is implemented on column 0 of the Toaster framework. The fields used to find the flow identifier are the diffserv code point, input interface number, output interface number, and layer-4 protocol. Once a flow identifier is computed, a lookup is made to the ICM. The flow identifier hashes into the ICM to give a queue number for the packet. The queue number is stored as the enqueue queue number in the control segment of the Toaster context and is used by the subsequent processing elements.

3.5.2   Conditioner

A conditioner is a component that is used to measure the adherence of a flow to its configured service rates and mark the packets belonging to it, appropriately. Conditioners are inherently based on the leaky bucket algorithm [11]. The conditioners defined in diffserv literature are the single-rate two-color marker (SRTCM) [7] and the two-rate three-color marker (TRTCM) [8]. A conditioner can take the form of a marker, dropper, or shaper [14]. A marker merely marks a packet based on adherence, while a dropper discards a packet based on the same property. The shaper delays the passage of a packet through the system to compel the flow to which it belongs to adhere to the configured rate.

The conditioner is implemented on column 1 of the Toaster framework and takes the form of a TRTCM algorithm [8]. The algorithm operates in color-aware mode. Every queue configured has an entry in a conditioner data structure. The conditioner marks the degree of compliance to configured rate. The action performed based on this check is configurable. In this system, the color code is marked in bits 5 and 6 of the DSCP.

3.5.3   Scheduler

The scheduler is a critical piece of the diffserv system. A scheduler is an algorithm that distributes resources among different consumers. In a router, the resources correspond to limited buffer space and output bandwidth. The resource consumers are the various queues that need to be serviced. There are several different classes of scheduling. The goal is to provide guaranteed delay and bandwidth to every queue being serviced.

A weighted round robin (WRR) scheduler is implemented on the simulator's Toaster framework. A WRR scheduler can prioritize service for a number of queues so that each queue may be serviced differently. At startup, a weight is associated with every active queue in the system. This weight is determined based on the mean packet size for the queue, the mean flow rate for packets belonging to the queue, and the maximum rate configured. A weight counter is associated with every queue. In every scheduling interval, all nonempty queues with nonzero weight counters receive service. The weight counter for a queue is decremented at every instance that the queue is serviced. Once the weight counter for the queue with the maximum weight reaches zero or the number of rounds of service reaches the maximum weight, all the weight counters are reset to their original values. The round number is a count of the number of times a check for serviceability has passed any queue in the system. Its reset value is the maximum of the weights of all currently active queues.

When implemented on a Toaster framework, several constraints play a role in the design. The implementation of the algorithm needs to be scalable and completely deterministic. While operating on a constrained cycle budget, it is not possible to query nondeterministically a number of queues until a serviceable queue is found. A serviceable queue is one that has packets in waiting and a weight counter that is nonzero. The baseline requirement is that the accesses to the queue structure holding the weight counter be optimized. In order to meet the requirement, the Toaster memory hierarchy is leveraged to implement a two-level system to deterministically compute queue serviceability.

The implementation of the WRR algorithm requires three basic structures:

1. *Serviceability.* This control variable indicates if a queue is eligible for service.

2. *Nonemptiness.* This control variable indicates if a queue has packets to send. A queue that is serviceable, yet empty, does not need to be served.

3. *Weight counter.* For every instance a queue is served, the corresponding weight counter needs to be decremented. When this counter reaches zero, the queue is no longer serviceable.

The serviceability and nonempty states are stored in the ICM, which has a low read latency compared to the XCM. These are organized as two parallel structures. Each queue has representative bits to indicate serviceability and nonempty states. These are organized as 32 elements, each 32 bits in width, as shown in Figure 3.4. These structures are called *tags*. A consolidated structure is maintained that aggregates the information in the 32 tags. This structure is called a *block*. There are two block-level structures to record aggregate serviceability and nonempty states. Each bit in these structures corresponds to a tag element of the same type—that is, a bit in the serviceability block references a serviceability tag.

The weight counter is placed along with other queue variables (original weight and queue statistics) in a queue structure. There is a queue structure associated with every queue. Memory constraints and the need for scalability direct that the queue structures be stored in the XCM.

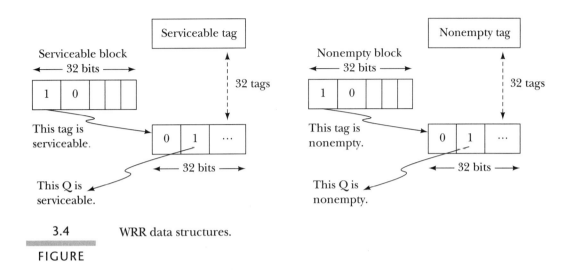

3.4

FIGURE

WRR data structures.

When the core implementing WRR processes a Toaster context, the serviceability and nonempty blocks are read from ICM. The logical AND of these structures provides a 32-bit computed block that indicates the presence of tag elements that are serviceable and nonempty. The bit location in the computed block corresponds to the location of tag elements referencing serviceable queues. The first tag element in the order of service is read from the ICM. The logical AND of serviceable and nonempty tag elements is used to determine the queue number to be serviced. The queue number corresponds to the first bit position of a serviceable and nonempty queue in the order of service. The corresponding queue structure is fetched from XCM and its weight counter updated. If the weight counter is reduced to zero, the queue is marked as nonserviceable. The service order is recorded as an integer quantity called *next_tag* or *next_q* as the case might be. When a queue is serviced, the next_q variable is incremented and stored along with the corresponding tag. Thus, in the next service round, the queue just serviced is ignored since the next_q quantity would cause it to be ignored. The next_tag quantity is used in an analogous manner but is associated with the block structure. At the end of a scheduling interval, the weight counters are not reset explicitly. Instead, a weight counter is reset if a referenced queue had been serviced in a prior scheduling interval. The same method is applied to the tag elements since it is inefficient to read every tag element and reset its serviceability bits. The serviceability block alone is reset at the end of the scheduling interval. The nonempty bit structures are controlled in parallel with the algorithm. It must be noted that the algorithm merely references the nonempty structure for information and does not manipulate its contents. The bits in the nonempty structure are set when a context corresponding to the queue referenced by the same bits passes through the framework. These bits are reset based on feedback information provided by the DMA component. This information is part of the control segment in the Toaster context.

A forced optimization that increases the efficiency of dequeue processing results in consecutive dequeues from the same queue. The optimization is forced since the update to the tag variable targeting a queue can occur only after the queue structure has been processed. The immediately adjacent core accesses the same tag structure, but the changes to the tag information are not visible to it. However, the queue structure itself is protected as it is read by the adjacent core late enough in a phase. In addition, a lock protects the queue structure. The new tag information will be visible to the third core in phase order. This ensures that the code does not spin on the same queue. The tag structure will reflect the correct state at the end of the second core's phase. In this situation, performance of high-rate queues will improve while that of low-rate queues may degrade. Low-rate queues that are dequeued consecutively are more likely to oscillate between empty and nonempty states. Dequeue requests to these are likely to be wasted since they are likely to occur when in an empty state.

3.6   ORGANIZATION AND CONFIGURATION

The organization of the simulator is intuitive and has three directories. The *trace* directory contains packet sequences generated using the *streamgen* shell script. The parameters for this script are minimum and maximum values for packet size, number of packets, and arrival rate (Mbps). A summary file (strlib.dat) is created during packet generation that is used by the dynamic component of the simulator. Files that are used in the setup of the dynamic component's applications are also generated during stream generation. The *source* directory contains all the source files for the simulator. Running *make* from this directory creates an executable called *sim*. Execution of the simulator is performed in the *test* directory, and output statistics are recorded in various files. The configuration of the simulator is managed by parameters defined in various header files in the source directory. Changes to the simulator parameters require a recompile of the source files in order to be visible.

3.7   EXPERIMENTS AND RESULTS

The experiments performed on the simulator seek to validate its implementation and the methodology. The results from two experiments are presented here. In the first experiment, the simulator is configured with four input interfaces, each at 622 Mbps (OC12). The results (see Table 3.1) show the queue performance metrics for identical tests run with an ideal and real Toaster shared memory system. The tests pass 100,000 packets through the simulator. The ideal memory system has zero latency and infinite bandwidth at the column level. This system eliminates scheduling conflicts and reduces lock contention. The number of packets, the total byte count, the average delay, and the average jitter are obtained for each stream. The average delay represents the average latency that a packet experiences from entry to exit. The average jitter is the average of difference in

Parameters		Ideal Toaster memory system				Real Toaster memory system			
Q number	Rate (Mbps)	Packets	Bytes	Average delay (ms)	Delay jitter (μs)	Packets	Bytes	Average delay (ms)	Delay jitter (μs)
56	510	5892	453684	5.76	7.82	5835	449295	14.93	12.88
120	510	6398	492646	7.65	7.72	6245	480865	16.88	11.79
144	610	1462	251464	1.57	4.79	1462	251464	2.70	6.48
184	510	7106	547162	5.11	7.25	7086	545622	12.58	13.14
248	510	7925	610225	4.67	6.58	8075	621775	10.49	8.93
521	550	6534	724032	12.19	9.10	5991	665889	21.31	12.31
533	550	3270	287760	2.81	9.28	3990	351120	5.21	16.13
543	500	5262	541986	17.32	9.05	4918	506554	27.15	15.60
585	550	5848	653734	18.15	9.70	5506	624664	26.92	14.25
597	550	2180	191840	1.96	8.27	2725	239800	4.48	12.26
607	500	3995	411485	5.61	7.90	4235	436205	11.80	12.07
649	550	5276	605114	16.91	10.15	5039	584969	25.90	15.29
661	550	2725	239800	2.19	9.05	3270	287760	4.32	15.11
671	500	4139	426317	7.83	9.84	4014	413442	17.51	14.77
713	550	4793	555230	16.13	10.56	4599	523026	25.27	14.46
725	550	2484	218592	2.81	9.92	3144	276672	5.58	18.52
735	500	3858	397374	14.27	9.89	3806	392018	23.67	14.87
798	580	4020	554760	5.95	9.82	4057	559866	14.99	13.75
862	580	5385	743130	8.77	9.56	5136	708768	18.37	14.36
926	580	4976	686688	5.87	9.70	4824	665712	15.34	17.16
990	580	6473	893274	8.93	8.72	6044	834072	18.71	13.38

3.1   Queue performance metrics on simulated Toaster models.

TABLE

Q number	Rate (Mbps)	Packets	Average delay (ms)
48	580	538	0.35
156	590	510	0.02
176	580	64	0.16
240	580	1423	0.11
522	590	527	0.01
561	550	457	1.00
569	590	85	0.52
588	570	1165	0.04
625	550	525	0.51
633	590	509	2.51
652	570	1026	0.30
689	550	1050	0.67
697	590	545	1.63
876	570	539	0.59
940	570	856	0.79
1004	570	182	0.99

Contexts passed 11577

3.2

TABLE

High-rate queue metrics.

latencies of any two consecutive packets on a particular queue. The results show the effect of the memory system on the latency and jitter characteristics. The effect of stall cycles due to imperfectly scheduled code and the need to maintain coherence of data is greatly reduced in the ideal memory system. The variation in the latency for queues within each simulation run is actually an increase in latency due to queuing delay as the simulation progresses.

In the second experiment, a large number of flows are configured. This test demonstrates that the performance of the system is affected by the configuration of input traffic vectors. The test has two parts with only the input traffic configuration being changed. The input ports are configured as OC12 interfaces. In the first test, the input traffic flows are of a high rate above 500 Mbps. The second test uses several low-rate flows whose average rates are about 100 Mbps. The test shows that the average latencies for the high-rate flows (see Table 3.2) are less than latencies for the low-rate flows (see Table 3.3). The total number of contexts passed through the Toaster cores is higher in the case of the low-rate flows. This difference in performance comes about due to the peculiarity of the implementa-

Q number	Rate (Mbps)	Packets	Average delay (ms)
137	100	1519	4.72
201	100	1520	4.72
523	100	176	7.94
561	100	424	0.01
562	100	160	8.11
583	100	207	3.65
625	100	424	1.23
626	100	158	8.14
651	100	177	7.89
711	100	206	3.64
715	100	178	7.81
753	100	424	0.01
754	100	161	8.03
781	100	159	7.64
802	100	304	7.34
833	100	569	3.98
860	100	224	7.28
874	100	879	4.06
897	100	572	3.94
909	100	159	7.52
930	100	301	7.39
938	100	880	4.03
988	100	220	7.51

Contexts passed 26508

3.3   Low-rate queue metrics.

TABLE

tion of the scheduling algorithm that tends to favor high-rate queues. Consecutive dequeues are better utilized by high-rate flows that tend to have nonempty queues.

The experiments show that a variation in the traffic patterns or the hardware architecture greatly influences the performance of the system. The same benefits cannot be realized by running a microkernel on a conventional processor since that would not include any of the parameters introduced by the traffic patterns and the memory system of the processor architecture. The same argument applies to the study of an application on this simulator. The environment for simulating the applications introduces realistic constraints on resource usage that would not be readily available on any generic simulator.

3.8   CONCLUSION AND FUTURE WORK

This paper presented a holistic methodology to study architectures for network processing. A cycle accurate simulator was implemented that will allow the study of the interactive nature of network traffic, algorithms, and hardware platforms. The implementation of a network processor architecture such as Toaster for use in the simulator was discussed. Diffserv applications were developed for the Toaster platform in the simulator, and an innovative implementation of the weighted round robin scheduling algorithm with support for 1024 queues was proposed. The development of the applications accounted for control memory design and optimization of memory references. The use of the simulator in studying the combined effects of network traffic, application, and architecture was shown. While the current generation of the simulator is decidedly Toaster specific, it has to be acknowledged that the holistic methodology used in this paper can find a role in the study of network hardware architectures. There are a wide variety of network processors in development today [17]. The range of systems and the need for accurate simulation precludes us from building an entirely generic simulator. Also, it is not possible to study a network processor in isolation. As demonstrated, the performance of a network processing system depends on the applications and the input traffic vectors.

The methodology used in this simulator could be extended to implement application code that may be compiled and executed on an execution-based processor simulator. The processor simulator could be combined with a system that can retrieve packets from traces and simulate their arrival. The design space in this case would include the application code, compiler, instruction set architecture, processor paradigms, memory system, and traffic generator.

The simulator can be used to verify and study performance of a network processor architecture using load experiments. Two types of experiments can be performed: The system can be tested for a specific traffic configuration to verify performance for a network processor system. The point at which the internal system buffers begin to overflow would indicate the maximum traffic load that can be handled by the system. The effect on the system's performance under incremental load can be studied by varying the traffic configuration.

REFERENCES

[1]   J. Balkman, P. Gupta, and N. McKeown, "Packet Lookup and Classification Simulator (PALAC)," *klamath.stanford.edu/tools/PALAC/SRC/*.

[2]   S. Blake, D. Black, M. Carlson, E. Davies, Z. Wang, and W. Weiss, "An Architecture for Differentiated Services," IETF RFC 2475, December 1998.

[3]   Cisco 7600 Optical Services Router (OSR), *www.cisco.com/warp/public/3/ca/press/us_opticalrouter.html*.

[4]   The Cooperative Association for Internet Data Analysis, *www.caida.org*.

[5]   P. Crowley, M. Fiuczynski, J. Baer, and B. Bershad, "Characterizing Processor Architectures for Programmable Network Interfaces," *Proceedings of the 2000 International Conference on Supercomputing*, May 2000.

[6]   S. Floyd, and S. Paxson, "Difficulties in Simulating the Internet," *IEEE/ACM Transactions on Networking*, 9(4), pp. 392–403, August 2001.

[7]   J. Heinanen, and R. Guerin, "A Single Rate Three Color Marker," IETF RFC 2697, September 1999.

[8]   J. Heinanen, and R. Guerin, "A Two Rate Three Color Marker," IETF RFC 2698, September 1999.

[9]   IBM Technical Library, Networking Technology White Papers, *www3.ibm.com/chips/techlib/techlib.nsf/productfamilies/Networking_Technology*.

[10]   Intel Internet Exchange Architecture, *developer.intel.com/design/ixa/whitepapers/ixapi.htm*.

[11]   S. Keshav, *An Engineering Approach to Computer Networking: ATM Networks, the Internet and the Telephone Network*, Addison-Wesley, 1997.

[12]   K. Key et al., Toaster2 Hardware Functional Specification, Cisco Systems, 2000.

[13]   G. Kramer, "Generator of Self-Similar Network Traffic," Networks Research Lab, Dept. of Computer Science, University of California, Davis, *wwwcsif.cs.ucdavis.edu/~kramer/code/trf_gen2.html*.

[14]   K. Narasimhan, "An Implementation of Differentiated Services in a Linux Environment," Masters thesis, North Carolina State University, December 2000.

[15]   K. Nichols, S. Blake, F. Baker, and D. Black, "Definition of the Differentiated Services Field (DS Field) in the IPv4 and IPv6 Headers," IETF RFC 2474, December 1998.

[16]   K. Park, and W. Willinger, "Self-similar network traffic: An overview," In K. Park and W. Willinger, editors, *Self-Similar Network Traffic and Performance Evaluation*, Wiley Interscience, 2000.

[17]   N. Shah, "Understanding Network Processors," *www-cad.eecs.berkeley.edu/~niraj/papers/UnderstandingNPs.pdf*, Version 1, September 2001.

[18]   D. Suryanarayanan, "A Methodology for Studying Network Processing Architectures," Masters thesis, North Carolina State University, July 2001.

[19]   UCB/LBNL/VINT Network Simulator—ns (version 2), *www-mash.cs.berkeley.edu/ns*.

[20]   T. Wolf, and M. Franklin, "CommBench—A Telecommunications Benchmark for Network Processors," *IEEE International Symposium on Performance Analysis of Systems and Software*, April 2000.

Design Space Exploration of Network Processor Architectures

**Lothar Thiele, Samarjit Chakraborty,
Matthias Gries, Simon Künzli**
Computer Engineering and Networks Laboratory,
Swiss Federal Institute of Technology (ETH), Zürich, Switzerland

Network processors usually consist of multiple processing units such as CPU cores, microengines, and dedicated hardware for computing-intensive tasks such as header parsing, table lookup, and encryption/decryption. Together with these, there are also memory units, caches, interconnections, and I/O interfaces. Following a system-on-a-chip (SoC) design method, these resources are put on a single chip and must interoperate to perform packet processing tasks at line speed. The process of determining the optimal hardware and software architecture for such processors includes issues involving resource allocation and partitioning, and the architecture design should take into account different packet processing functions, task scheduling options, information about the packet forms, and the QoS guarantees that the processor should be able to meet. The available chip area for putting the different components together might be restricted, imposing additional constraints. Further, network processors may be used for many different application scenarios such as those arising in backbone and access networks. Whereas backbone networks can be characterized by very high throughput demands but relatively simple processing requirements per packet, access networks show lower throughput demands but high computational requirements for each packet. The architecture exploration and evaluation of network processors therefore pose many interesting challenges and involve many tradeoffs and a complex interplay between hardware and software.

There are several characteristics that are specific to the packet processing domain, and these do not arise in other application areas such as classical digital signal processing (although both domains involve the processing of event streams). The packet processing case is concerned with the processing of interleaved flows of data packets, where for each flow a certain sequence of tasks must be executed (so there are usually no recurrent or iterative computations), the tasks are of high granularity, and they are often scheduled dynamically at runtime. Due to this difference with other known target domains for system-level design space exploration, several new questions arise: How should packet streams, task structures, and hardware and software resources be appropriately modeled? How can the performance of a network processor architecture be determined in the case of several (possibly conflicting) usage scenarios? Since the design space can be very large, what kind of strategy should be used to efficiently explore all options and to obtain a reasonable compromise between various conflicting criteria?

In this paper, we present a framework for the design space exploration of embedded systems operating on such flows of packets where we address the preceding issues. The underlying principles of our approach can be outlined as follows:

+ Our framework consists of a task and a resource model, and a *real-time calculus* [2, 20] for reasoning about packet flows and their processing. The task model represents the different packet processing functions such as header processing, encryption, and processing for special packets such as voice and video. The resource model captures the information about different available hardware resources, the possible mappings of packet processing functions to these resources, and the associated costs. There is also the information about different flows (e.g., their burstiness and long-term arrival rates), which are specified using their *arrival curves* [6] and possible deadlines within which the packets must be processed.

+ The design space exploration is posed as a multiobjective optimization problem. There are different conflicting criteria such as chip area, on-chip memory requirements, and performance (e.g., the throughput and the number of flow classes that can be supported). The output is a set of different hardware/software architectures representing the different tradeoffs.

+ Given any architecture, the calculus associated with the framework is used to analytically determine properties such as delay and throughput experienced by different flows, taking into consideration the underlying scheduling disciplines at the different resources. An exploration strategy comes up with possible alternatives from the design space, which are evaluated using our calculus, and the feedback guides further exploration.

To speed up the exploration, unlike previous approaches, we use several linear approximations in the real-time calculus so that the different system properties can be quickly estimated. We also show how different resources with possibly different scheduling strategies, and communication resources with different arbitration mechanisms, can be combined to construct a *scheduling network*, which allows us to determine, among other things, the size of shared as well as per-resource memory. Our multiobjective design space exploration takes into account the fact that there can be different scenarios in which the processor may be deployed, and this is modeled in the form of different *usage scenarios*. Lastly, the way we allocate the multiple processing units and the memory units, our optimization strategy also optimizes the load balancing between them.

Most of the previous work on modeling, performance evaluation, and design space exploration of network processors (such as [5] and [4]) relied on simulation techniques, where different architectures are simulated and evaluated using benchmark workloads. The work in [5] and [4] addresses issues related to identifying appropriate workloads and modeling frameworks to aid full system analysis and evaluation using simulation. An analytical performance model for network processors was proposed in [21] and [9]. Different network processor architectures can be evaluated on benchmark workloads using this analytical model. When the search space being explored is large, it might be too expensive to evaluate all the alternatives using simulation, or even by using performance models whose input is a benchmark workload. In contrast to these approaches, different architectures in our framework are evaluated on the basis of analytical models for both the input traffic (workload) and the performance of an architecture. Based on these models, we determine bounds on the resource requirements of a processor architecture (e.g., memory and cache sizes), and QoS parameters (e.g., delay experienced by packets). The focus here is on a high level of abstraction, where the goal is to quickly identify interesting architectures that can be further evaluated (e.g., by simulation) taking lower-level details into account.

Recent research on packet processors has dealt with task models [19], task scheduling [15], operating system issues [14], and packet processor architectures [10, 17]. All of these issues collectively play a role in different phases of the design space exploration of such devices, and the relevant ones in the context of our abstraction level have been considered in this paper.

Our previous attempts to perform system-level design space exploration of packet processing architectures have been described in [19] and [18]. In [19], the exploration is performed by an integer linear program and the estimation of the system properties is limited to very simple models. The complexity of the underlying optimization problem prevents the use of this method for realistic design problems. Moreover, the memory requirements are only analyzed for a shared memory architecture, and the overhead for communication between computational resources is not considered at all. Some of these shortcomings were overcome in [18] by using a multiobjective evolutionary algorithm for the design space exploration, instead of integer linear programming. In this paper, we extend the work presented in [18] first by modeling communication resources (e.g., buses and bus arbitration policies), and then by allowing for local memories to be associated with processing resources. We also present here a detailed design problem and show all the tradeoffs involved.

Related work on the design space exploration of SoC communication architectures includes [11] (and the references therein). However, in contrast to our approach, the methods used in these papers largely rely on simulation.

The next section formally describes the task and the resource structures, following which we describe the framework for analytically evaluating prospective candidate architectures in Section 4.2. Section 4.3 describes techniques for the multiobjective design space exploration, and a case study illustrating our methodology is presented in Section 4.4.

4.1 MODELS FOR STREAMS, TASKS, AND RESOURCES

In this section, we describe models for the workload generated by packet flows, and task structures associated with the processing of such flows. We then make use of these models to describe our network processor architectures.

4.1.1 Workload Generated by Packet Streams

A network processor operates on interleaved streams of packets that enter the device. In order to determine the load on the processing device, it is necessary to know the number of packets arriving per time unit. This information can be formalized using *arrival curves*, which allow us to derive deterministic bounds on the workload. Such arrival curves are commonly used in the networking area for characterizing traffic flows (e.g., the T-SPEC model [16] of the IETF).

Let $R(t)$ denote the number of packets that have arrived from a flow f during the time interval $[0, t]$.

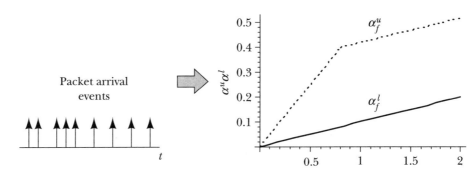

4.1

4.1   Representation of arrival curves.

FIGURE

Definition 4.1: Arrival Curves   For any flow f, the lower arrival curve α_f^l and the upper arrival curve α_f^u satisfy the relation

$$\alpha_f^l(t - s) \leq R(t) - R(s) \leq \alpha_f^u(t - s) \qquad \forall 0 \leq s \leq t$$

$\alpha_f^l(\Delta)$ gives a lower bound on the number of packets that might arrive from a flow f within any time interval of length Δ. Likewise, $\alpha_f^u(\Delta)$ gives an upper bound on the number of packets that might arrive from a flow f within any time interval of length Δ. Hence, for all $\Delta > 0$, $\alpha_f^l(\Delta) \leq \alpha_f^u(\Delta)$ and $\alpha_f^l(0) = \alpha_f^u(0) = 0$. Therefore, within any time interval of length $\Delta \in \mathbb{R}_{\geq 0}$, the number of packets arriving from a flow f is greater than or equal to $\alpha_f^l(\Delta)$, and less than or equal to $\alpha_f^u(\Delta)$.   ■

Arrival curves may be determined from service-level agreements (e.g., specified using T-SPECs), by analysis of the traffic source or by traffic measurement. Figure 4.1 shows an example of an arrival curve.

All packets belonging to the same flow are processed in the same way—that is, a fixed set of tasks are executed on each packet in a predefined order. This task structure characterizing packet processing functions can be described as follows.

Definition 4.2: Task Structure   Let F be a set of flows and T be a set of tasks. To each flow $f \in F$ there is an associated directed acyclic graph $G(f) = (V(f), E(f))$ with task nodes $V(f) \subseteq T$ and edges $E(f)$. The tasks $t \in V(f)$ must be executed for each packet of flow f while respecting the precedence relations in $E(f)$.   ■

Tasks associated with different flows can be combined into one *conditional task graph*, where, depending on the flow to which a packet belongs, the packet takes different paths through the graph (see Figure 4.12 for an example). Such tasks are implemented on *resources* that might be general CPUs, dedicated processors, and the like.

Definition 4.3: Deadlines and Requests   To each flow $f \in F$, there is associated an end-to-end deadline d_f, denoting the maximum time by which any packet of this flow has to be processed after its arrival. If a task t can be executed on a resource s, then it creates a "request," denoting the processing requirement due to task t processing a packet on the resource s. For example, this request might represent the number of processor cycles or instructions required for processing a packet with the function described by task t. Therefore, for all possible task-to-resource bindings, there exist a request $w(t, s) \in \mathbb{R}_{\geq 0}$.   ∎

As defined earlier, the end-to-end deadline d_f denotes the maximum allowed time span from the arrival of any packet from flow f until the end of the execution of the last task for that packet.

A network processor may be used in a variety of different *usage scenarios*, having different load conditions and delay constraints on the processing of packets. These different scenarios might lead to conflicting design objectives for the network processor. Our design space exploration scheme presented in this paper takes these conflicting goals into account and outputs all design tradeoffs (this is shown in Section 4.3). The set of packet flows belonging to each scenario might be different, and they might have different arrival curves. Additionally, for each scenario, there might be a different constraint on the memory available in the network processor (i.e., the maximum number of packets that might be stored in the processor at any point in time), and there might be different maximum allowable delays associated with each flow. These are formally defined in Section 4.3. Until then, unless otherwise mentioned, we assume that there is only one usage scenario.

4.1.2   System Architecture

Network processors are usually heterogeneous in nature, consisting of one or more CPU cores and dedicated processing units. Simple tasks with high data rate requirements are executed on dedicated or application-specific instruction set components, whereas more complicated tasks are implemented in software running on (homogeneous) multiprocessors. In the later case, runtime scheduling methods might be used to fairly share the available resources among packets be-

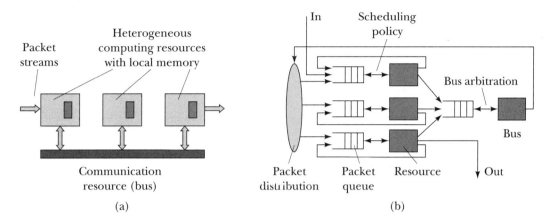

Example of a physical (a) and logical (b) structure of a network processor architecture.

longing to the different flows, and also to meet deadline requirements of real-time flows such as voice or video [3]. Each computation resource might make use of dedicated local memory such as on-chip embedded memory. If two neighboring tasks of a task graph are implemented on the same processing resource, then they do not suffer from any communication overhead. However, when such tasks are implemented on different resources, they must communicate using a communication resource (e.g., a bus). We would like to point out here that the task structure defined by Definition 4.2 may therefore also contain tasks that represent *communication tasks*. In contrast to tasks (e.g., header processing) where the load is defined by the number of packets, requests for communication tasks may be specified in terms of "number of bytes" involved in the transfer. Also note that the introduction of communication tasks requires the knowledge of the bindings of tasks to resources. How this is incorporated into our framework in a transparent way for the user is described in Section 4.2.3. Our consideration of buses and local memories in the architecture exploration allows for more realistic representation of typical network processors and generalizes the models presented in the previous work on this topic [18]. A sketch of a heterogeneous architecture with different packet processing paths is shown in Figure 4.2(a).

We describe the computation or communication capabilities of resources using *service curves*. These curves are similar to the arrival curves and denote the maximum and minimum possible "service" that can be offered by a resource over any time interval of a specified length. For example, let $C(t)$ denote the number

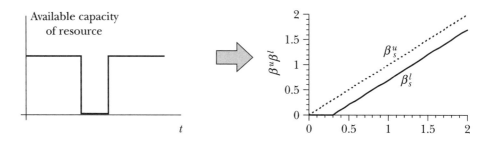

4.3

Representation of service curves.

FIGURE

of packets that can be processed by a resource s during the time interval $[0, t]$. Then the upper and lower service curves β_s^u and β_s^l corresponding to this resource satisfy the inequality:

$$\beta_s^l(t - s) \le C(t) - C(s) \le \beta_s^u(t - s) \qquad \forall 0 \le s \le t$$

and $\beta_s^l(0) = \beta_s^u(0) = 0$.

Definition 4.4: Service Curves   For any $\Delta \in \mathbb{R}_{\ge 0}$ and any resource s belonging to a set of available resources S, the lower service curve $\beta_s^l(\Delta)$ is a lower bound on the number of computing/communication units available from resource s over any time interval of length Δ. Similarly, the upper service curve $\beta_s^u(\Delta)$ denotes an upper bound on the number of computing/communication units available from resource s over any time interval of length Δ. Therefore, the computing/communication units available from resource s over any time interval of length Δ is always greater than or equal to $\beta_s^l(\Delta)$ and less than or equal to $\beta_s^u(\Delta)$.   ∎

Clearly, if a resource is loaded with the execution of certain tasks, then the available computing power after serving these tasks will be less than the power originally available; moreover, the computing power might vary over time intervals, depending on the executing pattern of the tasks. An example of $\beta_s^l(\Delta)$ and $\beta_s^u(\Delta)$ is shown in Figure 4.3.

Finally, the *set of available resources* and the task to resource mappings can be formally defined as follows.

Definition 4.5: Resources   We define a set of resource types S. To each type $s \in S$ there is associated a relative implementation cost $cost(s) \in \mathbb{R}_{\ge 0}$ and the number of available instances $inst(s) \in \mathbb{Z}_{\ge 0}$. To each resource instance there is associated a finite set of scheduling policies $sched(s)$ that the component supports, a lower service curve β_s^l, and an upper service curve β_s^u.   ∎

Definition 4.6: Task to Resource Mapping The mapping relation $M \subseteq T \times S$ defines possible mappings of tasks to resource types; that is, if $(t, s) \in M$, then task t could be executed on resource type s. ∎

If $(t, s) \in M$—that is, the task t can be executed on a resource of type s—then a *request* $w(t, s) \in \mathbb{R}_{\geq 0}$ is associated with this mapping (see Definition 4.3).

Therefore, our model of a feasible system architecture is based on the following:

✦ Available resource types including their processing or communication capabilities and performance described by service curves

✦ *Costs* for implementing a resource on the network processor, for example, the chip area required for the resource

✦ The scheduling/bus arbitration policies and associated parameters

The logical structure of a system architecture is shown in Figure 4.2(b). Here we see that the processing components have associated memories that store packets that are waiting for the next task to be executed on them. A scheduling policy associated with the processing component selects a packet and starts the execution. The processing of the current packet may be preempted in favor of a task for processing another packet. After the execution of a task, a packet may be reinserted into the input queue of the current resource, to be processed by the next task that also executes on the same resource. Alternatively, the packet may be redistributed to another resource using a bus. Without restricting the applicability of our approach, we limit the description of suitable architectures to a single bus in order to simplify the explanation.

4.2 ANALYSIS USING A SCHEDULING NETWORK

Although we have chosen a particularly simple cost model, it is not obvious how to determine for any resource the maximum number of stored packets in it waiting to be processed at any point in time. Neither is it clear how to determine the maximum end-to-end delays experienced by the packets since all packet flows share common resources. The computation time for a task t depends on its request $w(t, s)$, on the available processing power of the resource, that is, β_s^l and β_s^u, and on the scheduling policy applied. In addition, as the packets may flow from one resource to the next one, there may be intermediate bursts and packet jams, making the computations of the packet delays and the memory requirements nontrivial. Interestingly, we show that there exists a computationally efficient method to derive provably correct bounds on the end-to-end delays of packets and the required memory for each computation and communication.

We exploit the fact that characteristic chains of tasks are executed for each packet flow and that all the flows are processed independently of each other. Based on this knowledge, we construct a *scheduling network*, where the *real-time calculus* (based on arrival and service curves) is applied from node to node in order to derive deterministic bounds. Note that the execution of constant chains of tasks is one of the major characteristics in the network processing domain that cannot be found in any other domains (e.g., digital signal processing).

The basis for the determination of end-to-end delays and memory requirements is the description of packet flows in communication networks using a network calculus (see [6] for an introduction). Recently, this approach has been reformulated in an algebraic setting in [2]. In [20], a comparable approach has been used to describe the behavior of processing resources.

4.2.1   Building Blocks of the Scheduling Network

The basic idea behind our performance estimation (e.g., end-to-end delays experienced by packets when processed by a given architecture, and memory requirements of the architecture assuming a set of input traffic flows) is the provision for a network theoretic view of the system architecture. More precisely, packet flows and resource streams flow through a network of processing and communication resource nodes and thereby adapt their (output) arrival curves (of the packet flows) and (remaining) service curves (of the resources), respectively. Inputs to a network node are the arrival curves of packet flows and the service curves of the corresponding resource that the node is representing. The outputs describe the resulting arrival curves of the processed packet flows and the remaining service curves of the (partly) used resource. These resulting arrival and service curves can then serve as inputs to other nodes of the scheduling network. As an example, see Figure 4.16, which is explained in detail later.

In order to understand the basic concept, let us first describe a very simple example of such a node, namely, the preemptive processing of packets from one flow by a single processing resource. Following the discussion of Figure 4.2, a packet memory is attached to a processing resource that stores those packets that have to wait to be processed. In [19], the following theorem has been derived that describes the processing of a packet flow in terms of the already defined arrival and service curves.

Theorem 4.1   Given a packet flow described by the arrival curves α^l and α^u and a resource stream described by the service curves β^l and β^u, the following expressions bound the arrival curve of the processed packet flow and the remaining service of the resource node. $\alpha^{l'}$ and $\alpha^{u'}$ denote the lower and the upper arrival curve, respectively, of the processed flow, and $\beta^{l'}$ and $\beta^{u'}$ denote the lower and upper remaining service curve, respectively, of the resource node.

$$\alpha^{l'}(\Delta) = \inf_{0 \le u \le \Delta} \left\{ \alpha^l(u) + \beta^l(\Delta - u) \right\} \tag{4.1}$$

$$\alpha^{u'}(\Delta) = \inf_{0 \le u \le \Delta} \{ \sup_{v \ge 0} \left\{ \alpha^u(u + v) - \beta^l(v) \right\}$$

$$+ \beta^u(\Delta - u), \beta^u(\Delta) \} \tag{4.2}$$

$$\beta^{l'}(\Delta) = \sup_{0 \le u \le \Delta} \left\{ \beta^l(u) - \alpha^u(u) \right\} \tag{4.3}$$

$$\beta^{u'}(\Delta) = \sup_{0 \le u \le \Delta} \left\{ \beta^u(u) - \alpha^l(u) \right\} \tag{4.4}$$

■

Note that the arrival curve as used describes bounds on the *computing request* and *not* on the *number of packets*. In Figure 4.4, an example for remaining arrival and service curves is given. As we deal with packet flows in the system architecture, we need to convert packets to their corresponding computing requests. Given bounds on a packet flows of the form $[\overline{\alpha}^l, \overline{\alpha}^u]$, we can determine bounds on the related computing requests

$$[\alpha^l, \alpha^u] = [w\overline{\alpha}^l, w\overline{\alpha}^u] \tag{4.5}$$

considering the request w for each packet (representing the processing requirement for a packet). The notation $[\alpha^l, \alpha^u]$ represents the fact that α^l and α^u are lower and upper curves of the same flow.

The conversion for the output flow is more involved since we usually suppose that a next component can start processing after the whole packet has arrived.

$$[\overline{\alpha}^{l'}, \overline{\alpha}^{u'}] = [\lfloor \alpha^{l'}/w \rfloor, \lceil \alpha^{u'}/w \rceil] \tag{4.6}$$

The whole transformation is depicted in Figure 4.5.

4.2.2　Scheduling Policies

In this section, we describe how to extend the calculation of the resulting processed arrival curves (for packet flows) and the remaining service curves (for resource flows), to the case involving multiple flows and resources. As packets from several flows arrive at a resource, they are served in an order determined by the scheduling policy. The resulting arrival curves and remaining service curves

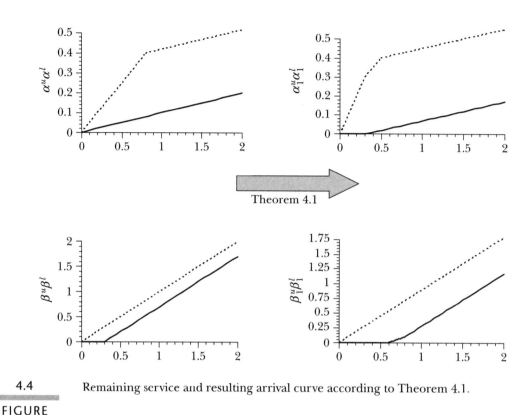

Theorem 4.1

4.4

FIGURE

Remaining service and resulting arrival curve according to Theorem 4.1.

are dependent on this scheduling policy. First, we give the results for the preemptive version of *fixed priority scheduling*, and then for the *generalized processor sharing scheduling*.

Fixed Priority Scheduling

For the fixed priority scheme, let us assume that there is a set of flows $f_1, \ldots, f_n$, and a resource s that serves these flows in the order of decreasing priority. Flow f_1 has the highest priority, and flow f_n the lowest. For each packet of the flow f_i, a task t_i must be executed on the resource s, and this creates a demand (or request) equal to $w(t_i, s)$ on s. We denote $w(t_i, s)$ by w_i. With each flow f_i is associated its upper and lower (packet) arrival curves $\overline{\alpha}_i^u$ and $\overline{\alpha}_i^l$. For the resource s, the flow f_i is served using the upper and lower service curves β_i^u and β_i^l, respectively. The resource s in its unloaded state is described by the service curves β^u and β^l.

Because of the fixed priority scheme, the resource s serves the flows in the order of decreasing priority, and the resulting arrival curves of the flows and the

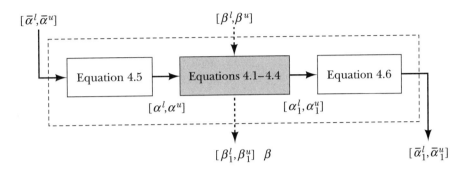

$[\bar{\alpha}^l, \bar{\alpha}^u]$ $[\beta^l, \beta^u]$

Equation 4.5   Equations 4.1–4.4   Equation 4.6

$[\alpha^l, \alpha^u]$ $[\alpha_1^l, \alpha_1^u]$

$[\beta_1^l, \beta_1^u]$ β $[\bar{\alpha}_1^l, \bar{\alpha}_1^u]$

4.5

FIGURE

Block diagram showing the transformation of packet flows and resource streams by a processing device. The dotted arrows represent the resource flow; the others show the flow of packets (or the corresponding requests).

remaining service curve of the resource is computed according to Theorem 4.1. In order to have compatible units, we need first to multiply the arrival curves with the demand for each task, namely w_i. Correspondingly, the flow leaving the resource must be divided by w_i. If the subsequent units that use the outgoing packets flowing out of s can start processing only after the whole task has been finished, then we need to apply the floor/ceiling function to the outgoing flows (depending on whether it is the lower or upper curve). Therefore, the outgoing arrival curves are transformed according to $\bar{\alpha}_i^{u'}(\Delta) = \lceil \alpha_i^{u'}(\Delta)/w_i \rceil$ and $\bar{\alpha}_i^{l'}(\Delta) = \lfloor \alpha_i^{l'}(\Delta)/w_i \rfloor$. The curves obtained provide the correct bounds since one can show that $\lfloor a \rfloor - \lfloor b \rfloor \leq \lfloor a - b \rfloor$ and $\lceil a \rceil - \lceil b \rceil \geq \lceil a - b \rceil$. In addition to the relations shown in Theorem 4.1 that have to be applied for all indices $1 \leq i \leq n$, we have the following equations describing how to obtain β_i^u, β_i^l ($1 < i \leq n$) from β_1^u and β_1^l as a result of the fixed priority scheduling. These equations along with the equations for scaling as described earlier can be given as follows:

$$\alpha_i^u(\Delta) = w_i \cdot \bar{\alpha}_i^u(\Delta) \quad , \quad \alpha_i^l(\Delta) = w_i \cdot \bar{\alpha}_i^l(\Delta)$$

$$\bar{\alpha}_i^{u'}(\Delta) = \lceil \alpha_i^u(\Delta)/w_i \rceil \quad , \quad \bar{\alpha}_i^{l'}(\Delta) = \lfloor \alpha_i^l(\Delta)/w_i \rfloor$$

$$\beta_1^u(\Delta) = \beta^u(\Delta) \quad , \quad \beta_i^u(\Delta) = \beta_{i-1}^{u}{}'(\Delta) \quad \forall 1 < i \leq n$$

$$\beta^{u'}(\Delta) = \beta_n^{u'}(\Delta)$$

$$\beta_1^l(\Delta) = \beta^l(\Delta) \quad , \quad \beta_i^l(\Delta) = \beta_{i-1}^{l}{}'(\Delta) \quad \forall 1 < i \leq n$$

$$\beta^{l'}(\Delta) = \beta_n^{l'}(\Delta)$$

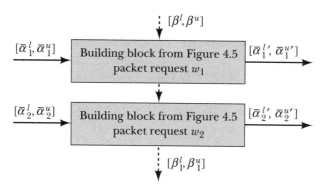

FIGURE

Representation of fixed priority preemptive scheduling of packet flows on a single processing resource. Flow 2 has a smaller priority than flow 1.

Figure 4.6 shows an example of fixed priority scheduling using two flows and one resource. Finally, note that the remaining service curves β' from the resource s (after it has processed the flows $f_1, \ldots, f_n$) can be used to service other flows, using possibly a different scheduling scheme, in a hierarchical manner. The processed flows with the resulting (packet) arrival curves $\overline{\alpha}_i^{u'}$ and $\overline{\alpha}_i^{l'}$ can now enter other resource nodes that are responsible for executing other tasks $t \in T$ or for performing communication tasks. In a later section, we show how these results can be used to estimate the delay experienced by packets and the memory requirements of the resource s to hold waiting packets.

Generalized Processor Sharing (GPS)

As a second example, we consider proportional share scheduling (GPS) [13]. In this case, with each flow f_i ($1 \leq i \leq n$), there is an associated weight ϕ_i with $\sum_{1 \leq i \leq n} \phi_i = 1$. A flow f_i receives a share $\phi_i / \sum_{j \in J(t)} \phi_j$ of the total available service given by β from the resource node. $J(t)$ is the set of indices of flows that are backlogged at time t. Here as well each flow is processed according to the model described in Theorem 4.1 and illustrated in Figure 4.5.

If the arrival curves associated with a flow f_i are given by $\overline{\alpha}_i^u$ and $\overline{\alpha}_i^l$, and a task t_i executing on packets of this flow makes a demand w_i on the resource, then we have the following scaled arrival curves as before:

$$\alpha_i^u(\Delta) = w_i \cdot \overline{\alpha}_i^u(\Delta) \quad , \quad \alpha_i^l(\Delta) = w_i \cdot \overline{\alpha}_i^l(\Delta)$$

$$\overline{\alpha}_i^{u'}(\Delta) = \lceil \alpha_i^u(\Delta)/w_i \rceil \quad , \quad \overline{\alpha}_i^{l'}(\Delta) = \lfloor \alpha_i^l(\Delta)/w_i \rfloor$$

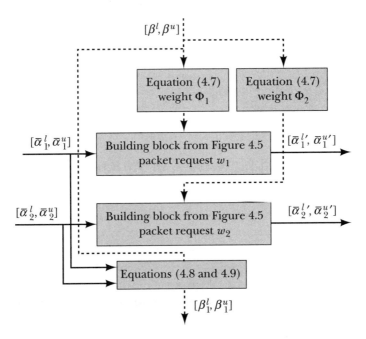

4.7

FIGURE

Deriving the resulting arrival curves and remaining service curves under the generalized processor sharing (GPS) scheduling discipline. Here two flows are scheduled on a single processing/communication resource.

Since a flow f_i is served using a service curve proportional to ϕ_i of the original service curve corresponding to the resource, we can obtain the following bounds:

$$\beta_i^l(\Delta) = \phi_i \cdot \beta^l(\Delta) \quad , \quad \beta_i^u(\Delta) = \beta^u(\Delta) \qquad \forall 1 \leq i \leq n \tag{4.7}$$

The remaining service curve after processing the packet flows can be given in accordance with Theorem 4.1.

$$\beta^{l'}(\Delta) = \sup_{0 \leq u \leq \Delta} \{\beta^l(u) - \sum_{1 \leq i \leq n} \alpha_i^u(u)\} \tag{4.8}$$

$$\beta^{u'}(\Delta) = \sup_{0 \leq u \leq \Delta} \{\beta^u(u) - \sum_{1 \leq i \leq n} \alpha_i^l(u)\} \tag{4.9}$$

Figure 4.7 shows an example with two flows. The case of nonpreemptive scheduling can be handled by shifting the service curves $\beta_i^l(\Delta)$ appropriately, that is, by replacing them with $\beta_i^l(\Delta - w_{\max})$ when $\Delta \geq w_{\max}$ and by $\beta_i^l(\Delta)$ when $\Delta \leq$

$w_{\max}$ where $w_{\max} = \max\{w_i : 1 \le i \le n\}$. Here $w_{\max}$ might represent the processing time of a packet.

Similar techniques can be used to describe other scheduling algorithms such as first-come-first-served or earliest deadline first. However, as pointed out in [2], the problem of determining accurate bounds for these scheduling disciplines is still an area of research.

4.2.3   Scheduling Network Construction

The scheduling network that enables the computation of performance parameters such as the end-to-end delays of packets and the memory requirements of the network processor, is constructed using the data from the specifications given in Section 4.1. These consist of a specification of the input packet flows, the processing functions associated with each flow (Section 4.1.1), and a specification of the system architecture, such as the types of the different processing and communication resources available (Section 4.1.2). In order to simplify the explanation, we restrict ourselves to the use of a fixed priority scheduling policy for all resource types, that is, $sched(s) = \{\text{fixedPriority}\}$ for all resource types $s \in S$. The basic idea is that the parameters describing the packet flows (i.e., the upper and lower arrival curves) pass from one resource to the next, and in the process get modified. Here the order is determined by the precedence relations in $E(f)$ in the task structure (see Definition 4.2) and the binding of tasks to resources. The parameters describing the *resource flows* (i.e., the capabilities of the resources described by the upper and lower service curves) also pass through the network and in the process get modified. The order here is determined by the priorities assigned to the packet flows (in the case of fixed priority scheduling) and the precedence relations in the task graph.

Definition 4.7: System Architecture   The allocation of resources can be described by the function $alloc(s) \in \mathbb{Z}_{\ge 0}$, which denotes the number of allocated instances of resource type s. The binding of a task $t \in T$ to a resource is specified by a relation $B \subseteq T \times S \times \mathbb{Z}_{\ge 0}$; that is, if $b = (t, s, i) \in B$ with $1 \le i \le alloc(s)$, then task t is executed on the ith instance of resource type s. The fixed priority scheduling policy is described by a function $prio(f) \in \mathbb{Z}_{\ge 0}$ that associates a priority to each stream f in a usage scenario.   ∎

Note that a system architecture is described not only by the type and the number of resource components, but also by the binding of the tasks to these components. This mapping may depend on the flow in which the task is active and on the scenario (see Section 4.1.1) under which the system architecture is evaluated.

In the target architecture, on the one hand, it is possible to have dedicated hardware modules for certain tasks with the resulting architecture being heterogeneous. On the other hand, we may have parallel resource instances of the same type (i.e., $alloc(s) > 1$) that may process a complete packet flow.

Now, we can describe the construction of a scheduling network for a given scenario. Note that in general we will have different scheduling networks for each usage scenario since the tasks, flows, and priorities might be different. Assuming that the user only specifies computation tasks since the definition of communication tasks mapped to communication resources requires the knowledge of a valid binding of the computation tasks on resources, a preparation step is required to introduce communication into our scheduling network. Again, we limit our description to a single bus.

◆ (Preparation to include communication.) For all flows f and all task dependencies $(t_i, t_j) \in E(f)$, if t_i and t_j are not bound to the same resource instance, add a communication task t_c to $V(f)$ and the edges (t_i, t_c), (t_c, t_j) to $E(f)$. Remove edge (t_i, t_j) from $E(f)$ and bind t_c to the communication resource $s_c \in S$.

◆ Include in the scheduling network one *source resource node* and one *target resource node* for each allocated instance of resource type $s \in S$. Include in the scheduling network one *source packet node* and one *target packet node* for each flow f present in the scenario.

◆ Construct an ordered set of tuples T_f that contains (t, f) for all flows f in the scenario and for all tasks $t \in V(f)$ in this flow. Order these tuples according to the priorities of the corresponding flows and according to the precedence relations $E(f)$. For each tuple (t, f) in T_f, add a scheduling node corresponding to that shown in Figure 4.5 to the scheduling network.

◆ For all flows f in the scenario, we add the following connections to the scheduling network:
  • For all task dependencies $(t_i, t_j) \in E(f)$, the packet flow output of scheduling node (t_i, f) is connected to the packet flow input of (t_j, f).
  • For each resource instance of any type $s \in S$, consider the scheduling nodes (t, f) where the task t is bound to that instance of s. If (t_i, f) precedes (t_j, f) in the ordered set T_f, then connect the resource stream output of (t_i, f) to the resource stream input of (t_j, f).

As a result of applying this algorithm, we get a scheduling network for a scenario containing source and target nodes for the different packet flows and resource streams, as well as scheduling nodes that represent the computations described in Figure 4.5. A scheduling network example is given in Figure 4.16.

Given the arrival curves for all the packet flows in the source nodes (i.e., $[\alpha_f^l, \alpha_f^u]$ for all flows f in a scenario), and the initial service curves for the allocated resource instances (i.e., $[\beta_{s,i}^l, \beta_{s,i}^u]$ for resource type s with $1 \leq i \leq alloc(s)$ allocated resources), we can determine the properties of all internal packet streams and resource flows in terms of their arrival and service curves. Now, it only remains to be seen how we can determine the end-to-end delays of the packets and the necessary memory required to hold packets waiting to be served.

4.2.4   System Properties

In order to estimate the properties of a system architecture for a network processor, we need bounds on the end-to-end delays experienced by the packets being processed and bounds on the memory requirements of the processor. Using well-known results from the area of communication networks (see, e.g., [6]), the bounds derived in Theorem 4.1 can be used to determine the maximum delays of the packets and the necessary memory required to store waiting packets.

$$delay \leq \sup_{u \geq 0} \left\{ \inf\{\tau \geq 0 : \alpha^u(u) \leq \beta^l(u+\tau)\} \right\} \tag{4.10}$$

$$backlog \leq \sup_{u \geq 0}\{\alpha^u(u) - \beta^l(u)\} \tag{4.11}$$

In other words, the delay can be bounded by the maximal horizontal distance between the curves α^u and β^l, whereas the backlog is bounded by the maximal vertical distance between them.

In the case of the scheduling network constructed earlier, we need to know which curves to use in the inequalities (4.10) and (4.11). The upper arrival curve is that of an incoming packet flow—that is, α_f^u of the flow f being investigated in the current scenario. The service curve β^l to be used in the inequalities (4.10) and (4.11) is the *accumulated* curve of all scheduling nodes through which the packets of flow f pass in the current scenario. As described in, for example, [2], this quantity can be determined through an iterated convolution. To this end, let us suppose that the packets of flow f pass through scheduling nodes $p_1, \ldots, p_m$, which have the lower service curves $\beta_1^l, \ldots, \beta_m^l$ at their resource stream inputs. Then β^l in (4.10) and (4.11) can be determined using the following recursion:

$$\overline{\beta}^l_1 = \beta^l_1 \tag{4.12}$$

$$\overline{\beta}^l_{i+1} = \inf_{0 \le u \le \Delta} \left\{ \overline{\beta}^l_i(u) + \beta^l_{i+1}(\Delta - u) \right\} \; \forall i > 1 \tag{4.13}$$

$$\beta^l = \overline{\beta}^l_{m+1} \tag{4.14}$$

As a result, using the scheduling network described, we can compute bounds on *delay* that give the maximum delay experienced by packets of a flow f, and the maximum shared memory *backlog* required by the flow. If we are interested in the memory requirements for an implementation with separate local memories as shown in Figure 4.2, we can generate the accumulated service curves for all sequences of tasks that are implemented on the same resource instance. There are several special cases, where we can make use of an accumulated service curve to determine tighter bounds, compared to independently deriving memory requirements for each node. For instance, suppose that a packet flow is processed first on a general-purpose component. For a certain task, the flow is then delegated to a more specialized unit. After being processed on that dedicated resource instance, the flow returns to the former component. An analysis using the accumulated service curve over all processing steps, including the ones on the specialized unit, may derive tighter memory bounds for the general-purpose component than two independent analyses of the first and second visits of the flow at that resource. We will not describe all the subcases here since the form of the equations (4.10) to (4.14) is not affected.

The memory requirements derived by an analysis of the communication resources must be assigned to the corresponding sending task (and therefore to the resource instance bound to that task). This memory requirement is visualized as an output queue before the communication resource in Figure 4.2.

4.2.5   Piecewise Linear Approximation

Clearly, the equations used in Theorem 4.1 are expensive to compute. It may also be noted that this set of equations has to be computed for all the scheduling nodes in a scheduling network. Moreover, when the design space exploration is based on schemes like evolutionary multiobjective algorithms [7], the performance of many candidate system architectures need to be estimated, and there might be several usage scenarios per system architecture.

To overcome this computational bottleneck, we propose a piecewise linear approximation of all arrival and service curves. Based on this, all the equations in Theorem 4.1 can be efficiently computed using symbolic techniques. We only

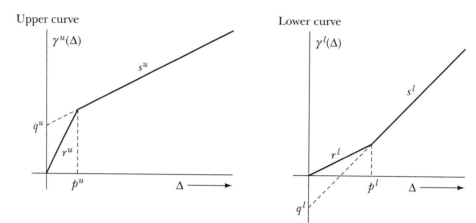

4.8

FIGURE

Simple representation of upper and lower curves.

describe the basic concepts here and give a few simple examples. Figure 4.8 shows how the arrival and service curves look when each curve is approximated by a combination of two line segments.

In this case, we can write

$$\gamma^u(\Delta) = \min\{r^u\Delta, q^u + s^u\Delta\}$$

$$\gamma^l(\Delta) = \max\{r^l\Delta, q^l + s^l\Delta\}$$

where

$$q^u \geq 0, \quad r^u \geq s^u \geq 0, \quad r^u = s^u \Leftrightarrow q^u = 0$$

$$q^l \leq 0, \quad 0 \leq r^l \leq s^l, \quad r^l = s^l \Leftrightarrow q^l = 0$$

As a shorthand notation, we denote curves γ^u and γ^l by the tuples $U(q, r, s)$ and $L(q, r, s)$, respectively. An example of a piecewise linear approximation of the remaining lower service curve $\beta^{l'}(\Delta)$ in Theorem 4.1 is given next.

Theorem 4.2   Given arrival curves and service curves $\alpha^u = U(q_\alpha, r_\alpha, s_\alpha)$, $\beta^l = L(q_\beta, r_\beta, s_\beta)$. Then the remaining lower service curve can be approximated by the curve

$$\beta^{l'} = L(q, r, s)$$

where

$$q = \begin{cases} q_\beta - q_\alpha & \text{if } s_\alpha \leq s_\beta \\ 0 & \text{if } s_\alpha > s_\beta \end{cases}$$

$$r = \max\{r_\beta - r_\alpha, 0\}$$

$$s = \max\{s_\beta - s_\alpha, 0\}$$

Proof   To see that $L(q, r, s)$ is a valid lower curve for the remaining service curve, it may be shown that

$$L(q, r, s)(\Delta) \leq \sup_{0 \leq u \leq \Delta} \{\beta^l(u) - \alpha^u(u)\}$$

Note that $\beta^l(\Delta) - \alpha^u(\Delta)$ and also $\sup_{0 \leq u \leq \Delta}\{\beta^l(u) - \alpha^u(u)\}$ are convex, since β^l and α^u are convex and concave, respectively. Therefore, a valid lower bound can be determined by considering the two cases $\Delta \to 0$ and $\Delta \to \infty$. If $\Delta \to 0$, we have

$$\sup_{0 \leq u \leq \Delta} \{\beta^l(u) - \alpha^u(u)\} = \sup_{0 \leq u \leq \Delta} \{r_\beta u - r_\alpha u\}$$

and therefore

$$r = \begin{cases} r_\beta - r_\alpha & \text{if } r_\beta > r_\alpha \\ 0 & \text{otherwise} \end{cases}$$

If $\Delta \to \infty$ and $s_\beta > s_\alpha$, then

$$\sup_{0 \leq u \leq \Delta} \{\beta^l(u) - \alpha^u(u)\} = \sup_{0 \leq u \leq \Delta} \{q_\beta + s_\beta u - q_\alpha - s_\alpha u\}$$

and therefore

$$s = \begin{cases} s_\beta - s_\alpha & \text{if } s_\beta > s_\alpha \\ 0 & \text{otherwise} \end{cases}$$

$$q = \begin{cases} q_\beta - q_\alpha & \text{if } s_\beta > s_\alpha \\ 0 & \text{otherwise} \end{cases}$$

∎

All the remaining equations on the curves can similarly be symbolically evaluated, including those that determine bounds on the delay and the backlog. Using these approximations, even for realistic task and processor specifications, hundreds of architectures can be evaluated within a few seconds of CPU time.

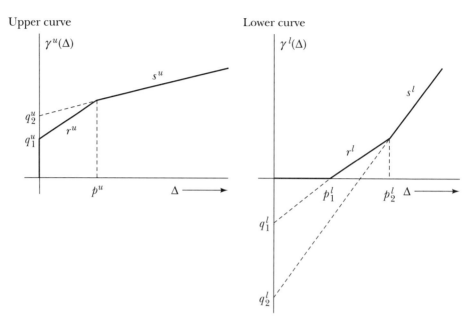

Improved approximation of upper and lower curves.

4.2.6   Improved Approximations

In this section, we show that it is possible to obtain improved approximations of the remaining arrival and service curves, by approximating these curves using three line segments instead of two as in Section 4.2.5. The resulting calculations, however, become more involved in this case. Figure 4.9 shows the resulting arrival and service curves. This allows us to exactly model an arrival curve in the form of a T-SPEC [16]. In the case of an arrival curve, q_1^u may represent the maximum possible workload involved in processing a single packet, r^u can be interpreted as the burst rate, and s^u the long-term arrival rate. In the case of communication resources, q_1^u represents the maximum size of a packet.

The upper and lower curves in this case can be written as

$$\gamma^u(\Delta) \quad = \quad \min\{q_1^u + r^u\Delta, q_2^u + s^u\Delta\}$$

$$\gamma^l(\Delta) \quad = \quad \max\{q_2^l + s^l\Delta, q_1^l + r^l\Delta, 0\}$$

where

$$q_2^u \geq q_1^u \geq 0, \quad r^u \geq s^u \geq 0, \quad r^u = s^u \Leftrightarrow q_1^u = q_2^u$$

$$q_2^l \leq q_1^l \leq 0, \quad 0 \leq r^l \leq s^l, \quad r^l = s^l \Leftrightarrow q_1^l = q_2^l$$

The values of p^u and p^l_1, p^l_2 (see Figure 4.9) can be calculated as

$$p^u = \begin{cases} \frac{q^u_2 - q^u_1}{r^u - s^u} & \text{if } r^u > s^u \\ 0 & \text{if } r^u = s^u \end{cases}$$

$$p^l_1 = \begin{cases} -\frac{q^u_1}{r^l} & \text{if } r^l > 0 \\ 0 & \text{if } r^l = 0 \end{cases}, \qquad p^l_2 = \begin{cases} \frac{q^l_2 - q^l_1}{r^l - s^l} & \text{if } r^l < s^l \\ p^l_1 & \text{if } r^l = s^l \end{cases}$$

We denote the curves γ^u and γ^l in this case by $U(q_1, q_2, r, s)$ and $L(q_1, q_2, r, s)$, respectively.

Theorem 4.3 Given the upper arrival and lower service curves $\alpha^u = U(q_{1\alpha}, q_{2\alpha}, r_\alpha, s_\alpha)$ and $\beta^l = L(q_{1\beta}, q_{2\beta}, r_\beta, s_\beta)$, respectively, the approximate remaining service curve $\beta^{l'} = L(q_1, q_2, r, s)$ can be given by the following four cases:

1. There exists a $\Delta' > 0$, such that $q_{2\beta} + s_\beta \Delta' = q_{2\alpha} + s_\alpha \Delta'$, and for all $\Delta < \Delta'$, $\alpha^u(\Delta) > \beta^l(\Delta)$. In this case, $r = 0$, $s = s_\beta - s_\alpha$ and $q_1 = 0$, $q_2 = q_{2\beta} - q_{2\alpha}$.

2. There exists a $\Delta' > 0$, such that $q_{1\beta} + r_\beta \Delta' = q_{2\alpha} + s_\alpha \Delta'$, and for all $\Delta < \Delta'$, $\alpha^u(\Delta) > \beta^l(\Delta)$. In this case, $r = r_\beta - s_\alpha$, $s = s_\beta - s_\alpha$ and $q_1 = q_{1\beta} - q_{2\alpha}$, $q_2 = q_{2\beta} - q_{2\alpha}$.

3. There exists a $\Delta' > 0$, such that $q_{1\beta} + r_\beta \Delta' = q_{1\alpha} + r_\alpha \Delta'$, and for all $\Delta < \Delta'$, $\alpha^u(\Delta) > \beta^l(\Delta)$. In this case, $r = r_\beta - r_\alpha$, $s = s_\beta - s_\alpha$ and $q_1 = q_{1\beta} - q_{1\alpha}$, $q_2 = q_{2\beta} - q_{2\alpha}$.

4. There exists a $\Delta' > 0$, such that $q_{2\beta} + s_\beta \Delta' = q_{1\alpha} + r_\alpha \Delta'$, and for all $\Delta < \Delta'$, $\alpha^u(\Delta) > \beta^l(\Delta)$. In this case, $r = s_\beta - r_\alpha$, $s = s_\beta - s_\alpha$ and $q_1 = q_{2\beta} - q_{1\alpha}$, $q_2 = q_{2\beta} - q_{2\alpha}$.

If $\alpha^u(\Delta) \geq \beta^l(\Delta)$ for all $\Delta \geq 0$, then $r = s = 0$ and $q_1 = q_2 = 0$.

Proof To prove that $\beta^{l'} = L(q_1, q_2, r, s)$ is a valid lower remaining service curve, we shall, as before, show that $L(q_1, q_2, r, s)(\Delta) \leq \sup_{0 \leq u \leq \Delta} \{\beta^l(u) - \alpha^u(u)\}$ for all $\Delta \geq 0$.

First, it may be noted that $\beta^l(\Delta)$ and $\alpha^u(\Delta)$ are convex and concave, respectively. Therefore, $\beta^l(\Delta) - \alpha^u(\Delta)$ and $\sup_{0 \leq u \leq \Delta} \{\beta^l(u) - \alpha^u(u)\}$ are convex. However, in contrast to our approximations with two segments in Section 4.2.5, here we have to consider four different cases.

Case 1 is when the last segment of $\beta^l(\Delta)$ intersects the last segment of $\alpha^u(\Delta)$, at, say, $\Delta = \Delta'$ (see Figure 4.10(a)). Therefore, for all $\Delta < \Delta'$, $\beta^l(\Delta) < \alpha^u(\Delta)$. Hence, $\sup_{0 \leq u \leq \Delta} \{\beta^l(u) - \alpha^u(u)\} \leq 0$ for all $\Delta \leq \Delta'$, and therefore

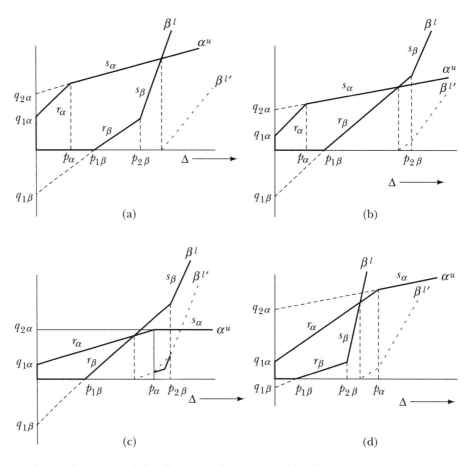

4.10

FIGURE
Approximate remaining lower service curves: (a), (b), (c), and (d) represent cases 1, 2, 3, and 4, respectively, in Theorem 4.3.

$r = 0$ and $q_1 = 0$. When $\Delta \to \infty$, $\sup_{0 \leq u \leq \Delta}\{\beta^l(u) - \alpha^u(u)\} = \sup_{0 \leq u \leq \Delta}\{q_{2\beta} + s_\beta u - q_{2\alpha} - s_\alpha u\}$. Therefore, we have $s = s_\beta - s_\alpha$ and $q_2 = q_{2\beta} - q_{2\alpha}$.

Case 2 is when the middle segment of $\beta^l(\Delta)$ intersects the last segment of $\alpha^u(\Delta)$. If this intersection is at $\Delta = \Delta'$, then for all $\Delta < \Delta'$, $\beta^l(\Delta) < \alpha^u(\Delta)$ and $\sup_{0 \leq u \leq \Delta}\{\beta^l(u) - \alpha^u(u)\} \leq 0$ for all $\Delta \leq \Delta'$. This case is shown in Figure 4.10(b). Clearly, $r = r_\beta - s_\alpha$, $s = s_\beta - s_\alpha$, $q_1 = q_{1\beta} - q_{2\alpha}$ and $q_2 = q_{2\beta} - q_{2\alpha}$.

Case 3 is when the middle segment of $\beta^l(\Delta)$ intersects the middle segment of $\alpha^u(\Delta)$ (see Figure 4.10(c)). In this case, $\sup_{0 \leq u \leq \Delta}\{\beta^l(u) - \alpha^u(u)\}$ is made up of four linear segments. But we approximate it using $L(q_1, q_2, r, s)(\Delta)$, which is made up of three segments. There can be two possible subcases: the first is when $p_{2\beta} \geq p_\alpha$ (as shown in Figure 4.10(c)), and the second is when $p_{2\beta} < p_\alpha$. If $\beta^l(\Delta)$ and $\alpha^u(\Delta)$ intersect at Δ', then the four segments that make up $\sup_{0 \leq u \leq \Delta}\{\beta^l(u) - \alpha^u(u)\}$ span the intervals $\Delta \in [0, \Delta')$, $[\Delta', p_\alpha)$, $[p_\alpha, p_{2\beta})$, $[p_{2\beta}, \infty)$ (as shown in Figure 4.10(c)) or $\Delta \in [0, \Delta')$, $[\Delta', p_{2\beta})$, $[p_{2\beta}, p_\alpha)$, $[p_\alpha, \infty)$ (in the case when $p_{2\beta} < p_\alpha$). To obtain $L(q_1, q_2, r, s)(\Delta)$, we neglect the segment of $\sup_{0 \leq u \leq \Delta}\{\beta^l(u) - \alpha^u(u)\}$ corresponding to the interval $[p_\alpha, p_{2\beta})$ in Figure 4.10(c) and the interval $[p_{2\beta}, p_\alpha)$ when $p_{2\beta} < p_\alpha$, and instead approximate this segment by the segments preceding and following it. It may be noted that $L(q_1, q_2, r, s)(\Delta)$ is a valid lower curve, since $L(q_1, q_2, r, s)(\Delta) \leq \sup_{0 \leq u \leq \Delta}\{\beta^l(u) - \alpha^u(u)\}$ for all $\Delta \geq 0$. Therefore, $r = r_\beta - r_\alpha$, $s = s_\beta - s_\alpha$, $q_1 = q_{1\beta} - q_{1\alpha}$, $q_2 = q_{2\beta} - q_{2\alpha}$.

Case 4 is when the last segment of $\beta^l(\Delta)$ intersects the middle segment of $\alpha^u(\Delta)$ (see Figure 4.10(d)). It can be seen that $r = s_\beta - r_\alpha$, $q_1 = q_{2\beta} - q_{1\alpha}$, and as before, $s = s_\beta - s_\alpha$ and $q_2 = q_{2\beta} - q_{2\alpha}$.

Lastly, if $\beta^l(\Delta) \leq \alpha^u(\Delta)$ for all $\Delta \geq 0$, then $\sup_{0 \leq u \leq \Delta}\{\beta^l(u) - \alpha^u(u)\} \leq 0$ for all $\Delta \geq 0$. Hence, $r = s = 0$ and $q_1 = q_2 = 0$. ∎

The approximations for all the remaining curves can be derived on the basis of similar techniques, and hence we omit them here.

4.3 MULTIOBJECTIVE DESIGN SPACE EXPLORATION

There are several possibilities for exploring the design space, one of which is a branch and bound search algorithm where the problem is specified in the form of integer linear equations [12]. For complicated examples where the design space can be very large, it is possible to use evolutionary search techniques [1], and this is the approach we describe here.

As already mentioned, we are faced with a number of conflicting objectives trading cost against performance, and there are also conflicts arising from the different usage scenarios of the processor. We illustrate this in the case study, which involves tradeoffs between the performance ψ_b in several different usage scenarios $b \in B$ and the cost of the system architecture. Recall from Section 4.1.1 that a usage scenario is defined by a certain set of flows F and by associated deadlines d_f. As a consequence, the binding of task to resource instances and the memory requirements may vary from scenario to scenario.

Definition 4.8: Cost Measure   The system cost is defined by the sum of costs for all allocated resource instances.

$$cost = \sum_{s \in S} alloc(s)\, cost(s) \qquad\qquad (4.15)$$

■

Definition 4.9: Performance Measure   Given a system architecture as defined in Definition 4.7, its performance under a scenario $b \in B$ is defined by a scaling parameter ψ_b that is the largest possible scaling of packet input flows according to $[\psi_b \alpha_f^l, \psi_b \alpha_f^u]$ for all flows f that are part of scenario b such that the constraints on end-to-end delays and memory can still be satisfied. In other words, given the scenario b, after the scaling we still have $delay \leq d_f$ for all flows f and $\sum_{f \in F} backlog \leq m(b)$ for a given shared memory constraint $m(b)$.   ■

As described in Section 4.2.4, we may also perform a refined per-instance memory analysis for each resource so that the (possibly weighted) sum of the local memories must be less than or equal to the memory constraint $m(b)$.

The basic approach is shown in Figure 4.11. The evolutionary multiobjective optimizer determines a feasible binding, allocation, and scheduling strategy based on the cost of the system architecture and the performance for each usage scenario. Based on this information, a scheduling graph is constructed for each usage scenario that enables the computation of the corresponding memory and delay properties. Then, the packet rates of the input streams are maximized until the delay and memory constraints as specified are violated. The corresponding scaling factors ψ_b of the input streams for each scenario $b \in B$ and the cost of system architecture $cost$ form the objective vector $v = (v_0, ..., v_{k-1})$, using $v_0 = cost$ and $v_i = 1/\psi_{b_i}$ for all $b_i \in B$, $i > 0$ to formulate a minimization problem. The goal is to determine implementations with *pareto-optimal* [8] objective vectors. The architectures associated with pareto-optimal objective vectors represent the tradeoffs in the network processor design.

Definition 4.10: Pareto-optimal   Given a set V of k-dimensional vectors $v \in \mathbb{R}^k$. A vector $v \in V$ dominates a vector $g \in V$ if for all elements $0 \leq i < k$ we have $v_i \leq g_i$ and for at least one element, say, l, we have $v_l < g_l$. A vector is called *pareto-optimal* if it is not dominated by any other vector in V.   ■

As can be seen, there are two optimization loops involved. The inner loop locally maximizes the throughput of the network processor in each scenario under the given memory and delay constraints. The outer loop performs the multiobjective design space exploration.

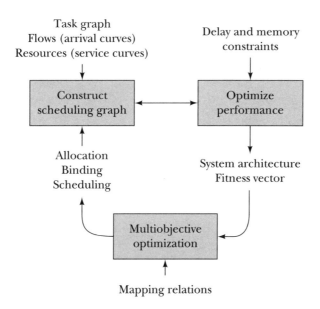

Basic concept for the design space exploration of packet processing systems.

We have used a widely used evolutionary multiobjective optimizer SPEA2 [7, 8] and incorporated some domain-specific knowledge into the search process. The optimizer iteratively generates new system architectures based on the already known set. These new solutions are then evaluated for their objective vector and fed into the optimizer to guide further search. It may be noted that due to the heuristic nature of the search procedure, no statements about the optimality of the final set of solutions can be made. However, there is experimental evidence that the solutions found are close to the optimum even for realistic problem complexities.

4.4   CASE STUDY

The purpose of this section is to give a complete design space exploration example. For the specification, we use the following set of traffic flows $F =$ {NRT_Forward, RT_Send, RT_Recv, NRT_Encrypt, NRT_Decrypt} and there are 25 computation tasks, that is, $|T| = 25$. The task graph with its dependencies is visualized in Figure 4.12.

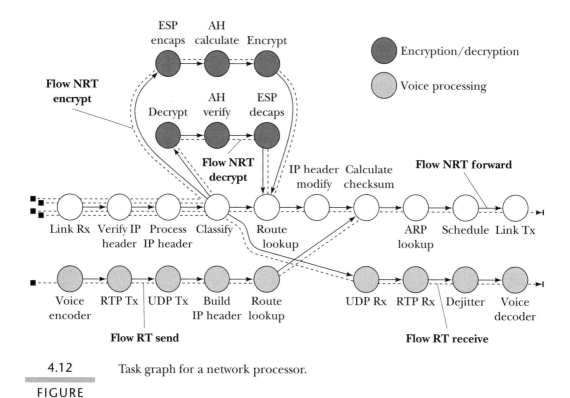

4.12   Task graph for a network processor.

FIGURE

Our goal is to optimize a network processor looking at two different scenarios. In the first usage scenario, we have just the flow NRT_Forward to model a forwarding functionality in the network backbone, whereas in the second scenario, all the flows in F are present, representing an access network environment with an increased per-packet processing requirement. We use eight different resource types with $S = \{$Classifier, PowerPC, ARM9, μEngine, CheckSum, Cipher, DSP, LookUp$\}$. Each type has different computational capabilities, and these are represented in the form of the mapping relation M (see Definition 4.6). A part of this specification is represented in Figure 4.13, including an example for the implementation cost $cost(s)$, the number of instances $inst(s)$ of a resource type, and a request $w(t, s)$ of a task. There are general-purpose resources like an ARM9 CPU that is able to perform all kinds of tasks, and very specialized ones like the classifier that can only handle a single task. The initial service curves are simply set to $\beta^l(\Delta) = \beta^u(\Delta) = c \cdot \Delta$, $c \in \mathbb{R}_{>0}$, for computation and communication resources, reflecting the fact that the resources are fully available for the processing of the tasks.

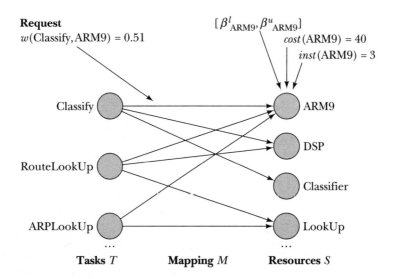

Request
$w(\text{Classify}, \text{ARM9}) = 0.51$

$[\beta^l_{\text{ARM9}}, \beta^u_{\text{ARM9}}]$

$cost\,(\text{ARM9}) = 40$

$inst\,(\text{ARM9}) = 3$

Classify

RouteLookUp

ARPLookUp

...

Tasks T

Mapping M

ARM9

DSP

Classifier

LookUp

...

Resources S

4.13

FIGURE

Graphical representation of a part of the mapping of tasks to resources.

It should now be obvious why the application of an evolutionary optimizer is advantageous for our setting. Looking at the access network scenario and considering all possible bindings of our task graph in Figure 4.12 to different resource types, we will have more than $4^{25} \cdot 5! > 10^{17}$ possible design points, assuming that all of the 25 tasks can at least be executed on the four general-purpose resource types (ARM9, PowerPC, μEngine, DSP) with varying requests. The factor 5! takes the choice of priorities for the five traffic streams into account. Note that this rough estimate does not even include the option to allocate several instances per resource type or several communication resources.

Using an evolutionary optimization algorithm, Figure 4.14 shows the final *population* of a design space exploration run after 300 generations of a population of 100 system architectures. This optimization takes less than 30 minutes to run on a Sun Ultra 10. Most parts of our software are written in Java, including the graphical editor for the specification of tasks, resources, and bindings, and the operators in evolutionary algorithm such as *mutation, crossover*, and *repair operators*. The evolutionary optimizer is written in C++. Each dot in Figure 4.14 represents a pareto-optimal system architecture. Each architecture includes (1) the set of allocated resources, (2) the binding of tasks to resource instances for each scenario, and (3) the scheduling priorities for each scenario. The three-dimensional design space is defined by the costs of resource allocations and the performance factors ψ for our two scenarios (backbone and access networks)

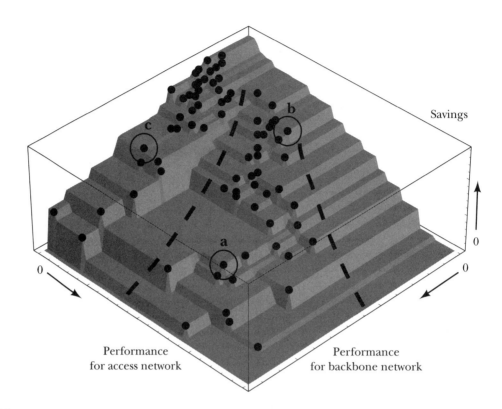

4.14

FIGURE

Final population of a design space exploration run. The three-dimensional space is defined by the performance (ψ) values for two usage scenarios and the savings in costs. All plotted designs are pareto-optimal.

that are bound by either the end-to-end deadlines associated with the streams or the maximum memory constraints (see Definition 4.9). For visualization purposes, we transformed the cost values *cost* by $cost := cost_{max} - cost$ (where $cost_{max}$ is the maximum cost value in the population) to have cheap solutions on top of the hill.

In this example, we can recognize two distinct regions of solutions. The region on the left includes solutions that are in particular good for the network backbone, whereas the region in the middle shows designs that can be used for both usage scenarios. Note that there are no solutions in the region on the right since architectures that show good performance for access networks must also inherently perform well for the backbone, because the flows for the backbone scenario are also included in the access network scenario. A major characteristic

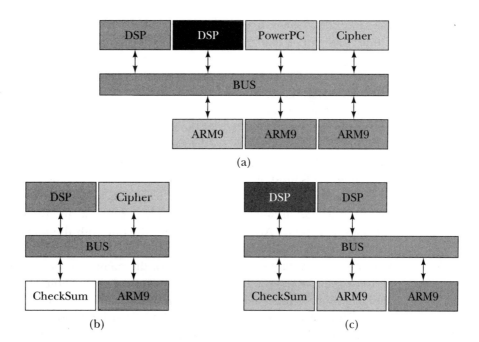

Examples for pareto-optimal resource allocations taken from Figure 4.14. Darker coloring means higher average utilization.

of the region in the middle is that allocations contained in this area require an expensive cipher unit to cope with the diverse set of flows in the access network scenario. Solutions in the left region, however, do not use a cipher component.

The allocations for three selected pareto-optimal design points are sketched in Figure 4.15 to show an example of the tradeoffs involved in a network processor design. A higher average utilization of a resource is denoted by a darker coloring in the figure. We bounded the exploration to a single communication instance where each allocation had a choice between two different bus types. The designs (b) and (c) in particular optimize the performance for one of the two usage scenarios at the same (moderate) costs, whereas design (a) performs even slightly better in both scenarios at more than double the cost. Depending on the targeted application domain, each of the solutions might be meaningful. Design (b), which performs well for the access network scenario, requires a relatively expensive cipher unit to cope with encryption and decryption. Design (c), which is aimed for IP forwarding in backbone networks, can however trade off the cost for an unnecessary cipher unit to allocate more general-purpose computing power at the same cost. Finally, design (a) is well suited for both scenarios and therefore requires an extensive allocation of resources, which actually is a mixture of the allocations for the designs (b) and (c). Note that all tasks that are bound to the relatively cheap CheckSum resource in the designs (b) and (c) are now bound to unexploited ARM resources in design (a).

Due to space limitations, we do not discuss the exact parameters for modeling our traffic streams, the costs, and the requests of tasks. For the same reason, we do not provide quantitative results for the memory consumption, but instead describe qualitative memory requirements. Design (c) aimed for the network backbone needs most of the memory for two resource instances only. About 60% of the memory space defined by the memory constraint (see Definition 4.9) is given to the DSP instance with the higher average load, and the remaining 40% are allocated to one ARM instance (again the one with the higher load value). Compared with that, design (b) targeted to access networks reverses the memory consumption by allocating one quarter of the memory space for the DSP, two-thirds for the ARM, and the remaining 8% for the cipher unit. For the expensive design (a), no simple memory consumption pattern can be recognized. If a network processor according to design (a) is alternately used for both scenarios (which would be a rather unlikely case), it would be interesting to note that the memory constraint must only be increased by 17.5% to accommodate for each resource instance the maximum required memory area of both the scenarios.

The performance of the allocation and the memory consumption are determined using our analytical approach based on the scheduling network. An example is given in Figure 4.16 for design (b), looking at a decryption traffic stream. Besides the order in which arrival and service curves are derived, we also recognize the allocation of resources and the binding of tasks to resources in the network.

ACKNOWLEDGMENTS

The work presented here was supported partly by IBM Research and partly by the National Competence Center in Research on Mobile Information and Communication Systems (NCCR-MICS), which is a center supported by the Swiss National Science Foundation under grant number 5005-67322. The authors are grateful to Andreas Herkersdorf from IBM Research in Zurich, for discussions that influenced the results presented here.

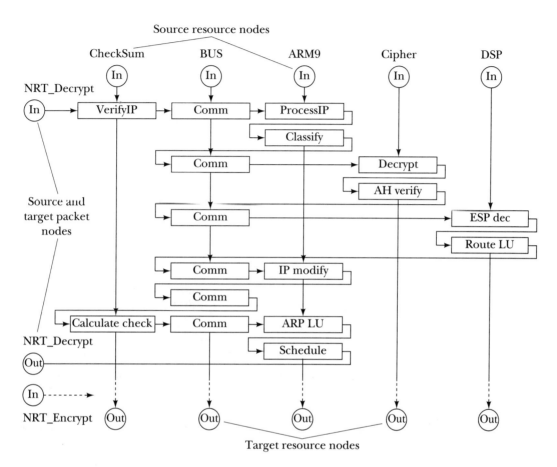

4.16

FIGURE

Scheduling network of one flow for architecture (b) in Figure 4.15. The scheduling policy for each resource is fixed priority. The internal scheduling nodes correspond to the basic blocks shown in Figure 4.5.

REFERENCES

[1]   T. Blickle, J. Teich, and L. Thiele, "System-level synthesis using evolutionary algorithms," *Design Automation for Embedded Systems*, 3(1):23–58, 1998.

[2]   J. L. Boudec and P. Thiran, *Network Calculus—A Theory of Deterministic Queuing Systems for the Internet*, LNCS 2050, Springer-Verlag, 2001.

[3]   G. Buttazzo, *Hard Real-Time Computing Systems—Predictable Scheduling Algorithms and Applications*, Kluwer Academic Publishers, 1997.

[4]   P. Crowley and J.-L. Baer, "A modeling framework for network processor systems," in *Proc. 1st Workshop on Network Processors, held in conjunction with the 8th International Symposium on High-Performance Computer Architecture*, Cambridge, Massachusetts, February 2002.

[5]   P. Crowley, M. Fiuczynski, J.-L. Baer, and B. Bershad, "Characterizing processor architectures for programmable network interfaces," in *Proc. International Conference on Supercomputing*, Santa Fe, 2000.

[6]   R. Cruz, "A calculus for network delay," *IEEE Trans. on Information Theory*, 37(1):114–141, 1991.

[7]   K. Deb, *Multi-objective optimization using evolutionary algorithms*, John Wiley & Sons, 2001.

[8]   M. Eisenring, L. Thiele, and E. Zitzler, "Handling conflicting criteria in embedded system design," *IEEE Design & Test of Computers*, 17(2):51–59, 2000.

[9]   M. Franklin and T. Wolf, "A network processor performance and design model with benchmark parameterization," in *Proc. 1st Workshop on Network Processors, held in conjunction with the 8th International Symposium on High-Performance Computer Architecture*, Cambridge, Massachusetts, February 2002.

[10]   E. Kohler, R. Morris, B. Chen, J. Jannotti, and M. Kaashoek, "The Click modular router," *ACM Transactions on Computer Systems*, 18(3):263–297, 2000.

[11]   K. Lahiri, A. Raghunathan, and S. Dey, "System level performance analysis for designing on-chip communication architectures," *IEEE Trans. on Computer Aided-Design of Integrated Circuits and Systems*, 20(6):768–783, 2001.

[12]   G. D. Micheli, *Synthesis and Optimization of Digital Circuits*, McGraw-Hill International Editions, New York, 1994.

[13]   A. Parekh and R. Gallager, "A generalized processor sharing approach to flow control in integrated services networks: the single-node case," *IEEE/ACM Transactions on Networking*, 1(3):344–357, 1993.

[14]   L. Peterson, S. Karlin, and K. Li, "OS support for general-purpose routers," in *Proc. 7th Workshop on Hot Topics in Operating Systems*, 1999.

[15]   X. Qie, A. Bavier, L. Peterson, and S. Karlin, "Scheduling computations on a software-based router," in *Proc. SIGMETRICS*, 2001.

[16]   S. Shenker and J. Wroclawski, "General characterization parameters for integrated service network elements," RFC 2215, IETF, September 1997.

[17]   T. Spalink, S. Karlin, L. Peterson, and Y. Gottlieb, "Building a robust software-based router using network processors," in *Proc. Symposium on Operating Systems Principles (SOSP)*, 2001.

[18]   L. Thiele, S. Chakraborty, M. Gries, and S. Künzli, "A framework for evaluating design tradeoffs in packet processing architectures," in *Proc. 39th Design Automation Conference (DAC)*, New Orleans, 2002. ACM Press.

[19]   L. Thiele, S. Chakraborty, M. Gries, A. Maxiaguine, and J. Greutert, "Embedded software in network processors—models and algorithms," in *First Workshop on Embedded Software*, Lecture Notes in Computer Science 2211, pp. 416–434, Lake Tahoe, California, 2001. Springer-Verlag.

[20]   L. Thiele, S. Chakraborty, and M. Naedele, "Real-time calculus for scheduling hard real-time systems," in *Proc. IEEE International Symposium on Circuits and Systems (ISCAS)*, Volume 4, pp. 101–104, 2000.

[21]   T. Wolf, M. Franklin, and E. Spitznagel, "Design tradeoffs for embedded network processors," Technical Report WUCS-00-24, Department of Computer Science, Washington University, St. Louis, 2000.

Compiler Backend Optimizations for Network Processors with Bit Packet Addressing

Jens Wagner
Computer Science XII Embedded Systems Group,
University of Dortmund

Rainer Leupers
Department of EE and IT Integrated Signal Processing Systems,
Aachen University of Technology

For modern general-purpose processors, most of the software development work is done in high-level languages (HLLs). High-level languages are platform independent, therefore software is portable between different architectures at low cost. The GNU C compiler, for example, supports nearly 100 different architectures and operating systems [1, 2]. Many software projects can be ported between different platforms simply by recompiling them. The availability of compilers is a main feature of a general-purpose system. Therefore, compilers are often assisted by processor features, for example, the instruction set of the Intel Pentium processor family supports function frame construction and destruction by the instruction set [3]. In other words, the machine language supports the semantics of the high-level language. Because development of compilers and processors goes hand in hand, the availability of compilers for such systems is very high. If an application has been developed in a high-level language once, it can easily be ported to another platform. If the software contains hardware-dependent code, in most cases only minor changes will be needed. A widespread example for portable software is the Linux operating system.

In contrast to general-purpose processors, there are also application-specific processors (ASIPs). These processors are optimized for a special application class that gives advantages in performance, power consumption, and/or cost. For instance, digital signal processors (DSPs) are optimized to process discrete mathematical algorithms in real time. A DSP is equipped with special data paths, instruction sets, and peripheral units. For example, the Micronas DSP MAS 3509F is optimized for a single application, MP3 audio decoding [4].

C compilers for such ASIPs have been successfully developed for many years. Specific optimizations focus on irregular data paths [5, 6, 7, 8, 9], address code optimization for DSPs [10, 11, 12, 13], and exploitation of multimedia instruction sets [14, 15, 16]. Experiments have shown that such highly machine-specific techniques are a promising approach in generating high-quality machine code, whose quality often comes close to handwritten assembly code. Naturally, this comes at the expense of increased compilation time in most cases.

However, there are important classes of ASIPs other than DSPs, where so far tool support is relatively weak. ASIPs for network protocol processing (*network processor units*, NPUs) are used to process high-speed communication protocols. NPUs are designed to be used in devices such as routers and switches for IP traffic as well as in telecommunication (e.g., ISDN and xDSL). A major system design problem in this area is that the required high bandwidth leaves only a very short time frame (as low as a few nanoseconds) for processing each bit packet arriving at a network node [17]. Even contemporary high-end programmable processors can hardly keep pace with the required real-time performance, not to mention the issue of computational efficiency in terms of MIPS/Watt. In [17], it is outlined that for packet handling in high-speed networks only a very small time frame exists. Even at the highest CPU cycle rates only a few instructions can be executed per packet. For instance, a 1 GHz processor applied to a 10 GBit core router can only execute 10 to 50 machine instructions per packet. This clearly shows the need for new NPU-like processor architectures.

It is common for high bandwidth wire-based applications like Ethernet communication to use data fields of a single constant length. Usually protocols employ 8-, 16-, or 32-bit wide data fields. In most cases, an NPU is chosen whose register width matches the length of the data fields in the protocol implementation to enhance processing speed. Very often, bandwidth of the channel (the cable) is wasted because bits of the data fields are not used. But the limitation of the overall system is still the processing time of the NPU. As long as it is the bottleneck, all optimizations should be done to enhance data processing in the NPU rather than the utilization of the channel bandwidth.

The opposite situation occurs if we focus on bandwidth limited networks like GSM or DSL. The bandwidth limitation is due to the channel bandwidth. Processors are fast enough to handle the data. To enhance the speed of the overall network, the usage of the channel has to be optimized. Therefore data has to be packed or compressed before crossing the channel. Packing demands variable field lengths, because frequently occurring information is encoded into smaller fields. Payload information does not consist of a number of words any longer,

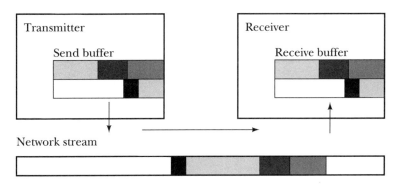

Communication via bitstream-oriented protocols.

but appears as a bitstream. Figure 5.1 shows the communication via a bitstream-oriented protocol.

Because network applications are often high-volume products, NPUs can be tuned to specific applications to reduce the power consumption or the price of an application, or to enhance its speed. Because the instruction set of an ASIP is designed for a single application domain, its high-level programming language support is usually low. The instruction set of an ASIP very often contains assembly commands of such high complexity that a number of HLL instructions are needed to describe them. An example for such machine instructions is the support of *bit packets*. The bitstreams in communication protocols consist of *packets* of different length; that is, there are variable length header packets and (typically longer) payload packets. Typical packet processing requirements include decoding, compression, encryption, or routing.

For a compiler, there are two different ways to handle this feature: (1) The complexity of the HLL can be enhanced. For this purpose, application domain–specific instructions are added. For example, in [18] this technique is used to handle bit-packed addressing from C. The disadvantage of this solution is that code reusability is very restricted. (2) A more clever way is to include dedicated algorithms into the compiler to match the behavior of the ASIP instruction set to a HLL program. The advantage of this is that the HLL is unchanged and therefore a main part of the software may stay unchanged if it needs to be ported to another system. Moreover, the developer of the HLL software needs less knowledge about the internal behavior of the target processor. The information about the customized hardware of the ASIP is transferred from the HLL into the compiler. Of course, such a compiler is often hand tailored to a special processor and is in itself not easily retargetable. In this paper, we focus on a compiler

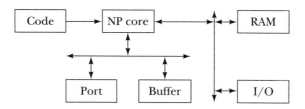

5.2

Infineon NPU architecture.

FIGURE

technique to support bit packet addressing. We will illustrate this technique on samples taken from GSM-kernel of the TU-Berlin [19].

We implemented the algorithm for the instruction set of an Infineon Technologies NPU [20]. Figure 5.2 shows a block diagram of the NPU. It supports instructions that allow subword-level data access, for example, move, load, and storage of bit packets, for highly efficient protocol processing code. The NPU instruction set permits the execution of these operations on bit packets not aligned at processor word boundaries. A packet may be stored in any bit index subrange of a register.

In order to enable packet-level addressing of unaligned data, the NPU instruction set permits the specification of offsets and operand lengths. The general instruction format is as follows:

```
CMD addr1.offset, addr2.offset, width
```

Code selectors based on integer size data flow analysis make only rare use of this class of instructions. One aim of this paper is to present a fast algorithm to detect bit packet operations. In a postpass phase, we insert bit packet instructions into the source code that make numerous instructions obsolete. A following dead code elimination phase will remove them.

We implemented an experimental version of this optimization and integrated it into an existing, fully operational ANSI C compiler for the Infineon NPU. We benchmarked our compiler with several test program fragments. We also compared the resulting code with hand-optimized code.

The remainder of the paper is structured as follows: In Section 5.1, we give an introduction to bit-level data flow analysis. In Section 5.2, we describe our code selection algorithm. In Section 5.3, we give an overview of a register allocation implementation optimized for handling bit packets in register arrays, and in Section 5.4, we present the idea of a dead code elimination using the information of a bit-level data flow analysis. In Section 5.5, we give further implementation details of the existing ANSI C compiler. In Section 5.6, we present experimental results, and in Section 5.7, we give conclusions and describe ideas for further work.

5.1   BIT-LEVEL DATA FLOW ANALYSIS AND BIT VALUE INFERENCE

A given HLL program can be represented as a data flow graph (DFG). A DFG contains all load, store, move, and data-manipulating operations, but no control flow–related aspects. A DFG is defined as a directed acyclic graph $G = (V, E)$, where each node represents an input, output, or operation. Each edge represents a definition-use (DEF-USE) dependency.

A standard representation for the dependencies between statement are DEF-USE chains. DEF-USE chains can be directly derived from the DFG [21]. Each machine operation of an instruction set should be defined by an instruction name and its parameters. Each operand of an instruction is one of the following: a constant number, the definition of a register content (DEF), the usage of a register content (USE), or both—the instruction uses and defines the same register parameter (USEDEF).

Related to the DFG, each used operand of a machine instruction may have one or multiple definitions, and each definition of an operand may have one or multiple uses. In very unusual cases, a USE without a DEF can happen if side effects are used: for instance, a push of any register is used to increment the stack pointer. Many instruction sets contain implicit operands, for example, flag manipulation through an addition. If an instruction contains only definitions that are never used, then the instruction is dead and can be removed from the program. DEF-USE chains work on entire registers; that is, DEF-USE dependencies are calculated on the full register bit width. In many cases, the results are suboptimal. Figure 5.3 shows an example where the fact that variable a does not affect the calculation of c would not be detected by the DEF-USE chain approach.

```
a = (* p1 & 0 x0F);
b = (* p2 & 0 xF0)|0 x0F;
c = a | b;
```

5.3   Bit-oriented data flow.

FIGURE

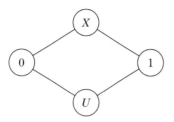

Lattice by Budiu and Goldstein.

FIGURE

An exact bit-level data flow analysis would give much more precise results. In recent years, this fact has been analyzed in different works. Yasuura, Tomiyama, and Inoue reported an analysis of the required register bank bit width for a given application [22]. If we expect that on a special ASIP only a single application is executed and we can furthermore calculate the complete bit-true data flow of the application, it is possible to reduce the size of the used data types. Therefore the power consumption of the CPU data paths and functional units can be reduced. However, this approach requires the user to determine the type information. In this paper, we will focus on algorithms without the need for user interaction.

Tool-based analysis is done in other work on bit-level data flow analysis. Brooks and Martonosi [23] proposed to replace the types of variables from integer to short to improve speed and to reduce the power consumption of a Pentium MMX processor. Impressive results are also shown by Budiu and Goldstein [24]. They pointed out that 20% of all the most significant bits of MediaBench and SpecINT95 are calculated unnecessarily. In both approaches, a bit value lattice is used. The order of the lattice is the information content of a bit. The elements are U for *no information*, 0 and 1 if a bit is a constant, and X for *don't care* if the value of a bit does not change the result of the operation. These elements form a lattice (Figure 5.4). Bit value lattices are extended to strings by concatenation.

We will extend the bit value inference approach by adding two further elements to the lattice: $\langle U_n \rangle$, *the content is unknown but we know the location*, and $\langle \bar{U}_n \rangle$, *the content is unknown but we know it is the negation of the content of a given location.* A location is a storage type (e.g., RAM, ROM, I/O) and an address. Figure 5.5 shows our lattice $\mathcal{L}$.

X is the top element ($\top$) and U the bottom element ($\bot$) of the lattice. This lattice gives us more information than the version from [24]. We will not give formal proof here, but a practical explanation later. Additionally, we need the location information later for the code selection phase in our compiler.

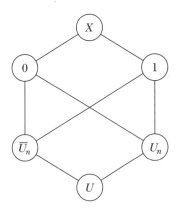

5.5

FIGURE

Extended lattice.

The bit inference is coupled to the DFG edges. For data flow analysis, we need to calculate how an operation changes the information content of a bit (or string of bits). Therefore, we define two transfer functions for each machine operation. One transfer function in the direction of the edges ($\downarrow$) that gives more information about the result of an operation (the defined parameters of a machine instruction). It calculates if/where the bits of the operators can be found in the result of an operation. This makes it easy to identify even complex combinations of *mask*, *shift*, and *move* operations. A bit packet isolation resulting from a number of such operations can be identified by looking for a consecutive number of bits from the same location in the result. Unused bits of the parameter can be identified by walking in the opposite direction to that of the edges ($\uparrow$). An example can be seen in Figure 5.9. All operand bits of an AND Operation will be $\langle X \rangle$ (*don't care*) if the bits at the same position of the other operand are $\langle 0 \rangle$. Asymmetric operations need a transfer function ($\uparrow$) for each operand.

A difficult situation occurs if two operands of an operation allow for an enhancement on the other operand, for example, $\langle 1 \rangle$ OR $\langle 1 \rangle$. Should the first or the second operand be enhanced to $\langle X \rangle$? As a first solution, we use a heuristic approach depending on the other bits of the operand.

Figures 5.6 and 5.7 give an example of a transfer function. To get as much information from the DFG as possible, we need to walk along the edges until we reach a fix point where we cannot add more information to the graph. For a loop-free DFG, this is achieved after each edge is changed by a single walk-down and walk-up. However, even for nested loops, the information about the bit content can only be improved at most four times because our lattice grid has a height

$\downarrow$	$\langle X \rangle$	$\langle 1 \rangle$	$\langle 0 \rangle$	$\langle U_n \rangle$	$\langle \bar{U}_n \rangle$	$\langle U \rangle$
$\langle X \rangle$	$\langle X \rangle$					
$\langle 1 \rangle$		$\langle 1 \rangle$	$\langle 1 \rangle$	$\langle 1 \rangle$	$\langle 1 \rangle$	$\langle 1 \rangle$
$\langle 0 \rangle$		$\langle 1 \rangle$	$\langle 0 \rangle$	$\langle U_n \rangle$	$\langle \bar{U}_n \rangle$	$\langle U \rangle$
$\langle U_n \rangle$		$\langle 1 \rangle$	$\langle U_n \rangle$	$\langle U_n \rangle$	$\langle 1 \rangle$	$\langle U \rangle$
$\langle \bar{U}_n \rangle$		$\langle 1 \rangle$	$\langle \bar{U}_n \rangle$	$\langle 1 \rangle$	$\langle \bar{U}_n \rangle$	$\langle U \rangle$
$\langle U \rangle$		$\langle 1 \rangle$	$\langle U \rangle$	$\langle U \rangle$	$\langle U \rangle$	$\langle U \rangle$

5.6

FIGURE

Transfer function ($\downarrow$) of an OR operation in the domain of $\mathcal{L}$.

of four ($|\mathcal{L}| = 4$)). Therefore in the worst case, $|\mathcal{L}| * 2$ changes will be needed until we cannot add any more information to a bit. We call this the *fix point*. After $|\mathcal{L}| * 2 * |E|$ iterations, any lattice bit reaches the top element ($\top$). To meet this low complexity, we accept only changes where at least a single bit in the DFG enhances its information content. Otherwise, it would be possible to construct a DFG where the analysis does not terminate. Figure 5.9 shows a simple example for a DFG, and Figure 5.8 shows the corresponding C program.

In the worst case, for a string S of bits with a length of $|S|$, a change can happen to a single bit only once during each iteration. A change is only valid for a graph if at least a single edge enhances its information content. In the worst case, a walk over all edges enhances each time a single bit in a single edge. That means the algorithm walks along the edges $|\mathcal{L}| * |S| * 2 * |E|^2$ times until a fix point solution is found, which gives a complexity of $O(n^2)$, where n is the number of the edges. We will use the information we get from a bit-true data flow analysis later to enhance the code quality of a given instruction sequence.

$\uparrow$	Changed operand					
	$\langle X \rangle$	$\langle 1 \rangle$	$\langle 0 \rangle$	$\langle U_n \rangle$	$\langle \bar{U}_n \rangle$	$\langle U \rangle$
Fix operand						
$\langle 1 \rangle$	$\langle X \rangle$	$\langle X \rangle$	$\langle X \rangle$	$\langle X \rangle$	$\langle X \rangle$	$\langle X \rangle$
All other	$\langle X \rangle$	$\langle 1 \rangle$	$\langle 0 \rangle$	$\langle U_n \rangle$	$\langle \bar{U}_n \rangle$	$\langle U \rangle$

5.7

FIGURE

Transfer function ($\uparrow$) of an OR operation in the domain of $\mathcal{L}$.

```
a = (b & 0 x0F);
```

5.8   Simple DFG example.

FIGURE

5.2   CODE SELECTION

Code selection uses the data flow analysis information of a basic block (BB), where a BB is a sequence of statements with one entry and one exit point. Figure 5.10 shows a BB of C statements, and Figure 5.11 the corresponding DFG.

Each machine operation of a given instruction set can be considered a small pattern. Code selection can be conceived as a complete coverage of a DFG with instruction patterns. This code selection technique is called *pattern matching*. Optimal pattern matching on graphs is NP hard [25]. The common solution for this problem is to break up the graph into a forest of trees and to perform the pattern matching on each tree separately. Figure 5.12 shows the resulting trees for the preceding example. Optimal tree pattern matching can be done in linear time with respect to the number of nodes and a constant factor given by the grammar definition, but it may cause additional machine instructions compared to optimal graph-based code selection. However, for existing homogenous machines, the code quality is similar.

In this paper, we use the *Olive* tree parser generator [26]. Olive produces from an extended Backus-Naur grammar specification a tree parser C source code as output. Figure 5.13 shows a short example of an Olive tree grammar.

The tree pattern matching algorithm is based on two phases: first, a bottom-up phase, where for each node all possible match patterns are calculated. For

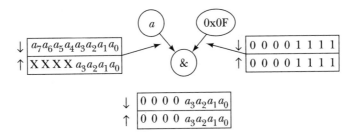

5.9   DFG representation of Figure 5.8.

FIGURE

```
a = * p + 4;
b =   a * 3;
c =   a * 7;
```

C example for a basic block.

each node, the code selector generated by Olive computes the optimal cover with respect to a given cost function. The second phase is top-down, where the machine code is emitted. Every node of the tree is visited twice by the algorithm. Therefore, the complexity is linear in the number of nodes and a constant factor given by the grammar. In this paper, we will use tree pattern matching to postoptimize the assembly output of our compiler.

5.2.1   Ertl's Tree Pattern–Matching Grammar Composition

Ertl shows in [27] that certain optimizations can be achieved virtually for free if a given tree pattern–matching grammar is extended by additional nonterminals and the according rules. The artifice behind this is that an operation is not emitted

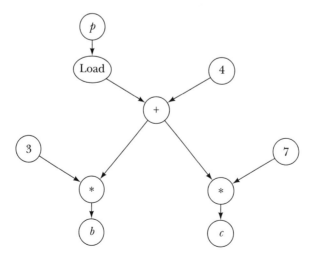

DFG example.

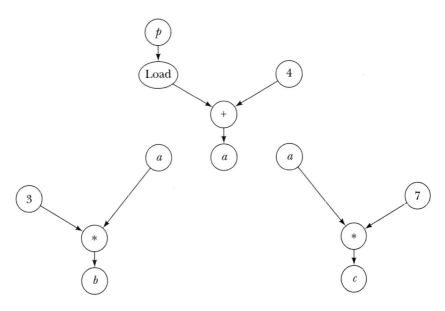

5.12

FIGURE
Decomposed forest of data flow trees.

in place, but "remembered" by an additional nonterminal. Other operations
on the way up the tree may make the operation obsolete or can do the same
computation with less cost. The example in Figure 5.14 shows an Ertl composition.
Rules 4 to 7 are the necessary rules to match Negation and the AND and OR
expressions (~, &, |). Rules 8 to 13 are an Ertl composition, whereas rules 8 and 13
remember the bitwise negation of a register for later application in the additional
nonterminal *negreg*. Rules 8 and 9 propagate the negation by transforming a
negreg into a *reg*, and vice versa. At this point, they are not affected by our
grammar extension because rules 8 and 11 are exactly equivalent to rule 5, and
also rules 9 and 10 are equivalent to 5. But rules 12 and 13 develop *De Morgan's*

```
#No non-terminal: Production              #Cost#Code Assembly
  1    reg      : Load(reg1)              #    1# LD reg, *reg1
  2    reg      : Add(reg1, const)        #    1# Add reg, reg1, const
  3    reg      : Mul(reg1, const)        #    1# Mul reg, reg1, const
```

5.13

FIGURE

Example of a short-form tree-parsing grammar.

```
#No non-terminal: Production        #Cost#Cost Assembly
 4     reg : REG                    #  0 #
 5     reg : NEG(reg1)              #  1 # NEG(reg, reg1)
 6     reg : AND(reg1, reg2)        #  1 # AND(reg, reg1, reg2)
 7     reg : OR(reg1, reg2)         #  1 # OR(reg, reg1, reg2)
#Ertl composition
 8 negreg : NEG(reg1)               #  0 #
 9    reg : NEG(negreg1)            #  0 #
10 negreg : reg1                    #  1 # NEG(negreg, reg1)
11    reg : negreg1                 #  1 # NEG(reg, negreg1)
12 negreg : AND(negreg1,negreg2) #  1 # OR(negreg,negreg1, negreg2)
13 negreg : OR(negreg1,negreg2)  #  1 # AND(negreg,negreg1, negreg2)
```

5.14

FIGURE

Example of a tree-parsing grammar with Ertl's extensions.

theorem—(Equation 5.1)—as an optimization to the grammar. Equation 5.2 is an example for an application of rule 12, and Equation 5.3 applies rule 13. Another application of rule 13 is Equation 5.4. Figure 5.15 outlines a data flow tree that is covered by usage of rule 13. In Figure 5.15(a), a standard grammar needs the cost of rule 5 twice and rule 6 once, which gives an overall cost of 3. In Figure 5.15(b), rules 8, 9, 11, and 12 are used, which gives costs of 2 because rules 8 and 9 are free. Figure 5.16 displays the resulting assembly code with and without usage of the Ertl composition in Figure 5.14, which saves one of three machine operations. Ertl [27] also shows examples for advanced constant folding, flag optimization, and optimization of unary operators. In some cases, Ertl gives some impressive results of 50% code-sized reduction for small trees.

$$\overline{a \vee b} = \bar{a} \wedge \bar{b}$$

$$\overline{a \wedge b} = \bar{a} \vee \bar{b} \tag{5.1}$$

$$\bar{a} \vee \bar{b} = \overline{a \wedge b} \tag{5.2}$$

$$\bar{a} \wedge \bar{b} = \overline{a \vee b} \tag{5.3}$$

$$\overline{\bar{a} \wedge b} = \bar{\bar{a}} \vee \bar{b} = a \vee \bar{b} \tag{5.4}$$

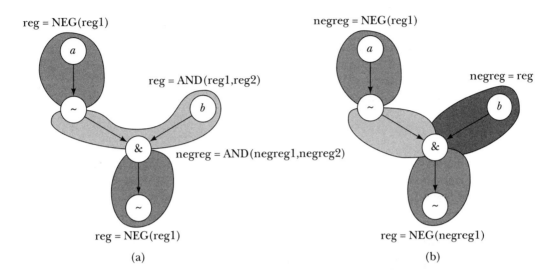

reg = NEG(reg1)

reg = AND(reg1,reg2)

negreg = AND(negreg1,negreg2)

reg = NEG(reg1)

(a)

negreg = NEG(reg1)

negreg = reg

reg = NEG(negreg1)

(b)

5.15

FIGURE

Tree pattern matching using standard grammar (a) and standard grammar extended by Ertl's composition (b).

5.2.2   Dynamic Cost Functions

In order to enforce a selection between a number of rules that match the same pattern in runtime, Olive allows for *dynamic cost functions*. To this point, we have assumed the cost of a pattern to be constant. But Olive allows the costs of a pattern to be calculated. Hence the costs of a pattern can be dependent on its parameters.

Figure 5.17 shows a constant folding example. If one parameter of the OR operation is equal to zero, the pattern 14 with no code emission is selected, but

```
NEG(R1,a)          NEG(R1,b)
AND(R2,R1,b)       OR(R2,a,R1)
NEG(R3,R2)
```

(a)   (b)

5.16

FIGURE

Resulting assembly code of the DFT (Figure 5.15) using standard grammar (a) and grammar extended by Ertl's composition (b).

```
#No non-terminal: Production#Production Cost        # Assembly
   14 reg : OR(reg1, reg2)    #(reg1==0||reg2==0)?0:∞#
   15 reg : OR(reg1, reg2)    #                 1 # OR(reg1, reg2)
```

5.17   Example of a dynamic cost function.

FIGURE

if both parameters are unequal to zero, the pattern 15 is chosen. Of course, this is only a simple example for dynamic cost functions. In Section 5.2.3, we will use more advanced functions.

5.2.3   Bit Packet Detection and Integer Instruction Substitution

In this section, we outline how extended bit-level data flow analysis, Ertl's composition on tree pattern matching, and dynamic cost functions work together in an algorithm to find a replacement for a given sequence of statements by a special bit packet operation.

We assume that all parameters and the result (all edges) of a pattern are labeled with a lattice string of a previous data flow analysis. We introduce the following nonterminals to distinguish between three different types of parameters:

+ *bp.* A bit packet, the parameter contains a number of consecutive bits of a source (a register). All other bits of the parameter are constant or *don't care* ($\langle X \rangle$, $\langle 0 \rangle$, $\langle 1 \rangle$).

+ *conBP.* The parameter can be assumed as a concatenation of two bit packets or the insertion of a bit packet into an integer. The result is a register that contains a bit packet and the remaining part of the integer.

+ *reg.* A register can be assumed as a complete integer with any value including the other two cases.

To detect these nonterminals, we define two functions that will be used in dynamic cost functions: *isBP(reg)*, which returns **true** if the register is a bit packet, and *isConBP(reg)*, which returns **true** if the register is a concatenation of two bit-packets as defined earlier.

```
#No non-terminal: Production #                    Cost#Cost Assembly
16  bp       : reg            #                       0 #
17  bp       : AND(bp, const) #       (isBP(bp))?0:∞ #
18  bp       : SHL(bp, const) #                       0 #
19  conBP    : OR(bp, bp)     # (isConBP(conBP))?0:∞ #
20  reg      : conBP          #                       1 #
                                   movBP(reg,src1,off1,src2,off2,width)
```

5.18   Part of a tree pattern–matching grammar to detect bit packet operations.

FIGURE

Figure 5.18 illustrates a part of a tree pattern–matching grammar that detects a bit packet insertion into an integer. Rules 16, 17, and 18 match the isolation of the bit packet and remember the bit packet in the *bp* nonterminal. Rule 19 gives an example for the insertion of a bit packet into an integer. To enhance code quality "no code" is emitted in this rule. If the result is needed somewhere, as a register, rule 20 would be activated where a bit packet move instruction is inserted into the assembly code.

Figure 5.19 shows a typical bit packet insertion in ANSI-C. The resulting assembly code is outlined in Figure 5.20. If we use a bit-true data flow analysis, we detect that the result r is built from three bit packets: the constant 0 at position 7, the bit packet a_0 at position 6, and the bit packet $b_7 \ldots b_2$ at position $5 \ldots 0$. Therefore only three operations (instead of nine) are needed: r needs to be set to the constant, the insertion of a_0 and the insertion of $b_7 \ldots b_2$. Figure 5.21 outlines the data flow analysis.

```
t1 = (a & 1)<<3;
t2 = t1 | ((unsigned)b >> 5);
t3 = t2 << 3;
t4 = ((unsigned)b >> 2) & 7;
r  = t3 | t4;
```

5.19   C example for bit packet insertion.

FIGURE

```
AND (t1, a, 1)
SHL (t1, t1, 3)   ;t1 = (a & 1)<<3

SHR (t2, b, 5)
AND (t2, t2, 0x7);((unsigned)b >> 5)

OR  (t2, t1, t2);t2=t1|((unsigned)b>>5)
SHL (t3, t2, 3)   ;t3=t2 << 3

SHR (t2, b, 2)
AND (t2, t2, 0x7);((unsigned)b >> 2)&7

OR  (r, t3, t4)   ;r  = t3 | t4
```

5.20

Assembly code example for bit packet insertion.

FIGURE

5.3 REGISTER ALLOCATION CONSIDERING REGISTER ARRAYS

Although the NPU shows a RISC-like basic architecture, the classical graph coloring approach to global register allocation [28] cannot be used directly. The reason is that the NPU allows us to address registers indirectly with the use of a special pointer register. The pointer register contains not only the integer address of a register, but it stores the packet offset, too. With a single clock operation, it can be incremented by the width of a packet to point to a new integer address and offset. We call a number of registers in a given order a *register array*. Register arrays arise from indirect addressing in C programs, where unaligned bit packets are traversed within loops. As a consequence, virtual registers containing (fragments of) bit packet arrays have to be assigned to contiguous windows in the physical register file.

In order to achieve this, the register allocator maintains two sets of virtual registers: one for scalar values and one for register arrays. All virtual registers are indexed by a unique number, where each register array gets a dedicated, unique, and contiguous index range. As usual, register allocation starts with a lifetime analysis of virtual registers. Potential conflicts in the form of overlapping life ranges are represented in an *interference graph*, where each node represents a

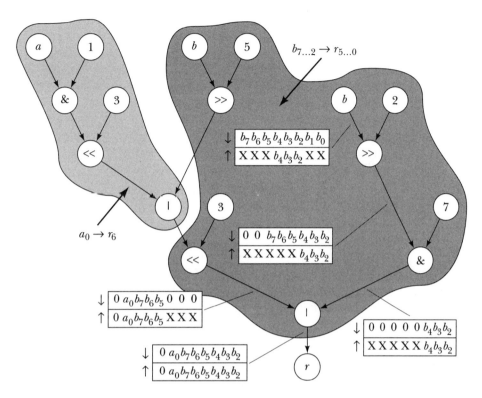

5.21

FIGURE

DFT representation and two covers.

virtual register and each edge denotes a lifetime overlap. The lifetime analysis is based on a DEF-USE analysis of virtual registers.

Due to the allocation constraints imposed by register arrays, the mapping of virtual registers to physical registers is based on a special multilevel graph coloring algorithm. Physical registers are assigned first to those virtual registers that belong to register arrays. This is necessary since register arrays present higher pressure for the register allocator than scalar registers.

First, any node set in the original interference graph that belongs to a certain register array is merged into a *supernode*. Then the interference graph is transformed into a *super-interference graph* (SIG), while deleting all edges within each supernode and all scalar virtual register nodes and their incident edges (Figure 5.22).

Next, a weight is assigned to each supernode n, which is equal to the number of internal virtual registers of n plus the maximum number of internal virtual

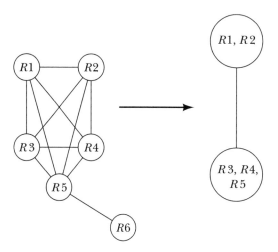

Construction of the SIG: in this example, the virtual register sets $\{R1, R2\}$ and $\{R3, R4, R5\}$ represent two register arrays, while $R6$ refers to a scalar variable.

registers of n's neighbors in the SIG. The supernodes are mapped to physical registers according to descending weights. This heuristic is motivated by the fact that supernodes of a lower weight are generally easier to allocate because they cause less lifetime conflicts. Furthermore, in case of a conflict, it is cheaper to locate a smaller array of bit packets in memory instead of a larger one. For any supernode n with r internal virtual registers, a contiguous range in the register file is assigned. Since there may be multiple such windows available at a certain point in time, the selection of this range is based on the best fit strategy in order to ensure a tight packing of register arrays in the register file.

The size of arrays of bit packets is restricted by the size of the register array. Therefore, the compiler needs to reject code where no register allocation can be done. In such a case, the compiler uses static register access and stores packets into memory. Note that for such code it would be impossible to find an equivalent assembly code even manually. Such a case can be encountered for too large register arrays or by a control flow that gives multiple definitions of a pointer variable to multiple register arrays. In such a case, all possibly accessed register arrays must be assumed to be live at the same time. Therefore, the register file has to be large enough to hold all of them simultaneously.

After register allocation for the supernodes, all remaining virtual registers in the original interference graph are mapped to physical registers by traditional graph coloring, inserting spill code whenever required.

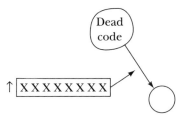

5.23

Dead code identification by bit-true data flow analysis in a special case.

FIGURE

5.4   DEAD CODE ELIMINATION

Bit-true data flow analysis gives us a more accurate impression of the data flow of a program than integer-based data flow analysis. This may be used in other optimizations other than bit packet detection. Dead code elimination, for instance, removes code that does not have any effect on the results of a program. We defined $\langle X \rangle$ as a bit that has no effect in the calculation of the result. In the expression $a = (b \,\&\, 0x0F)$; none of the bits except the four least significant bits have an effect on the result. In a special case (Figure 5.23), if all bits of an edge are set to $\langle X \rangle$, all nodes above the edge do not change the result. Therefore all these nodes are dead code and can be removed from the program, if they are not needed as common subexpressions somewhere else.

In this special case, we use the characteristic of the integer $\{\langle X \rangle \ldots \langle X \rangle\}$ that it can be replaced by anything without changing the result. In a more general case, we can remove the nodes between two edges e_1 and e_2 if edge e_2 can be replaced by e_1 without changing the result. In general: if edge e_1 can substitute edge e_2, e_1 is a subset of e_2 or e_1 is equal to e_2 ($e_1 \subseteq e_2$), and n_2 postdominates n_1, then the nodes between e_1 and e_2 are dead code.

We define the *subset equality* relation ($\subseteq$) for $\mathcal{L}$. An integer represented by i_1 is a *subset* of or equal to another integer represented by i_2 if each bit of the integer represented by i_1 is a *subset* of or equal to the bit at the same position of the integer represented by edge i_2. Figure 5.24 defines the *subset equality relation* in $\mathcal{L}$. If a crosspoint is marked with a plus, the bits are identical or a subset; if it is marked with a minus, they are not. Note that $\langle U \rangle \neq \langle U \rangle$ because the value of *both* bits cannot be predicted. For located unknown bits, however, we can assume that both bits are equal if the locations are the same ($\langle U_n \rangle = \langle U_m \rangle$; if $n = m$). Of course, anything is a subset of or equal to $\langle X \rangle$.

Figure 5.25 shows the location of dead code between two edges in a general example.

⊆	$\langle X \rangle$	$\langle 1 \rangle$	$\langle 0 \rangle$	$\langle U_n \rangle$	$\langle \bar{U}_n \rangle$	$\langle U \rangle$
$\langle X \rangle$	+	−	−	−	−	−
$\langle 1 \rangle$	+	+	−	−	−	−
$\langle 0 \rangle$	+	−	+	−	−	−
$\langle U_n \rangle$	+	−	−	+	−	−
$\langle \bar{U}_n \rangle$	+	−	−	−	+	−
$\langle U \rangle$	+	−	−	−	−	−

5.24

FIGURE

Definition of the subset equality relation of 2 bits in $\mathcal{L}$.

5.5   IMPLEMENTATION

To test our optimization, we extend an already existing *Infineon NP C compiler* described in [18] with our optimization. Like almost all compilers, our compiler is subdivided into a frontend and a backend. As a frontend, we use the LANCE compiler system developed at the University of Dortmund. This frontend is largely device independent and is used in many compiler projects [29]. Our backend, built on a retargetable tool suite, is described in [30]. Because our backend is based on an intermediate representation, where tools like code selection, optimizations, and register allocation are used as plugins, we are easily able to integrate a new optimization. Our optimization uses the intermediate representation and the processor description provided by the toolset as interface. Therefore

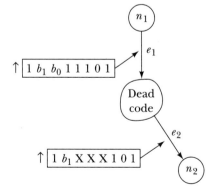

5.25

FIGURE

Dead code identification by bit-true data flow analysis in a general example.

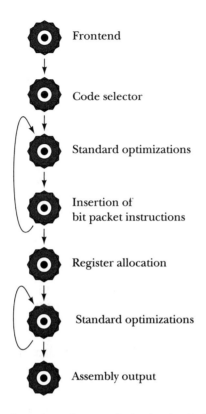

Frontend

Code selector

Standard optimizations

Insertion of
bit packet instructions

Register allocation

Standard optimizations

Assembly output

5.26   Location of our optimization in the Infineon NP C compiler.

FIGURE

it is retargetable with low effort to any architecture that supports bit packet operations. We placed the optimization into the loop of prepass optimizations before the register allocation because it lowers the register pressure (Figure 5.26). The advantage of this location is that the code for the address generation is visible because it is located after the code-generation phase. Furthermore, there is no need to replace obsolete code. The bit-packed operations are inserted into the assembly code and afterward an already available dead code elimination is reused to remove the obsolete code. Our optimization also profits from the earlier running backend optimizations that simplify the data flow of a given assembly program.

The implementation of our optimization is only experimental. We noticed that especially the grammar for tree pattern matching needs to be extended to detect a high percentage of bit packet transfers in larger benchmarks.

5.6   RESULTS

For benchmarking of our optimization, we used an existing compiler where we plugged in an additional optimization. Therefore we saved time on implementation. On the other hand, we had the problem that the interface to the intermediate representation is not optimized to our needs. For example, there is only a limited number of tools in the compiler where a bit-oriented data flow analysis is used. This may cause new problems in the compiler backend. For instance, the insertion of bit-oriented instructions may override existing, integer-based optimizations. In our test cases, the insertion of bit packet operations enhances the code quality significantly, but we noticed that the effect is lowered by the impeding of existing tools.

In order to obtain results, we compared three cases: compilation with the existing compiler, compilation with additional use of bit packet operation insertion, and hand-optimizing compiler-generated code. We decided not to generate code completely by hand. Even hand-optimizing small code fragments is extremely time-consuming. Therefore, at this early stage, we only present five small code examples. The benchmarks are created from the GSM-kernel source code [19]:

✦ *ins1*. Encoding: Insertion of bit packets smaller than an integer into an existing stream

✦ *ins2*. Encoding: Insertion of bit packets overlapping an integer

✦ *extr1*. Decoding: Extraction of bit packets from a stream into an integer

✦ *extr2*. Decoding: Extraction from overlapping integers

✦ *mem*. Bit packet memory-to-memory data transfers

Figure 5.27 shows the benefit of bit packet operation insertion and hand-optimized code as against the compiler output without bit packet operation insertion in percentage of cycles.

Name	Bit packet insertion	Hand-optimized code
ins1	−12%	−15%
ins2	−8%	−19%
extr1	−15%	−27%
extr2	−8%	−22%
mem	−14%	−45%

5.27   Benefit in percentage of cycles.

FIGURE

ACKNOWLEDGMENTS

This work was supported by the Informatik Centrum Dortmund (ICD), Infineon Technologies, and Agilent Technologies. The authors would also like to thank Jörg Eckart, Robert Pyka, and Luis Gomez, who significantly contributed to the tool implementation and test. We also thank Lars Wehmeyer for his help and suggestions.

REFERENCES

[1]   The GNU CC Project, Free Software Foundation, 2001, *www.gnu.org/software/gcc/gcc.html*.

[2]   R. M. Stallman, *Using and Porting GNU CC for Version 2.95*, Free Software Foundation, 1999.

[3]   "Instruction Set Reference," in *Intel Architecture Developer's Manual*, Vol. 2, order no. 243191, Intel Corporation, 1999, pp. 3–158, 3–355.

[4]   "Short Information MAS 3509 Compressed-Audio Decoder," order no. 6251-505-2SI, Micronas, 1999.

[5]   B. Wess, "Automatic Instruction Code Generation based on Trellis Diagrams," in *Proc. IEEE Int. Symp. on Circuits and Systems (ISCAS)*, 1992, pp. 645–648.

[6]   G. Araujo and S. Malik, "Optimal Code Generation for Embedded Memory Non-Homogeneous Register Architectures," in *Proc. 8th Int. Symp. on System Synthesis (ISSS)*, 1995, pp. 36–41.

[7]   S. Liao, S. Devadas, K. Keutzer, S. Tjiang, and A. Wang, "Code Optimization Techniques for Embedded DSP Microprocessors," in *Proc. 32nd Design Automation Conference (DAC)*, 1995, pp. 593–598.

[8]   A. Timmer, M. Strik, J. van Meerbergen, and J. Jess, "Conflict Modeling and Instruction Scheduling in Code Generation for In-House DSP Cores," in *Proc. 32nd Design Automation Conference (DAC)*, 1995, pp. 593–598.

[9]   S. Bashford and R. Leupers, "Constraint Driven Code Selection for Fixed-Point DSPs," in *Proc. 36th Design Automation Conference (DAC)*, 1999, pp. 817–822.

[10]   D. H. Bartley, "Optimizing Stack Frame Accesses for Processors with Restricted Addressing Modes," in *Software—Practice and Experience*, Vol. 22(2), 1992, pp. 101–110.

[11]   S. Liao, S. Devadas, K. Keutzer, S. Tjiang, and A. Wang, "Storage Assignment to Decrease Code Size," in *Proc. ACM SIGPLAN Conference on Programming Language Design and Implementation (PLDI)*, 1995, pp. 186–195.

[12]   R. Leupers, and F. David, "A Uniform Optimization Technique for Offset Assignment Problems," in *Proc. 11th Int. System Synthesis Symposium (ISSS)*, 1998, pp. 3–8.

[13]   E. Eckstein, and A. Krall, "Minimizing Cost of Local Variables Access for DSP Processors," in *Proc. ACM Workshop on Languages, Compilers, and Tools for Embedded Systems (LCTES)*, 1999, pp. 20–27.

[14]   R. J. Fisher, and H. G. Dietz, "Compiling for SIMD within a Register," in *Proc. 11th Annual Workshop on Languages and Compilers for Parallel Computing (LCPC98)*, 1998, pp. 290–304.

[15]   R. Leupers, "Code Selection for Media Processors with SIMD Instructions," in *Design Automation & Test in Europe (DATE)*, 2000, pp. 4–8.

[16]   S. Larsen, and S. Amarasinghe, "Exploiting Superword Level Parallelism with Multimedia Instruction Sets," in *Proc. ACM SIGPLAN Conference on Programming Language Design and Implementation (PLDI)*, 2000, pp. 145–156.

[17]   P. Paulin, "Network Processors: A Perspective on Market Requirements, Processors Architectures, and Embedded S/W Tools," in *Design Automation & Test in Europe (DATE)*, 2001, pp. 420–427.

[18]   J. Wagner, and R. Leupers, "C Compiler Design for a Network Processor," in *IEEE Trans. on CAD of Integrated Circuits and Systems (TCAD)*, Vol. 20, No. 11, 2001, pp. 1302–1308.

[19]   J. Degener, and C. Bormann, "GSM: Implementation of the 13 kbps GSM speech coding standard," 2001, *file://tub.cs.tu-berlin.de/pub/tubmik/gsm-1.0.tar.Z*.

[20]   X. Nie, L. Gazsi, F. Engel, and G. Fettweis, "A New Network Processor Architecture for High-Speed Communications," in *IEEE Workshop on Signal Processing Systems (SiPS)*, 1999, pp. 548–557.

[21]   A. W. Appel, *Modern Compiler Implementation in C*, Cambridge, New York: Cambridge University Press, 1998.

[22]   H. Yasuura, H. Tomiyama, A. Inoue, and F. N. Eko, "Embedded System Design Using Soft-Core Processor and Valen-C," in *Proc. of Asia Pacific Conf. on Hardware Description Languages*, 1997, pp. 121–130.

[23]   D. Brooks, and M. Martonosi, "Dynamically Exploiting Narrow Width Operands to Improve Processor Power and Performance," in *Proc. of HPCA-5*, 1999.

[24]   M. Budiu, and S. C. Goldstein, "Bit Value Inference: Detecting and Exploiting Narrow Bitwidth Computations," in *Proc. of 6th International Euro-Par Conference*, 2000.

[25]   A. V. Aho, S. C. Johnson, and J. D. Ullman, "Code Generation for Expressions with Common Subexpressions," in *Journal of the ACM*, Vol. 24, No. 1, 1977.

[26]   S. Tjiang, *An Olive Twig*, technical report, Synopsys Inc., 1993.

[27]   M. A. Ertl, "Optimization During Tree-Parsing Code Selection," talk given at The Dagstuhl Seminar on Code Optimization, 2000.

[28]   P. Briggs, *Register Allocation via Graph Coloring*, Doctoral thesis, Dept. of Computer Science, Rice University, Houston, 1992.

[29]   R. Leupers, *Code Optimization Techniques for Embedded Processors—Methods, Algorithms, and Tools*, Kluwer, 2001.

[30]   J. Wagner, and R. Leupers, "A Fast Simulator and Debugger for a Network Processor," in *Proc. of Embedded Intelligence Conference*, 2002.

6

CHAPTER

A Network Processor Performance and Design Model with Benchmark Parameterization

Mark A. Franklin
Departments of Computer Science and Electrical Engineering
Washington University in St. Louis

Tilman Wolf
Department of Computer Science
Washington University in St. Louis

Two design considerations are important for contemporary network processors (NPs). One is the flexibility to adapt to new functional requirements; another is the ability to provide scalable performance in response to increasing line rates. Such requirements can lead to a host of potential architectures, as can be seen when examining the multitude of commercial designs available.

While commercial designs have a number of common characteristics, we focus on just three of these. First, to deal with high line rates, NPs employ parallel processors. Network workloads inherently lend themselves to high levels of parallelism due to independence between different packet flows. Second, to reduce the latency effects of off-chip instruction and data access, the processors employ on-chip caches and multithreading techniques. Third, various state information (e.g., routing tables) and packet data is stored in separate off-chip memories, which require an on-chip memory interface.

In this paper, we develop a performance model to quantify the design alternatives associated with these three architectural elements and optimize the design to maximize overall processing power per area. This represents a starting point for developing a coherent approach and theory of NP architecture design.

The idealized single-chip NP architecture that is used in our work is shown in Figure 6.1. It contains a number of identical multithreaded general-purpose processors, each having its own instruction and data caches. To satisfy off-chip

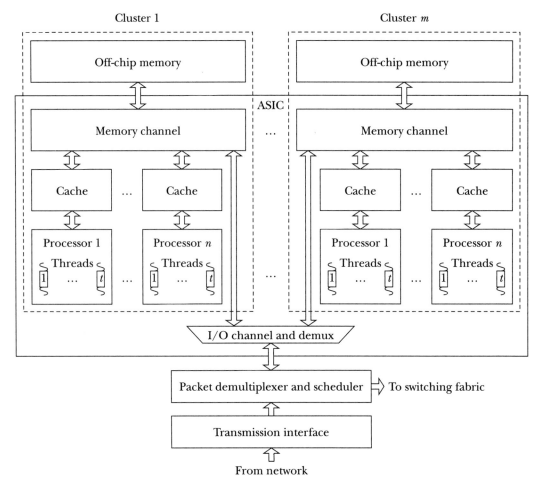

6.1 Overall network processor architecture.

FIGURE

memory bandwidth requirements, groups of processors are clustered together and share a memory interface. A scheduler assigns packets from independent flows to the different processors, thus achieving speedup by exploiting parallelism. Thus, after assignment of a flow to a processor, all packets of the same flow are routed to the same processor. More detail on the architecture can be found in [8]. Packet scheduling issues in this environment are considered in [7].

6.1 THE PERFORMANCE MODEL

The system parameters used in the performance model are listed in Table 6.1. The entire system has m clusters with n RISC processors in each cluster. Each cluster has a single memory interface with an area (in units of mm^2) of $s(mchl)$, and the entire chip has a single I/O interface with an area of $s(io)$. Each processor has an area of $s(p_j, k)$ and has its own instruction and data caches of size c_i and c_d bytes and chip areas of $s(c_i)$ and $s(c_d)$, respectively.

Component	Symbol	Description
Processor	clk_p	Processor clock frequency
	t	Number of simultaneous threads on processor
	ρ_p	Processor utilization
Program a	f_{load_a}	Frequency of load instructions
	f_{store_a}	Frequency of store instructions
	$mi_{c,a}$	I-cache miss probability for cache size c_i
	$md_{c,a}$	D-cache miss probability for cache size c_d
	$dirty_{c,a}$	Probability of dirty bit set in d-cache of size c_d
	$compl_a$	Complexity (instruction per byte of packet)
Caches	c_i	Instruction cache size
	c_d	Data cache size
	$linesize$	Cache line size of i- and d-cache
Off-chip memory	τ_{DRAM}	Access time of off-chip memory
Memory channel	$width_{mchl}$	Width of memory channel
	clk_{mchl}	Memory channel clock frequency
	ρ_{mchl}	Load on memory channel
I/O channel	$width_{io}$	Width of I/O channel
	clk_{io}	Clock rate of I/O channel
	ρ_{io}	Load on I/O channel
Cluster	n	Number of processors per cluster
ASIC	m	Number of clusters and memory channels
	$s(x)$	Actual size of component x, with $x \in \{ASIC, p, c_i, c_d, io, mchl\}$

6.1 System parameters.

TABLE

Each cache is shared among the t threads that can be supported in hardware by each processor. We assume that context switching is done in hardware with zero cycle overhead. This means that if one thread stalls on a memory miss, another thread can immediately start processing with no cycle delay. The processor is a typical RISC processor that ideally executes one instruction per cycle when no hazards are present. We also assume that the on-chip SRAM cache can be accessed in a single cycle.

The goal of our work is to find the "optimal" configuration of a network processor for a given workload. Optimal, in this context, means obtaining the maximum processing power per chip area. In the remainder of the paper, we develop analytic expressions for the processing power, *IPS* (instructions per second), and the area, *area*, associated with a given architecture configuration (number of processors, sizes of caches, etc.). From these expressions, we can obtain *IPS / area* and find its maximum as a function of the various configuration parameters, thus developing a near optimal architecture. In the remainder of this section, we discuss obtaining *IPS* and *area* in terms of system and workload characteristics.

6.1.1   Processing Performance

For a single processor, processing power can be expressed as the product of the processor's utilization, ρ_p, and its clock rate, clk_p. The processing power of the entire NP can be expressed as the sum of processing power of all the processors on the chip. Thus, with m clusters of processors and n processors per cluster,

$$IPS = \sum_{j=1}^{m} \sum_{k=1}^{n} \cdot \rho_{p_{j,k}} \cdot clk_{p_{j,k}} \tag{6.1}$$

If all processors are identical and run the same workload, then on average the processing power is

$$IPS = m \cdot n \cdot \rho_p \cdot clk_p \tag{6.2}$$

A key question is how to determine the utilization of the processors. In the extreme case where there are a large number of threads per processor, large caches that reduce memory misses, and low memory miss penalties, the utilization approaches 1. However, a large number of thread contexts and larger caches require more chip area. Our goal is to find the optimal configuration of these parameters in terms of processing power per chip area. Thus, we need to develop a cost function for different configurations that reflect the required chip area.

6.1.2   Chip Area

The on-chip area equation for an NP configuration in our general architecture is

$$area_{NP} = s(io) + \sum_{j=1}^{m}(s(mchl) + \sum_{k=1}^{n}(s(p_{j,k}, t) + s(c_{i_{j,k}}) + s(c_{d_{j,k}}))) \qquad (6.3)$$

This is the summation over all the system component areas shown in Figure 6.1. With identical processor configurations, this can be simplified to

$$area_{NP} = s(io) + m \cdot (s(mchl) + n \cdot (s(p, t) + s(c_i) + s(c_d))) \qquad (6.4)$$

The processor size, $s(p, t)$, depends on the number of hardware threads and is therefore expressed as $s(p, t)$, a function of t. We model the processor size in terms of two components: The first component, size $s(p_{basis})$, is independent of the number of supported threads. It represents the basic processor logic (ALU, pipeline control, branch prediction, etc.). The second component, size $s(p_{thread})$, relates to logic associated with a thread (thread context registers, associated logic, etc.). This thread component is modeled as increasing linearly with the number of threads, t. While this might be optimistic for large numbers of threads, it is a reasonable assumption for the relatively small number of threads considered here. Thus, the processor size is

$$s(p, t) = s(p_{basis}) + t \cdot s(p_{thread}) \qquad (6.5)$$

The size of a memory or I/O bus also consists of a basis area plus the on-chip area of the pin drivers and pads. The total size depends on the width of the bus.

$$s(mchl) = s(mchl_{basis}) + width_{mchl} \cdot s(mchl_{pin}) \qquad (6.6)$$

The number of pins depends on the bus clock, clk_{mchl}, and the required bus bandwidth, bw_{mchl}. Thus,

$$s(mchl) = s(mchl_{basis}) + \left\lceil \frac{bw_{mchl}}{clk_{mchl}} \right\rceil \cdot s(mchl_{pin}) \qquad (6.7)$$

with the equivalent equation being used for the I/O channel.

Equation 6.4 and the subsequent Equations 6.5 through 6.7 define the space of available architecture configurations (n, m, t, etc.) and determine the network processor chip area. However, before this can be used in the evaluation of the overall performance metric $IPS/area_{NP}$, the processor utilization must be determined so that IPS from Equation 6.2 can be evaluated. In particular, the processor utilization, ρ_p, depends on the performance of the memory system.

6.1.3   Memory System

The performance of the network processor is determined by the utilization of the individual processing engines. A processor is fully utilized as long as memory misses do not cause a processor stall. Other stalls due to hazards, such as branch misprediction, are not considered here since, with modern processor and compiler designs, they generally have a relatively small effect compared to the effects of cache misses. Using the model proposed and verified by Agarwal [1], the utilization $\rho_p(t)$ of a multithreaded processor is given as a function of the cache miss rate p_{miss}, the off-chip memory access time τ_{mem}, and the number of threads t as

$$\rho_p(t) = 1 - \frac{1}{\sum_{i=0}^{t} \left(\frac{1}{p_{miss} \cdot \tau_{mem}}\right)^i \frac{t!}{(t-i)!}} \tag{6.8}$$

To illustrate the overall trend in this equation, we can simplify Equation 6.8 by ignoring the second and higher-order terms of the summation. Thus,

$$\rho_p(t) = \frac{t}{(t + \tau_{mem} \cdot p_{miss})} \tag{6.9}$$

Note from this expression that, as expected, the utilization decreases with increasing miss rates and with increasing miss penalties for off-chip memory accesses. However, the larger the number of threads, t, the less the impact of τ_{mem} and p_{miss} since more threads are available for processing and processor stalls are less likely. In the limit $\lim_{t \to \infty} \rho_p(t) = 1$. While it is desirable to run processors at high utilization, there is an area cost with this as indicated in Equation 6.5. This impacts overall performance since the added processor area due to more thread contexts leads to less area available for caches and thus can lead to higher miss rates. On the other hand, more threads can also help mask cache misses and thus can be beneficial. There is a design tradeoff here, which can be understood more fully only after expressions for the memory access time, τ_{mem}, and the cache miss rate, p_{miss}, are obtained.

Off-Chip Memory Access

We assume the memory channel implements a FIFO service order on the memory requests in such a way that they can be interleaved in a split transaction fashion. The total off-chip memory request time, τ_{mem}, thus has three components: the bus access time, τ_Q; the physical memory access time, τ_{DRAM}; and the cache line transmission time, $\tau_{transmit}$ (all represented in terms of numbers of processor clock cycles).

$$\tau_{mem} = \tau_Q + \tau_{DRAM} + \tau_{transmit} \tag{6.10}$$

The DRAM access time and the cache line transmission time are straightforward to determine. The queuing time, however, depends on the load on the memory channel, which depends on the number of processors that share the memory channel, the number of threads per processor, and the cache miss rates. This system component can be simply modeled as a single server queuing system with n processors that generate requests. The request distribution can be modeled as geometrically distributed random variables (as suggested in [1]). Based on the average cache miss rate of a thread (see Equation 6.14), the parameter of the geometric random variable is p_{miss}. The number of requests per processor is limited to t, which corresponds to the situation where all the processor threads are stalled and the processor is idle until a memory request is served. The service time for the memory channel is taken to be deterministic with parameter $1/\tau_{transmit}$.

This model can be slightly modified to make it more suitable for the analytical evaluation. Instead of considering n processor sources each providing up to t requests, we model the system as a single finite source having up to $n \cdot t$ requests. Since each of the n sources generates requests at a mean rate p_{miss}, the single source model generates requests at a rate $n \cdot p_{miss}$.

Assuming an exponential distribution rather than a geometric one and ignoring the limit of $n \cdot t$ customers, the queuing system can be approximated by an M/D/1 queuing system. The request rate is $\lambda = n \cdot p_{miss}$, and the deterministic service rate is $\mu = 1/\tau_{transmit}$.

The M/D/1 model is a reasonable approximation of the real system, which has a finite source population. Figure 6.2 shows the average queue length for the simulated real finite source system and the analytic result for the M/D/1 system. The number of threads in this example is $t = 8$, the number of processors is $n = 4$, and the service time $\tau_{transmit} = 40$. The M/D/1 model has no constraint on the maximum number of requests and therefore reaches a much larger queue length for very high loads (i.e., $> 90\%$). For a more typical load of $\rho_{mchl} = 0.5 \ldots 0.9$, the difference between M/D/1 and the other model is relatively small. Furthermore, below 50% load the queue length is small enough for both models to have relatively little effect on the overall performance. Therefore we will use the M/D/1 model for an approximation of the queuing time τ_Q.

The bus access time, τ_Q, is then given by the queuing time of the M/D/1 system, which is

$$\tau_Q = \frac{\rho_{mchl}^2}{2(1 - \rho_{mchl})} \cdot \frac{linesize}{width_{mchl}} \cdot \frac{clk_p}{clk_{mchl}} \tag{6.11}$$

With a fixed DRAM access time, τ_{DRAM}, and a transmission time of

$$\tau_{transmit} = \frac{linesize}{width_{mchl}} \cdot \frac{clk_p}{clk_{mchl}} \tag{6.12}$$

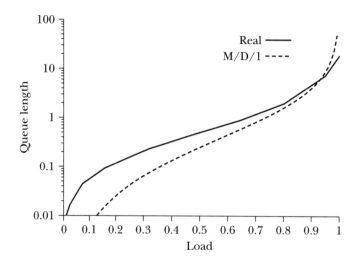

6.2   Comparison of average memory queue length for different queuing models.

FIGURE

we can substitute in Equation 6.10 to obtain the memory access time.

$$\tau_{mem} = \tau_{DRAM} + \left(1 + \frac{\rho_{mchl}^2}{2(1 - \rho_{mchl})}\right) \cdot \frac{linesize}{width_{mchl}} \cdot \frac{clk_p}{clk_{mchl}} \tag{6.13}$$

On-Chip Cache

The remaining component needed to evaluate the utilization expression (Equation 6.8) is the cache miss rate p_{miss}. For a simple RISC-style load–store processor running application a, the miss probability is given as [4]:

$$p_{miss,a} = mi_{c,a} + (f_{load_a} + f_{store_a}) \cdot md_{c,a} \tag{6.14}$$

where $mi_{c,a}$ and $md_{c,a}$ are the instruction and data cache miss rates, and f_{load_a} and f_{store_a} are the frequency of occurrence of load and store instructions associated with application a. The instruction and data cache miss rates depend on the application, the cache sizes that have been implemented, and the effects of cache pollution due to multithreading.

Cache pollution from multithreading reduces the effective cache size that is available to each thread. On every memory stall, a thread gets to request one new cache line (replacing the least recently used line). While the thread is stalled, $t - 1$ other threads can replace one line. In steady state, each thread can use $\frac{1}{t}$ of the available cache. If the working set size of a thread is very small, its effective cache usage could be less than $\frac{1}{t}$ (and the other threads could use slightly more). In a network processor, we expect the cache sizes to be smaller than the working set size due to chip area constraints, which leads to equal sharing of the available cache between threads. Thus, the effective cache size that is available to a thread is

$$c_{i,eff} = \frac{c_i}{t}, \qquad c_{d,eff} = \frac{c_d}{t} \tag{6.15}$$

The application characteristics that are necessary for evaluating Equation 6.14 are derived from a communications benchmark that is discussed in Section 6.2.

6.1.4 Memory and I/O Channels

The expression for miss rate p_{miss} (Equation 6.14) and for total memory access time τ_{mem} (Equation 6.10) can now be substituted into Equation 6.8 to obtain processor utilization. In order to do this, we need to fix the memory channel load, ρ_{mchl}, because τ_Q depends on ρ_{mchl}. Thus, with the memory channel load given, we can determine the utilization of a single processor. This gives us the memory bandwidth, $bw_{mchl,1}$, required by a single processor

$$bw_{mchl,1} = \rho_p \cdot clk_p \cdot linesize \cdot (mi_c + (f_{load} + f_{store}) \cdot md_c \cdot (1 + dirty_c)) \tag{6.16}$$

In this equation, we have to consider the case where a dirty cache line needs to be written back to memory. The probability of the dirty bit being set on a cache line is $dirty_c$. In Equation 6.14, considering dirty cache lines was not necessary, since a write-back does not stall the processor. In practice, the write-back only increases the required memory bandwidth slightly and Equation 6.16 can be approximated by

$$bw^*_{mchl,1} = \rho_p \cdot clk_p \cdot linesize \cdot p_{miss} \tag{6.17}$$

The number of processors n in a cluster is then the number of processors that can share the memory channel without exceeding the specified load.

$$n = \left\lfloor \frac{width_{mchl} \cdot clk_{mchl} \cdot \rho_{mchl}}{bw_{mchl,1}} \right\rfloor \tag{6.18}$$

This gives us a complete cluster configuration for all ranges of cache sizes and thread contexts. Finally, we need to determine the bandwidth that is required for the I/O channel. The I/O channel is used to send packets to the processing engines and back out. Thus, each packet traverses the I/O channel twice. From Equation 6.21, we get a relation between the number of instructions executed in processing a packet and the size of the packet. This "complexity" is a parameter that is characteristic for each application. The I/O channel is operated at a load of ρ_{IO}; thus, the I/O channel bandwidth for the entire network processor is

$$bw_{IO} = 2 \cdot \frac{IPS}{compl \cdot \rho_{IO}} \tag{6.19}$$

Finally, the network processor is limited in the number of pins that the package can have. As a rough estimate, we add the number of pins required by the I/O and memory channels, which depends on their respective width, to the control pins for the network processor:

$$pins_{NP} = pins_{IO} + m \cdot pins_{mchl} + pins_{control} \tag{6.20}$$

We can see later that, for our basic architecture, the number of pins that can be supported do not pose a practical limit on the network processor.

6.1.5   Optimization

With the performance and area of the network processor expressed in terms of cache configurations, application characteristics, and memory channel load, we can find the maximum $IPS/area$. Since the optimization space is discrete (other than the memory channel load) and relatively small, we can do this by exhaustive search.

6.2   WORKLOAD AND SYSTEM CHARACTERISTICS

Before we can optimize the network processor configuration, we have to define the workload and system parameters.

6.2.1   CommBench Benchmark

To properly evaluate and design network processors, it is necessary to specify a workload that is typical of that environment. This has been done in the development of the benchmark CommBench [6]. CommBench applications have been selected to represent typical workloads for both traditional routers (focusing on header processing) and programmable routers (performing both header and stream processing). Thus, the applications can be divided into two groups: *header-processing applications* (HPA) and *payload-processing applications* (PPA). HPAs process only packet headers, which in general makes them computationally less

Name	Type	Application	Kernel
RTR	HPA	Radix tree routing	Lookup on tree data structure
FRAG	HPA	IP header fragmentation	Packet header checksum computation
DRR	HPA	Deficit round robin	Queue maintenance
TCP	HPA	TCP filtering	Pattern matching on header fields
CAST	PPA	Encryption	Encryption arithmetic
ZIP	PPA	Data compression	Compression arithmetic
REED	PPA	Reed-Solomon FEC	Redundancy coding
JPEG	PPA	JPEG compression	DCT and Huffman coding

6.2   Benchmark applications.

TABLE

demanding than PPAs, which process all of the data in a packet. A list of the applications is given in Table 6.2.

A desirable property of any application in a benchmark is its representativeness of a wider class of applications in the domain of interest. Therefore, the key focus is on the "kernels" of the applications, which are the program fragments containing the set of dynamically and frequently used instructions. We determine the kernel of a program statistically by identifying the set of instructions that constitutes the majority of all instruction executions. If the kernel of an application is computationally similar to a wide class of applications, we can assume that the derived characteristics of the benchmark applications are representative for this class. For example, the tree-based lookup in the RTR program is representative of many routing algorithms as well as packet classification schemes. The discrete cosine transform performed in the JPEG program is the basis of all JPEG and MPEG coding schemes. The application kernels are also shown in Table 6.2.

For each application, the properties required for the performance model have been measured experimentally: computational complexity, load and store instruction frequencies, instruction cache and data cache miss rate, and dirty bit probability.

The complexity of an application can be obtained by measuring the number of instructions that are required to process a packet of a certain length:

$$compl = \frac{instructions\ executed}{packet\ size} \tag{6.21}$$

Table 6.3 shows the computational complexity for the CommBench applications. Payload processing applications are inherently more complex since they process the entire packet payload.

HPA a	$compl_{a,64}$	$compl_{a,1536}$	PPA a	$compl_{a,\infty}$ **(enc)**	$compl_{a,\infty}$ **(dec)**
TCP	10.3	.4	REED	603	1052
FRAG	7.7	.3	ZIP	226	35
DRR	4.1	.2	CAST	104	104
RTR	2.1	.1	JPEG	81	60

6.3

TABLE

Computational complexity of CommBench applications.

The cache properties were obtained with a processor and cache simulator (Shade [2] and Dinero [3]) for cache sizes ranging from 1 kB to 1024 kB. A two-way associative write-back cache with a linesize of 32 bytes was simulated. The cache miss rates were measured such that cold cache misses were amortized over a long program run. Thus, they can be assumed to represent the steady-state miss rates of these applications.

Compared to the SPEC CPU benchmark [5], which is the established benchmark for workstation processors, CommBench applications are about one order of magnitude smaller in terms of static and dynamic code size. Also, cache miss rates for CommBench are much smaller than for SPEC applications. This supports the notion of network processing applications being simpler and more focused than workstation workloads. As a result, simple RISC cores with small caches can perform better on network processor workloads (see Section 6.3). More details on CommBench application characteristics can be found in [6].

6.2.2   Network Processor Workload

We aggregate the application parameters from CommBench into two workloads that we consider for the evaluation of our analysis:

✦ Workload A: Header processing applications

✦ Workload B: Payload processing applications

These workloads are such that there is an equal distribution of processing requirements over all applications within each workload. Table 6.4 shows the aggregate complexity and load and store frequencies of the workloads. Note that the complexity of payload processing is significantly higher than for header processing. This is due to the fact that payload processing actually touches every byte of the packet payload (e.g., transcoding, encryption). Header processing typically only reads few header fields and does simple lookup and comparison operations. The aggregate cache miss rates for instruction and data cache are shown in Figure 6.3.

Workload W	$compl_W$	$f_{load,W}$	$f_{store,W}$
A—HPA	9.1	0.2319	0.0650
B—PPA	249	0.1691	0.0595

6.4

TABLE

Computational complexity and load and store frequencies of workloads.

The x-axis corresponds to the effective cache size available to a thread as given in Equation 6.15. Both workloads achieve instruction miss rates below 0.5% for cache sizes of 8 kB or more. The data cache miss rate for workload A also drops below 0.5% for 8 kB. For workload B, though, the data cache miss rate only drops below 1% for 32 kB or larger caches.

6.2.3 System Parameters

The system parameters for the network processor are listed in Table 6.5. The values for the on-chip area of different components are approximated for .18μm CMOS technology. It should be noted that exact values are hard to obtain from industrial sources. The performance model can of course be used with more accurate parameter sets.

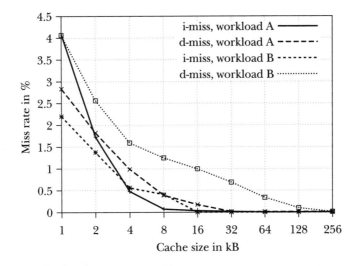

6.3

FIGURE

Aggregate cache performance of workloads.

Parameter	Value(s)
clk_p	200 MHz ... 800 MHz
t	1 ... 16
c_i	1 kB ... 1024 kB
c_d	1 kB ... 1024 kB
$linesize$	32 byte
τ_{DRAM}	60 ns
$width_{mchl}$	16 bit ... 64 bit
ρ_{mchl}	0 ... 1
$width_{io}$	up to 72 bit
ρ_{io}	0.75
clk_{mchl}, clk_{io}	200 MHz
$s(p_{basis})$	1 mm^2
$s(p_{thread})$	0.25 mm^2
$s(c_i)$, $s(c_d)$	0.10 mm^2 per kB
$s(mchl_{basis})$, $s(io_{basis})$	10 mm^2
$s(mchl_{pin})$, $s(io_{pin})$	0.25 mm^2
$s(ASIC)$	up to 400 mm^2

6.5

TABLE

System parameters for optimization.

6.3   DESIGN RESULTS

This section presents and discusses the optimization results and performance trends for various system parameters.

6.3.1   Optimal Configuration

Table 6.6 shows the best overall configuration for both workloads. There are several important points that can be seen from this table:

✦ The optimal number of threads in both cases is $t = 2$, which indicates that it is not necessary to have a large number of threads to obtain good performance.

✦ The cache sizes are in the range of 16 kB to 32 kB, which yields an effective cache size of 8 kB to 16 kB per thread. These values correspond to knees in the i-miss curves in Figure 6.3. Note that for the d-cache of workload B, a

Parameter	Workload A	Workload B
clk_p	800 MHz	800 MHz
t	2	2
m	2	3
c_i	16 kB	32 kB
c_d	16 kB	16 kB
$width_{mchl}$	64 bit	64 bit
ρ_{mchl}	0.91	0.89
p_{miss}	0.187%	0.286%
τ_{mem}	137.6	121.6
ρ_p	0.974	0.957
n	31	20
$width_{io}$	71	3
$pins_{NP}$	$199+pins_{control}$	$195+pins_{control}$
IPS	48324 MIPS	45934 MIPS
area	272 mm^2	322 mm^2
IPS/area	178 MIPS/mm^2	142 MIPS/mm^2

6.6   Optimal configurations.

TABLE

small cache size gives better results since there is no clear knee in the curve that makes a larger cache pay off.

◆ Both configurations use the fastest processor because there is no cost in the model associated with higher clock rates. Also the widest memory channel is used because it amortizes the basis cost $s(mchl_{basis})$ over a wider channel.

◆ The number of processors per cluster, n, is 31 and 20. This is relatively high because a wider memory channel with more processors sharing it amortizes the basis cost better. When limiting the width of the memory channel to smaller sizes (e.g., 48 bits), the same configuration as in Table 6.6 with a smaller n (e.g., 24) and a larger m (e.g., 3) is the best overall. The IPS/area value for this configuration is slightly lower (e.g., 173 MIPS/mm^2).

◆ The number of clusters per system is two or three, which is limited by the overall chip area and the I/O channel width. With smaller memory channels and smaller n, the number of possible clusters increases.

◆ The width of the I/O channel is much higher for workload A because the processing complexity is much smaller for header processing applications.

Therefore data moves more quickly into and out of the network processor. For payload processing, the data remains on the processor for a longer time. Thus, the width of the I/O channel is smaller.

✦ The overall processing power for both workloads is about the same (although workload B uses more chip area). Due to the lower complexity of header processing, this translates into a much larger throughput for workload A.

Note that these results are optimistic and do not account for certain factors. For example, packet classification is assumed to be done off-chip and no resources are consumed in maintaining and managing memories and routing tables.

6.3.2 Performance Trends

The optimal configurations of the network processor are very specific to a particular workload. To get more general results, we now look at the impact of different system parameters on the overall performance by varying them. Unless noted otherwise, parameters are fixed to $t = 2$, $clk_p = 800$ MHz, $m = 1$, $c_i = 16$ kB, $c_d = 16$ kB, $width_{mchl} = 64$ bit, and workload A. Note that these parameters correspond to the optimal configurations for workload A shown in Table 6.6. Also, ρ_{mchl} is chosen to be such that it yields the maximum performance. When using the term *performance*, we mean *IPS/area* (not *IPS*). Some of the configurations discussed next exceed the limits on total chip area, width of the I/O channel, and pin count. They are still shown because they might become feasible in the future.

Memory Channel

One critical parameter for the memory channel performance is the load, ρ_{mchl}. Figure 6.4 shows the performance of the network processor depending on the chosen load. It also shows the queue length given by the M/D/1 queuing model. For high loads, the queuing time is so high that it impacts the performance of the processors. For most configurations, the best load is about $\rho_{mchl} = 0.9$.

The width of the memory channel also affects the performance of the network processor. Figure 6.5 shows that for one thread, the memory channel performance does not impact the overall performance because the system is mostly limited by τ_{DRAM} and τ_Q. For two or more threads, a fourfold increase in memory channel bandwidth (from 16 bit to 64 bit) yields up to twice the performance.

Processor

The processor can be analyzed in terms of clock rate and the number of thread contexts. Figure 6.6 shows the performance gains for higher clock rates over

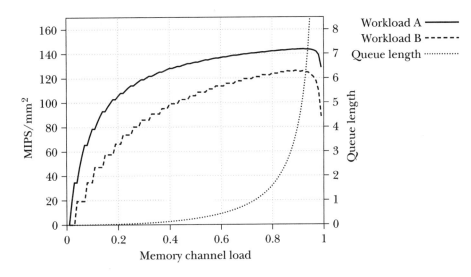

6.4

FIGURE

Performance depending on memory channel load.

different numbers of threads. For one or two threads, the performance increases almost linear with clock speed. For larger numbers of threads, the amount of available cache per thread is less, which leads to more cache misses and possible memory stalls. Thus, the increase in performance is limited by off-chip memory accesses that cause processor stalls.

The performance impact of the number of available thread contexts can also been seen in Figures 6.5 and 6.6. In both graphs, the optimal number of threads is two. For a larger number of threads, there are two factors that limit their benefits: one is the higher cache miss rate due to memory pollution; the other is the additional area cost for the thread context.

To illustrate the impact of the cache pollution, Figure 6.7 shows the optimal number of threads for a given i-cache and d-cache configuration. This shows that if larger caches were available, more threads could be used for optimal performance. This indicates that with advances in on-chip memory technology, it can be expected that the number of threads in a processing engine will increase in the future.

Cache Memory

The size of on-chip caches is also an important configuration parameter. Since on-chip SRAM is expensive in terms of area cost, the amount of memory should be

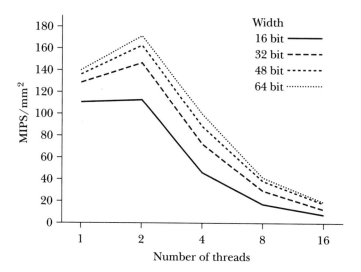

6.5

FIGURE

Performance depending on memory channel width and number of threads.

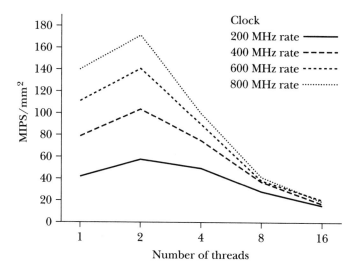

6.6

FIGURE

Performance depending on processor clock rate and number of threads.

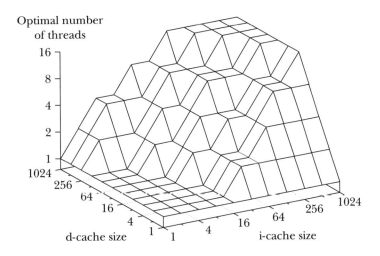

Optimal number
of threads

16

8

4

2

1

1024
    256
        64
        16
            4
                1   1   4   16   64   256   1024

d-cache size   i-cache size

Optimal number of threads for cache configuration.

minimized, while still maintaining good cache hit rates to allow efficient execution
of applications. Figures 6.8 and 6.9 show the performance of different cache
configurations for both workloads. The performance is low for small caches due
to high miss rates. It is also low for very large caches since much chip area is used.
The optimum for workload A lies at $c_i = 16$ kB and $c_d = 16$ kB. The optimum for
workload B is at $c_i = 32$ kB and $c_d = 16$ kB. With $t = 2$, each thread uses effectively
half of the available cache.

Another observation is that the performance is relatively sensitive to devia-
tions from the optimal i-cache size. The d-cache size is less sensitive but still has
much impact on the overall performance. This leads to the conclusion that it is important to configure the memory system of network processors for the particular
workload.

Chip Area Usage

Finally, to give a rough idea of how the chip area of a network processor is used,
we evaluate what fraction of the total area is used for the processor (including
thread contexts), the cache, and the memory and I/O channels. Figure 6.10 shows
the fraction of processor area versus the fraction of cache area. The remaining
fraction (to add up to 1) is the memory and I/O channel area. The top 1% (= 531)
of all configurations are shown. Thus, the processor area typically makes up 25%–
40% of the chip area. The cache area accounts for 20%–60%, and the memory

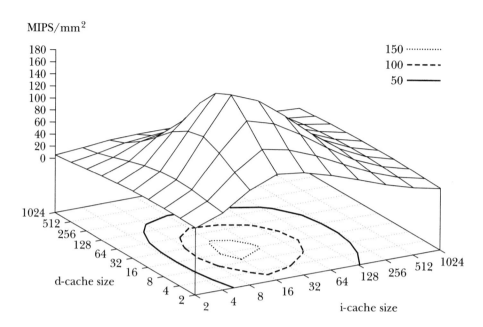

6.8

FIGURE   Performance depending on cache configuration (workload A).

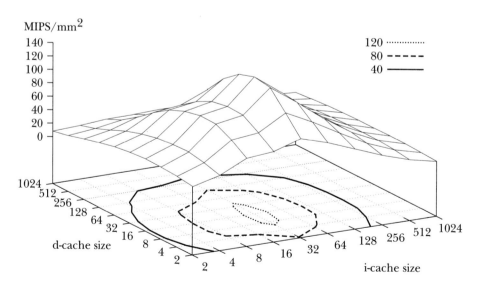

6.9

FIGURE   Performance depending on cache configuration (workload B).

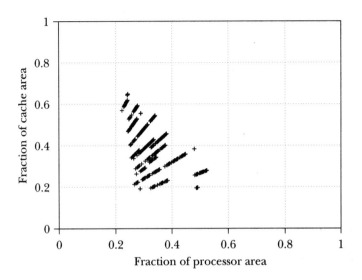

Chip area distribution for top 1% of configurations.

and I/O channel area for 20%–60%. The centroid lies at 34% for processors, 38% for cache, and 27% for memory and I/O channel.

6.3.3   Summary of Results

The results of our performance model can be used to extract a few general design guidelines for network processors:

- ✦ The cache configuration has a big impact on the overall performance, which is sensitive to the workload.

- ✦ Two to four hardware contexts for threads is optimal. With large on-chip caches, more threads perform better.

- ✦ Higher processor clock rates and memory channel bandwidths are directly related to performance improvements for four or fewer threads.

- ✦ The chip area is roughly evenly split between processors, caches, and memory interfaces.

These results are somewhat dependent on the particular workload and system parameters that are used. The main contribution of this work are not the design results per se but rather the performance model that can be used with other workloads and system parameters.

6.4   CONCLUSION

The network processor model and the associated performance expressions represent an attempt at developing a coherent approach to designing NPs. The approach is driven by the requirements of applications, the constraints associated with technology, and the selection of design alternatives within a general architecture. While the presented architecture is relatively simple, it could handle line rates on the order of Gbps given current ASIC technology.

Several extensions to the model can be pursued to account for trends in commercial network processor design:

- ✦ *Specialized co-processors and instruction sets:* Certain time-consuming networking tasks occur frequently. To deal with such tasks, it is often worthwhile to develop customized logic for use with specialized processor instructions or co-processors.

- ✦ *More sophisticated memory management:* In the current model, every packet is transmitted to a processing engine and back. For header processing applications, only the header of the packet is needed. Many commercial NPs store part of the packet (i.e., the header) in faster on-chip SRAM and the payload in off-chip DRAM.

- ✦ *Trace-driven simulation instead of mean value analysis:* The proposed model provides a first step toward understanding design tradeoffs. Using actual packet and instruction traces for a system simulation is the next step toward more accurate results.

These extensions are currently work in progress. We believe that this work will help formalize NP design and provide a method for fast and accurate exploration of the vast network processor design space.

REFERENCES

[1]   A. Agarwal, "Performance tradeoffs in multithreaded processors," *IEEE Transactions on Parallel and Distributed Systems*, 3(5):525–539, September 1992.

[2]   R. F. Cmelik, and D. Keppel, "Shade: A fast instruction-set simulator for execution profiling," in *Proc. of ACM SIGMETRICS*, Nashville, May 1994.

[3]   J. Edler, and M. D. Hill, *Dinero IV Trace-Driven Uniprocessor Cache Simulator*, 1998. *www.cs.wisc.edu/~markhill/DineroIV/*.

[4]   J. L. Hennessy, and D. A. Patterson, *Computer Architecture—A Quantitative Approach*, Second ed., Morgan Kaufmann, San Francisco, 1995.

[5]   Standard Performance Evaluation Corporation, *SPEC CPU95—Version 1.10*, August 1995.

[6]   T. Wolf, and M. A. Franklin, "CommBench—A telecommunications benchmark for network processors," in *Proc. of IEEE International Symposium on Performance Analysis of Systems and Software (ISPASS)*, pp. 154–162, Austin, Texas, April 2000.

[7]   T. Wolf, and M. A. Franklin, "Locality-aware predictive scheduling for network processors," in *Proc. of IEEE International Symposium on Performance Analysis of Systems and Software (ISPASS)*, pp. 152–159, Tucson, November 2001.

[8]   T. Wolf, and J. S. Turner, "Design issues for high performance active routers," *IEEE Journal on Selected Areas of Communication*, 19(3):404–409, March 2001.

A Benchmarking Methodology for Network Processors

Mel Tsai, Chidamber Kulkarni, Niraj Shah, Kurt Keutzer
University of California, Berkeley

Christian Sauer
Infineon Technologies, CPR ST, Munich

The number of network processors has grown at an astonishing rate; there are currently more than 30 network processor unit (NPU) vendors that have collectively achieved over 500 design wins [1]. Although this rapid growth has spawned many new network processor alternatives, it also presents a host of new problems. Indeed, network processors have widely disparate microarchitectures, memory architectures, and system interfaces that make evaluation and comparison very difficult [2]. Furthermore, NPU vendors target applications with widely different requirements, from low-speed switches to high-end Internet core routers. Because one of the primary tasks of a system architect is to choose the best network processor for a particular application, a fair comparison and evaluation of network processors is needed.

Recent work in network processing benchmarks [3, 4, 5, 6] has focused on functionality, largely neglecting architectural concerns. As a result, these approaches are unable to effectively adapt to rapid changes in network processor architectures. Hence, a disciplined approach to network processor *benchmarking* is required.

Two important goals of NPU benchmarks are

+ They must provide results that are *comparable* across network processors.

◆ They must provide results that are *representative* and *indicative* of real-world application performance.

Though not the focus of this paper, benchmarking also plays a critical role in the architectural development process of application-specific instruction processors (ASIPs). In the development of a network processor, architects can apply a benchmarking methodology that facilitates the evaluation of a prospective architecture and thus enables efficient exploration of the space of potential architectures.

To meet the goals of NPU benchmarking, we present a methodology that allows benchmark results to be comparable, representative, and indicative of real-world application performance. Comparability of results is achieved by precise specification and separation of benchmark *functionality*, *environment*, and means of *measurement*. Functionality captures the important aspects of the benchmark's algorithmic core. In contrast, the environment supplies the normalizing test bench in which the functionality resides and allows results to be compared across NPUs. Finally, guidelines for the measurement of performance ensure that quantitative results are consistently measured across implementations.

The specification of benchmark functionality, environment, and means of measurement is only one part of the methodology. For benchmarks to be representative of real-world NPU applications, a correct way to *select* benchmarks is important. Thus, not only does our methodology describe how to select a realistic suite of benchmarks based on an application domain analysis of network processors, but also how to choose the appropriate granularity of a benchmark so that results will be indicative of real-world performance.

To specify our benchmark functionality and environment, we augment an English-language description with an executable specification in the Click Modular Router framework [7]. Click is a parallel language that naturally communicates the benchmark specification and is superior to approaches that merely include a reference implementation (with little notion of system-level aspects) in a serial programming language.

The rest of this paper is organized as follows: In Section 7.1, we summarize previous and ongoing work relating to NPU benchmarks. Next, in Section 7.2, we describe our generalized benchmarking methodology and apply it to the network processor domain. Section 7.3 presents our proposed NPU benchmarking suite and includes a benchmark specification example for IPv4 packet forwarding. We demonstrate results for the Intel IXP1200 network processor in Section 7.4. Finally, in Sections 7.5 and 7.6, we suggest future work and then summarize and identify some limitations of our benchmarking methodology.

7.1   RELATED WORK

Popular benchmarking approaches such as SPEC [8], Dhrystone [9], and Media-Bench [10] work well because their intended architectural platforms are homogeneous. In other words, these and other related approaches focus solely on the functional characteristics of the application and do not emphasize the system-level aspects (e.g., interfaces) of the architectural platform. As a result, these approaches do not work well for application domains with widely heterogeneous architectures.

We are aware of five primary benchmarking efforts related to NPUs: Comm-Bench, EEMBC, NetBench, NPF Benchmarking Working Group, and Intel Corporation. In general, these approaches do not emphasize the system-level interfaces of a network processor. Because the performance of a network processor is heavily dependent on system-level interfaces such as the network and control interfaces, it is crucial to account for such differences in a network processor benchmarking methodology. For example, how does one compare the Motorola C-Port C-5 (which contains a programmable and flexible on-chip MAC unit) to the Intel IXP1200 (which does not contain an on-chip MAC unit)? Without special consideration of these environmental issues, fair comparisons between the C-Port C-5 and the IXP1200 cannot be drawn.

As shown later, benchmarking also requires a specification methodology, an executable description, a method for performance measurement, and a motivation for the selection of benchmarks.

7.1.1   CommBench

CommBench [5] specifies eight network processor benchmarks, four of which are classified as header processing applications and the other four as payload processing applications. CommBench motivates their choice of benchmarks but provides no methodology of specification or consideration of system-level interfaces. In addition, the implementation and analysis of CommBench currently targets general-purpose uniprocessors [5], and it is unclear how their benchmark suite can be applied in the context of network processors.

7.1.2   EEMBC

The Embedded Microprocessor Benchmark Consortium [4] (EEMBC) defines a set of 34 application benchmarks in the areas of automotive/industrial, consumer, networking, office automation, and telecommunication domains. In the networking domain, EEMBC defines only three simple benchmarks (Patricia route lookup, Dijkstra's OSPF algorithm, and packet flow between queues) with little notion of a methodology that can be applied to network processors.

7.1.3   NetBench

NetBench [6] defines and classifies a set of nine network processor benchmarks according to microlevel, IP-level, and application-level granularities. By using this classification, NetBench acknowledges the heterogeneous aspects of network processor microarchitectures and has initial results for the SimpleScalar [11] simulator and three results for the Intel IXP1200. However, as with [4] and [5], NetBench does not provide a methodology that considers the heterogeneity of network processor interfaces.

7.1.4   NPF Benchmarking Working Group

The NPF Benchmarking Working Group [3] (NPF-BWG) defines benchmarks based on microlevel, function-level, and system-level applications. Although NPF-BWG has previewed examples of each type of these classifications, as of this writing they have produced only an IPv4 routing benchmark. They are currently working on a draft specification for an MPLS benchmark.

NPF-BWG attempts to address some environment- and system-related NPU benchmarking issues (through their notion of a system-test configuration). However, we have seen little discussion or published work on what defines a system-test configuration, and it is unclear whether network interface issues have been fully addressed.

7.1.5   Intel Corporation

Intel's [12] benchmarking approach focuses on the IXP1200 network processor. They define a four-level benchmark hierarchy: hardware level, microlevel, function level, and system level. Hardware-level benchmarks are designed to test functionality specific to a particular NPU (e.g., memory latencies). They provide some results for IPv4 forwarding on the Intel IXP1200. Intel's executable description and method for performance measurement are specific to the IXP1200.

Intel's work recognizes the need for benchmark comparability by describing a "benchmarking reference platform." This model wraps black-box functionality (the network processor, co-processors, and memory) with a set of media, fabric, and control interfaces. However, these interfaces are left unspecified so that customers can modify the reference platform to suit their particular needs. As we will argue later, these interfaces must be appropriately specified because they are critical for benchmark comparability. Intel's published work does not indicate whether they provide a methodology for benchmark specification.

7.1.6   Other Work

Nemirovsky [13] recognizes the needs and requirements of network processor benchmarking. Although Nemirovsky provides insight into the methods for quantifying network processor performance, he does not provide precise information about a viable benchmarking approach.

Crowley et al. [14] present an evaluation of theoretical network processor architectures based on a programmable network interface model and detailed workload analysis. However, their model does not include many aspects of current target systems for network processors. Also, their model does not fully separate functional and environmental concerns.

7.1.7   Summary of Existing Approaches

In Table 7.1, we compare existing approaches to network processor benchmarking. As this table shows, none of the existing approaches meets all the requirements of a network processor benchmarking methodology. In particular, there are a number of deficiencies, including lack of specification methodology, lack of consideration of interfaces, and little support for design space exploration.

	CommBench	NetBench	EEMBC	NPF-BWG	Intel
Specification methodology	No	No	No	Unknown	Not specified
Executable description	Yes	Yes	Yes	Unknown	IXP1200-specific
Method for performance measurement	No	No	Yes	Yes	IXP1200-specific
Consideration of interfaces	No	No	No	Unknown	Yes
Methodology for benchmark choice	Yes	Yes	No	Yes	Yes
Facilitates design space exploration	No	No	No	No	No

7.1   Characteristics of existing approaches.

TABLE

7.2   A BENCHMARKING METHODOLOGY

In this section, we motivate and present principles of a generalized benchmarking methodology that apply not only to network processors, but to other application domains as well. Next, we demonstrate these principles for network processors. Finally, we illustrate our methodology on an IPv4 packet forwarding benchmark.

Before introducing our methodology, we first define a benchmark,

> A benchmark *is a mechanism that allows quantitative performance conclusions regarding a computing system to be drawn.*

7.2.1   Principles of a Generalized Benchmarking Methodology

Complete benchmarking methodologies produce benchmark results that are comparable, representative, indicative, and precisely specified.

Comparable

A quantitative performance claim that a benchmark provides is not enough. Benchmarks also need to be comparable across system implementations with heterogeneous interfaces. Thus, the benchmark specification cannot simply be a functional representation of the application; it must also model the system environment.

  1. Quantitative benchmark results must be comparable across a range of system implementations.

Representative

To properly characterize a particular application domain, a benchmark suite must cover most of the domain and provide results that correlate to real-world performance. While the number of benchmarks chosen should adequately represent the application domain, the usefulness and feasibility of implementation is questionable for large benchmark suites. Thus, a suite of benchmarks must be chosen based on careful *application domain analysis*.

  2. A set of benchmarks must be representative of the application domain.

Indicative

A representative benchmark will not necessarily produce results that are indicative of real-world application performance. For benchmark results to be indicative, the benchmark must be specified with the right *granularity*. The granularity of a benchmark is its relative size and complexity compared to other applications in a particular domain. NetBench and NPF-BWG, for example, implement benchmarks according to three different granularities: small (microlevel), medium (IP or function level), and large (application or system level).

The right benchmark granularity is determined by finding the *performance bottlenecks* of the application and architecture. In some cases, a particular subset of the application (i.e., a small application kernel) may dominate the performance of the larger application. However, in many cases bottlenecks are not easily identified or are heavily influenced by the architecture on which the application is implemented. In such cases, choosing a benchmark granularity that is too small may lead to performance results that are not indicative of real-world application performance.

3. The granularity of a benchmark must properly expose application and architectural bottlenecks of the domain.

Precisely Defined

A key component of our methodology is the precise specification of a benchmark. A benchmark specification requires functional, environment, and measurement specifications communicated in both an English and an executable description.

To separate concerns of benchmarking, we distinguish between functional, environment, and measurement specifications. The *functional specification* describes the algorithmic details and functional parameters required for the benchmark. This specification is architecture independent. In contrast, the *environment specification* describes the system-level interface for a specific architectural platform. This ensures comparability of results across multiple architectural platforms. The environment specification also defines the test bench functionality, which includes traffic generation. The *measurement specification* defines applicable performance metrics and the means to measure them. At a minimum, a method to determine functional correctness should be provided.

These specifications should be communicated in two forms: an English description and an executable specification. The *English description* should provide all of the necessary information to implement a benchmark on a particular system. This description also provides implementation guidelines such as acceptable memory/speed tradeoffs (e.g., it may be unreasonable for a benchmark to consume all on-chip memory), required precision of results, and acceptable use of special hardware acceleration units. Besides the English description, the specification includes an *executable description*. This allows rapid initial evaluation and precise functional validation, and facilitates unambiguous communication of the requirements. Note that neither description eliminates the need for the other.

Thus we summarize the final tenet of our benchmarking methodology:

4. Each benchmark should include functional, environment, and measurement specifications in both an English and an executable description.

7.2.2   A Benchmarking Methodology for NPUs

Because of the heterogeneity of NPU architectures, it is necessary to separate benchmarking concerns to ensure comparability of results. In this section, we present our benchmarking methodology for network processors that separates the functional, environment, and measurement specifications.

Functional Specification

The role of the functional specification for our NPU benchmarking methodology is threefold:

1. First, it must specify the benchmark requirements and constraints, such as the minimum allowable routing table size supported by the implementation, the minimum quality of service (QoS) that must be maintained, or restrictions on where tables can be stored. Requirements and constraints may vary significantly across the suite of benchmarks.

2. Second, the functional specification must describe the core algorithmic behavior of the benchmark along with any simplifying assumptions in an English description.

3. Finally, the functional specification should include an executable description written in the Click Modular Router Language [7]. While the algorithmic and functional behavior of a benchmark can be unambiguously communicated using standard languages such as C or C++, Click is a parallel, modular, and natural language for the rapid prototyping of network applications. Click allows the programmer to connect network router elements (application building blocks such as IP routing table lookups, queues, and packet sources/sinks) and run simulations on these element collections to design and verify network applications. Click is also an extensible language; new elements can be added into the element database to serve the needs of different applications.

Environment Specification

Previous approaches to NPU benchmarking lack environment specifications that are critical for comparability. We present different models to specify the environment: the NPU line card model, the gateway model, and the NIC model. These models overcome many of the difficulties associated with comparing benchmark results from different network processors.

Currently, a major target of network processors is core and edge network equipment. In these segments, routing and switching are the most common tasks, and these tasks are performed by systems based on line cards with switched back-plane architectures. Thus, a close examination of how a network processor sits in a line card will help us define the boundary between functionality and environment. Later we will illustrate the gateway model, more suited to the low-end access segment of network equipment.

Line cards manage the physical network interfaces of a router. Typical router architectures such as the one presented in Figure 7.1 contain a variable number of router line cards [15, 16]; up to 16 or more line cards are included in larger

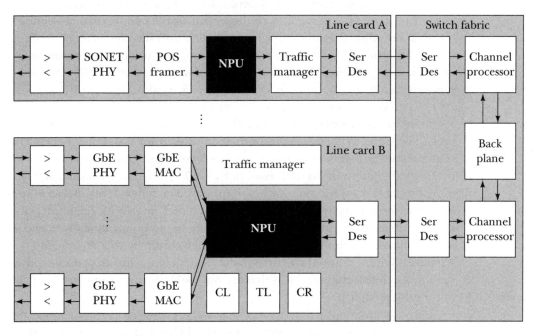

7.1   An example of a router architecture.

FIGURE

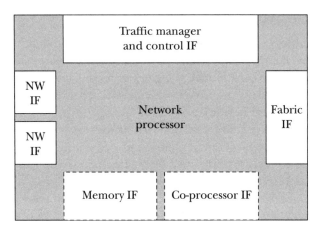

Network processor interfaces.

routers. Each line card is also connected to a switch fabric that allows packets to
pass to other line cards and control processors.

Figure 7.1 demonstrates two different line card deployment scenarios. The
network processor in line card A is configured in a serial fashion to its surrounding
components, while the network processor in line card B is connected to multiple
Gigabit Ethernet MAC units in a parallel fashion. Network processors within line
cards may have different interface configurations. In our example, line card A
supports an OC-192 packet-over-SONET interface, while line card B supports
10×1 Gigabit Ethernet interfaces.

In the environment specification, it is vital to capture interface differences between line cards. Without capturing these aspects, comparability of benchmark
results is not ensured because the network processor is not doing the same work if
its line card configuration is different. In Figure 7.2, the system-level and architectural interfaces of an NPU are further illustrated. The system-level interfaces consist of the network (physical and fabric) and control interfaces; these interfaces
directly influence the benchmark specification due to their tremendous impact
on benchmark functionality and performance. Accordingly, this paper focuses on
system-level network interfaces of an NPU. The memory and co-processor interfaces are architectural interfaces that are not visible at the system level, and are
not considered here.

Based on an examination of more than 20 NPU interfaces [2], we found two
major distinguishing characteristics: (1) some NPUs integrate network interfaces,
while others do not; and (2) of those that do, the supported interfaces vary

greatly. For instance, some network processors contain integrated MAC units for Ethernet interfaces, and some do not. If the network processor does not include an integrated MAC unit, one must be added to the hardware or software simulator. If the network processor includes an integrated MAC, it must be configured to conform to the specification. The MAC unit(s) must support the required per-port data rate and number of ports. Further, network interface restrictions may be specified by individual benchmarks (e.g., buffer size limits).

For the environment specification, the network interfaces in Figure 7.2 have three important parameters: the number of ports, the type of ports, and the speed of each port. The functional specification must also be made aware of these parameters since they directly impact functionality; the number and type of active ports in the system must be specifically defined in order to program where, when, and how packets flow within the network processor. In most cases, optimal performance cannot be achieved without customization of the benchmark software to suit a particular port configuration. For example, a programmer of an Intel IXP1200 must treat "slow" ports (i.e., 10/100 Fast Ethernet) significantly differently than "fast" ports (i.e., Gigabit Ethernet) [17].

Line card configurations from router vendors such as Cisco [15] and Juniper Networks [16] have a wide range of performance requirements, as shown in Table 7.2. Hence, we propose two classes of line card port configurations: one that targets lower-performance line card deployment scenarios and one that targets higher-performance scenarios. For this reason, each benchmark should specify two valid port configurations: one that models a "low-end" line card configuration and one that models a "high-end" configuration.

While each benchmark may specify its own port configuration, a uniform configuration should ease implementation complexity. A standardized port configuration also facilitates the understanding of the overall performance of a network processor.

For the low-end line card configuration, we recommend a standard configuration of 16 Fast Ethernet ports, a relatively low-bandwidth configuration supported by many router vendors. For the high-end line card configuration, we recommend a standard configuration of four OC-48 packet-over-SONET ports (10 Gbps of aggregate bandwidth). OC-48 interfaces are common in high-end line card configurations [18].

While the NPU line card model is a realistic environment for the core and edge segments, it does not accurately represent equipment within the access segment. In the access segment, rich application services such as line termination, DHCP, network address translation, and firewall security are common. These types of functions are performed by a *gateway*. The gateway acts as the boundary between the external network (i.e., the Internet) and the internal home or office

Number of ports	Type of ports	Maximum bandwidth (aggregate) in Mbps
16	Fast Ethernet	100 (1,600)
24	Fast Ethernet	100 (2,400)
48	Fast Ethernet	100 (4,800)
8	Gigabit Ethernet	1,000 (8,000)
16	Gigabit Ethernet	1,000 (16,000)
8	OC-3 POS	155 (1,242)
4	OC-12 POS	622 (2,488)
4	OC-12 ATM	622 (2,488)
1	OC-48 POS	2,488 (2,488)
4	OC-48 POS	2,488 (9,953)
1	OC-192	9,953 (9,953)

7.2   Common router line card configurations.

TABLE

network. Thus, to represent this type of functionality and environment, we have defined the gateway deployment scenario, presented in Figure 7.3. Currently, a handful of network processors target home and office gateway equipment [19, 20, 21].

The network processor inside the gateway acts as a centralized connection point for internal network devices to the local loop interface. The gateway connects multiple interface media such as wireless (e.g., 802.11b) and wireline (e.g., Ethernet) devices to an external broadband connection (e.g., xDSL or cable).

Based on Figure 7.3, three important distinctions can be drawn between the gateway deployment scenario and the line card deployment scenario. First, in the gateway, the internal network interfaces are heterogeneous. Second, in addition to packet data, the gateway must also support nonpacketized data from interfaces such as USB, IEEE 1394, or even analog phone line connections. Third, NPUs designed for gateway applications such as those from Brecis [20] include payload-processing accelerators to support DSP (e.g., voice over IP) and encryption (e.g., 3DES) tasks. A network processor that does not include these accelerators or co-processors may be unable to perform such tasks at all. Thus, comparing network processors using the gateway model will not only require accounting for interface differences, but also differences in payload accelerators and co-processors.

In the future, a potential application of network processors is the network interface card (NIC). An NIC connects a PC or workstation to the LAN and has two primary interfaces: the network interface and the PC bus interface. Today,

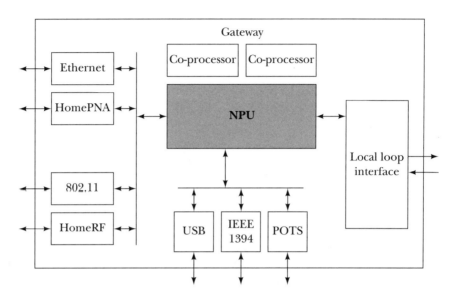

7.3

FIGURE

Gateway environment model.

NICs are low-cost ASIC-based products designed for simple buffering and data transfer. However, evolving applications such as virtual private networks (VPNs) at large data rates (> 1 Gbps) may place greater processing requirements on the PC. Thus, offloading of tasks to the NIC may be a necessary result of tomorrow's network processing requirements. An area of future work will be to develop the NIC environment model for network processors.

Additional considerations of the environment specification are the packet *sources* and *sinks*. The IETF Benchmarking Methodology Workgroup recommends exercising network equipment using the following test setup: a "tester" supplies the device under test (DUT) with packets, which in turn sends its output back to the tester [22]. In this case, the tester serves as both a packet source and sink. Alternately, a packet "sender" (source) supplies packets to the DUT, whose output is fed into a packet "receiver" (sink) for analysis. Either approach will serve the needs of our benchmarking methodology, as long as the packet traces meet the requirements of the benchmark environment specification.

According to the IETF, the data set for network interconnected devices such as routers and switches must include a range of packet sizes, from the minimum to maximum allowable packet size according to the particular application or network medium (i.e., Ethernet). Specifically, they recommend using evenly distributed Ethernet packet sizes of 64, 128, 256, 512, 1024, 1280, and 1518 bytes [22].

For protocols that use variable-sized packets, network processor vendors often report packet throughput using minimum-sized packets. Because many network applications operate primarily on fields in the packet header, more processing must be performed on a large group of minimum-sized packets than on a small group of large packets. Using only minimum-sized or maximum-sized packets can test the corner cases of benchmark performance, but these are not realistic indicators of overall performance, and we defer to the IETF's recommendations and Newman's work for packet sizes.

Newman [18] observed packet sizes based on live Internet samples from the Merit network over a two-week period. The top four IP packet sizes, according to the author, were 40, 1500, 576, and 52 bytes (56%, 23%, 17%, and 5% of the total, respectively). Newman uses this proportion of packet sizes to develop a traffic pattern called the *Internet mix* (*Imix*).

Applications are still evolving in the gateway deployment scenario. Benchmarking for the gateway deployment scenario requires workload characterization and remains an open problem.

Measurement Specification

A benchmark implementation must be functionally correct before performance can be measured. In many cases, functional correctness can be observed by comparing the trace output of the network processor to the output of a reference implementation (i.e., the Click executable description). However, this may not be sufficient for functional correctness; other measures of functional correctness (e.g., real-time constraints or allowable packet drop rate) may also be specified by the benchmark.

Once a benchmark implementation is shown to be functionally correct, its quality of results can be measured. For many network processor benchmarks, line speed (throughput) is the most important measurement of performance.

There are two different units used to measure line speed: packets per second and bits per second. While the former provides insight into computational performance, the latter provides a clearer understanding of throughput. However, with knowledge of the packet size distribution, one can be converted to the other.

According to RFC 1242 [23], throughput is defined as "the maximum rate at which none of the offered [packets] are dropped by the [device]." However, for our methodology, we extend this definition to include the possibility that some packets *should* be dropped in accordance with the benchmark specification.

The measurement of throughput is challenging. According to [22], throughput is measured by sending packets to the DUT at a specific rate. If packets are incorrectly dropped by the DUT, the rate is successively throttled back until packets are no longer dropped. Using this procedure in our methodology ensures that the measurement of throughput is consistent across implementations.

Besides line speed, there are other useful performance metrics. For example, in a benchmark with real-time constraints, packet latency may be an important performance metric. Derived metrics such as cost effectiveness (i.e., performance/cost) may also be important. The notion of time is central to the measurement of many of these metrics. At the very least, a cycle-accurate software simulator of the network processor architecture is required.

First introduced by NPF-BWG [3] and discussed by Nemirovsky [13], the concept of *headroom* is loosely defined as the amount of available processing power that could be used by other tasks in addition to the core application. In theory, headroom is useful to evaluate support for additional functionality on top of the core application. Unfortunately, headroom is difficult to define and measure.

7.2.3 A Benchmark Specification Example

To illustrate our methodology, we present a benchmark specification for IPv4 packet forwarding. Using our template for network processor benchmarks shown in Figure 7.4, we motivate and summarize the specification for this benchmark.

Functional specification

    Requirements and constraints

    Behavior

    Click implementation

Environment specification

    Network interface

    Control interface

    Traffic mix and load distribution

    Click implementation

Measurement specification

    Functional correctness

    Quality of results

7.4   Template for NPU benchmarking.

FIGURE

Functional Specification

Our functional specification of this benchmark is based on RFC 1812, Requirements for IP Version 4 Routers [24]. Because the entire English description is too long to fit in this paper, we list the main points:

+ A packet arriving on port P is to be examined and forwarded on a different port P'. The next-hop location that implies P' is determined through a longest prefix match (LPM) on the IPv4 destination address field. If $P = P'$, the packet is flagged and forwarded to the control plane.

+ Broadcast packets, packets with IP options, and packets with special IP sources and destinations are forwarded to the control plane.

+ The packet header and payload are checked for validity and packet header fields checksum and TTL are updated.

+ Packet queue sizes and buffers can be optimally configured for the network processor architecture unless large buffer sizes interfere with the ability to measure sustained performance.

+ The network processor must maintain all nonfixed tables (i.e., tables for the LPM) in memory that can be updated with minimal intrusion to the application.

+ Routing tables for the LPM should be able to address any valid IPv4 destination address and should support next-hop information for up to 64,000 destinations simultaneously.

In addition to the written description, Figure 7.5 shows the graphical representation of the accompanying Click description. This Click description also includes components of the environment specification.

Environment Specification

For the network interfaces, we require the recommended 16 Fast Ethernet ports for the low-end configuration and 4 OC-48 POS ports for the high-end configuration. A simplifying assumption of our benchmark is that it is a stand-alone configuration. As a result, we do not require a fabric interface.

We define a simple control interface that drops all incoming control packets and does not generate any control packets.

The traffic mix for our benchmark contains destination addresses evenly distributed across the IPv4 32-bit address space. Packet sizes are evenly distributed across 64, 128, 256, 512, 1024, 1280, and 1518 bytes, and 1% of the packets

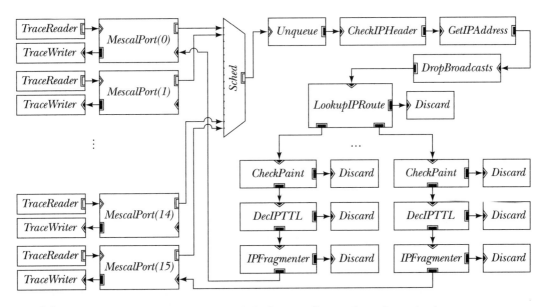

IPv4 packet forwarding Click diagram (low-end configuration).

are hardware broadcast packets [22]. In addition, 1% of the packets generate IP errors.

There is a single packet source for each input port that generates an evenly distributed load. Also, the range of destination addresses and associated next-hop destinations provide an evenly distributed load on every output port.

Figure 7.5 contains packet sources and sinks that model network interfaces of the low-end configuration.

Performance Measurement

To prove the functional correctness of a benchmark implementation, one must compare all output packets (including error packets) from the Click description to that of the DUT.

Overall performance should be measured as the aggregate packet-forwarding throughput of the network processor such that no valid packets are dropped. This is measured by successively lowering the bandwidth at which packets are sent to each MAC port simultaneously until the network processor does not drop valid packets. This measurement is obtained by using packet traces and port loads specified by the environment.

7.3　　THE BENCHMARK SUITE

Before we present our suite of benchmarks for network processors, we discuss benchmark granularity for our methodology.

7.3.1　　Granularity

As introduced earlier, the appropriate benchmark granularity must be chosen after careful application domain analysis and the identification of performance bottlenecks. Previous benchmarking approaches often choose benchmarks with relatively small granularities (e.g., microlevel). In our experience, typical applications running on a network processor must perform a large number of diverse tasks on packets. Nearly all such applications must perform microlevel operations such as input queuing, table lookups, bit field replacements, filtering rule application, appending bytes to packets (resizing), and checksum calculations. While it is possible that any one of these functions may become a performance bottleneck, it is virtually impossible to determine a priori which microlevel tasks will dominate a particular application on a particular network processor. As an example, Figure 7.6 shows a microlevel breakdown of IPv4 packet-forwarding benchmark on the IXP1200 for packet traces consisting only of 64-byte packets. Even when processing small packets (which heavily stresses the header processing ability of a network processor), LPM routing lookup consumes only 18% of the processing time on an IXP1200 microengine. As Figure 7.6 shows, no single microlevel task dominates execution time, thereby supporting the chosen granularity of this benchmark.

We believe the performance bottlenecks of network applications are not appropriately represented by microlevel or function-level benchmarks. Hence, network processor benchmarks should be specified at the application level.

7.3.2　　Choosing the Benchmarks

Some existing approaches to NPU benchmarking define criteria for differentiating the characteristics of benchmarks (i.e., header versus payload) and choose benchmarks based on these criteria. However, we strongly believe that the choice of benchmarks should be driven by an application domain analysis. For this analysis, we created a classification of applications based on network equipment and chose benchmarks that were characteristic of these classes. This equipment-centric view provides a representative set of applications to evaluate system architectures.

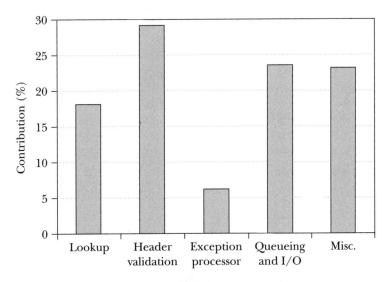

7.6

FIGURE

Profile for IPv4 packet forwarding on the IXP1200 (64-byte packets).

We identify three major segments within the network application domain. First, equipment designed for the Internet *core* segment is generally the highest throughput devices found in networking. Core equipment is usually responsible for routing high-speed WAN/MAN traffic and handling Internet core routing protocols such as BGP.

Second, the network *edge* segment comprises equipment that operates at lower speeds (with shorter links) than equipment in the core. These devices include a variety of midrange MAN packet processors such as routers, switches, bridges, traffic aggregators, layer-3 to -7 devices (e.g., Web switches and load balancers), and VPNs/firewalls.

Finally, the network *access* segment usually comprises low- to high-speed LAN equipment. This segment includes equipment such as LAN switches (Fast Ethernet, Gigabit Ethernet, FDDI, Token Ring, etc.), wireless devices (802.11 a and b), integrated access devices, access concentrators, and cable modems.

Based on this classification, we identify five major application categories in which network processors are likely to play a role. Ten benchmarks were chosen based on their relative significance within the network:

✦ LAN/WAN packet switching
  1. Ethernet bridge
  2. IPv4 packet forwarding

    3. ATM switch

    4. MPLS label edge router

✦ Layer 3+ switching

    5. Network address port translation (NAPT)

    6. HTTP (layer-7) switch

✦ Bridging and aggregation

    7. IP over ATM

    8. Packet-over-SONET framer

✦ QoS and traffic management

    9. IPv4 packet forwarding with QoS and statistics gathering

✦ Firewalls and security

    10. IPv4 packet forwarding with tunneling and encryption

7.4　PRELIMINARY RESULTS

To date, we have completed three benchmark specifications: IPv4 packet forwarding, MPLS, and NAPT. These benchmarks were implemented in assembly language on the Intel IXP1200 network processor.

In our experience, describing network processor benchmarks using Click is advantageous. First, the intended functionality of the benchmark can be verified using Click's Linux-based simulation tools. Second, the extensibility of Click allowed us to write a number of new elements and tools. For example, we have written a "port" element that models the ports of a router line card. Port elements are used in conjunction with new elements that read and write packet trace files (in a format similar to TCPDump [25]) and supply the Click simulator with realistic packet data from our packet generation utility (written in C).

The same packet trace interface used by the Click simulator is used for the network processor simulation environment, which aids verification of benchmark functionality. In our benchmark experiments with the IXP1200, a Windows dynamic-linked library was written to interface with the IXP1200 Developers Workbench tools.

Performance on the IXP1200 was measured using version 2.0 of the Developer Workbench software assuming a microengine clock rate of 200 MHz and an IX bus clock rate of 83 MHz. Intel's IXF440 MAC devices are modeled within the Developer Workbench and configured for 16 Fast Ethernet ports.

Figure 7.7 shows the results for IPv4 packet forwarding. A variety of packet sizes were tested, including the mix of packet sizes recommended by the IETF

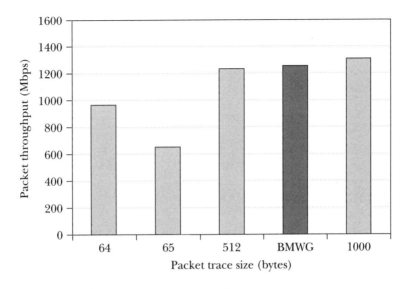

IPv4 packet forwarding on the IXP1200.

Benchmarking Methodology Workgroup (BMWG) in [22]. With 16 100 Mbps ports, the maximum achievable throughput is 1600 Mbps, yet for the range of packet sizes, the IXP1200 cannot sustain this throughput due to the computational complexity of the benchmark specification.

As shown in Figure 7.8, the IXP1200 achieves noticeably higher packet throughput for the range of packet sizes on Network Address Port Translation (NAPT). Incoming packet headers are used to hash into an SRAM-based session table, an operation that benefits greatly from the IXP1200's on-chip hash engine.

As shown in Figure 7.9, the IXP1200 achieves the highest performance on our MPLS benchmark. This is due to the lower computational requirements of our MPLS specification compared to the IPv4 and NAPT benchmarks. This benchmark exercises all three modes of an MPLS router (ingress, egress, and transit) in a distributed fashion.

In theory, as packet size increases, packet throughput should also increase. In practice, we observe a reduction in throughput between 64- and 65-byte packets, 128- and 129-byte packets, and so on across all three benchmarks. This is due to the 64-byte alignment of the receive and transmit FIFOs on the IXP1200. Extra processing and transmission time are required for nonaligned packct segments. This type of information provides insight into the architectural nuances of network processors.

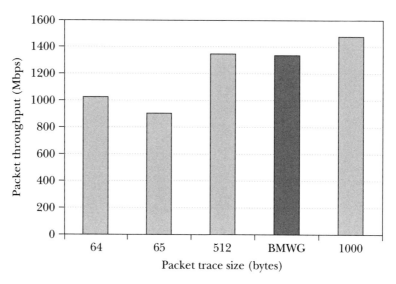

7.8

FIGURE

NAPT on the IXP1200.

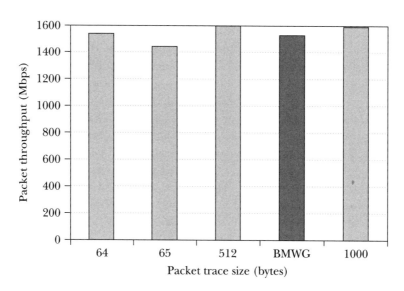

7.9

FIGURE

MPLS on the IXP1200.

7.5   CONCLUSION AND FUTURE WORK

In this paper, we present four principles of a generalized benchmarking methodology. The methodology defines a template for a benchmark consisting of functional, environment, and measurement specifications. We tailor this methodology to the specific requirements and goals of network processor benchmarking. However, other application domains (e.g., telecommunications, multimedia, automotive) may also benefit from this work.

Our key contributions are the emphasis of the network-level interfaces for NPUs based on our line card model, the utility of a Click executable description, motivation for application-level benchmarks, and a disciplined approach to identifying a set of benchmarks.

While this approach addresses many of the weaknesses of previous and ongoing projects, it is a work in progress. That our benchmarks are *indicative* and that our approach enables *comparability* still needs to be demonstrated. In addition, we have only specified and implemented a fraction of our benchmark suite. Finally, our method of measuring functional correctness requires further refinement. In summary, we believe we have identified a number of key issues in benchmarking NPUs and have made steps toward embodying them in a benchmarking methodology.

For our benchmark methodology to show NPU comparability, we need to develop benchmark implementations for network processors other than Intel's IXP1200. We are working to develop IPv4 packet forwarding and MPLS benchmark implementations on other network processors, including the Motorola C-Port C-5. We also need to correlate our benchmark results with entire application implementations on NPU-based line cards to illustrate the indicativeness of our benchmark suite. Third, we have to develop specifications for the remaining benchmarks in our suite. Based on further implementation insights, additional issues related to control, memory, and co-processor interfaces need to be investigated.

Our gateway deployment scenario for network processor benchmarking requires further development. As more network processors target the low-end access segment, this environment model will become increasingly important. New benchmarks and a workload characterization must be developed for the gateway model.

It would also be interesting to determine other metrics and measurements such as robustness. This issue gains further significance as our methodology is used in the design of network processor architectures.

REFERENCES

[1]   C. Matsumoto, "Technical trial-by-fire awaits NPUs," *EE Times,* CMP Media LLC, December 27, 2001.

[2]   N. Shah, *Understanding Network Processors*, Master's thesis, Dept. of Electrical Engineering and Computer Sciences, University of California, Berkeley, 2001.

[3]   S. Audenaert, and P. Chandra (NPF Benchmarking Working Group co-chairs), "Network Processors Benchmark Framework," *NPF Benchmarking Workgroup, www.npforum.org/.*

[4]   Embedded Microprocessor Benchmark Consortium (EEMBC), *www.eembc.org/.*

[5]   T. Wolf, and M. Franklin, "CommBench—A Telecommunications Benchmark for Network Processors," *IEEE International Symposium on Performance Analysis of Systems and Software*, Austin, Texas, April 2000, pp. 154–162.

[6]   G. Memik, B. Mangione-Smith, and W. Hu, "NetBench: A Benchmarking Suite for Network Processors," *International Conference on Computer-Aided Design (ICCAD)*, November 2001.

[7]   E. Kohler, R. Morris, B. Chen, J. Jannotti, and M. Kaashoek, "The Click Modular Router," *ACM Transactions on Computer Systems*, (18)3, August 2000, pp. 263–297.

[8]   Standard Performance Evaluation Corporation (SPEC), *www.spec.org/.*

[9]   R. Weicker, "Dhrystone Benchmark: Rationale for Version 2 and Measurement Rules," *SIGPLAN Notices*, Vol. 23, No. 8, August 1988.

[10]   C. Lee, M. Potkonjak, and W. Mangione-Smith, "MediaBench: A tool for evaluating and synthesizing multimedia and communications systems," in *Proceedings of the 30th Annual International Symposium on Microarchitecture*, December 1997, pp. 330–335.

[11]   D. Burger, and T. Austin, "The SimpleScalar Tool Set, Version 2.0," *Technical Report CS-TR-97-1342*, University of Wisconsin, June 1997.

[12]   P. Chandra, F. Hady, R. Yavatkar, T. Bock, M. Cabot, and P. Mathew, "Benchmarking Network Processors," in *Proceedings of the 2002 Workshop on Network Processors (NP-1)*, held in conjunction with *HPCA8.*

[13]   A. Nemirovsky, "Towards Characterizing Network Processors: Needs and Challenges," *XStream Logic* (now *Clearwater Networks*), white paper, November 2000.

[14]   P. Crowley, M. Fiuczynski, J. Baer, and B. Bershad, "Characterizing Processor Architectures for Programmable Network Interfaces," in *Proceedings of the 2000 International Conference on Supercomputing*, Sante Fe, New Mexico, May 2000.

[15]   Cisco Systems, "Technology of Edge Aggregation: Cisco 1000 Series Edge Services Router," product data sheet, March 2001.

[16]   Juniper Networks, "M160 Internet Backbone Router," *product data sheet*, December 2001.

[17]   Intel Corporation, "Intel IXP1200 Network Processor Family: Hardware Reference Manual," Revision 8, pp. 225–228, August 2001.

[18] D. Newman, "Internet Core Router Test," *Light Reading* (*www.lightreading.com/*), March 2001.

[19] Infineon Technologies, "Harrier-XT Network Processor," *product brief*, 1999.

[20] Brecis Communications, "MSP5000 Multi-Service Processor," *product brief*, 2002.

[21] Intel Corporation, "IXP425 Network Processor Family," *product brief*, 2002.

[22] S. Bradner, and J. McQuaid, "A Benchmarking Methodology for Network Interconnect Devices," *Request for Comments—2544*, Internet Engineering Task Force (IETF), March 1999.

[23] S. Bradner, "Benchmarking Terminology for Network Interconnection Devices," *Request for Comments—1242*, Network Working Group, July 1991.

[24] F. Baker, "Requirements for IP Version 4 Routers," *Request for Comments—1812*, Network Working Group, June 1995.

[25] S. McCanne, C. Leres, and V. Jacobson, Tcpdump 3.4 documentation, 1998.

8

CHAPTER

A Modeling Framework for Network Processor Systems

Patrick Crowley, Jean-Loup Baer
Department of Computer Science and Engineering,
University of Washington

Network processors provide flexible support for communications workloads at high-performance levels. Designing a network processor can involve the design and optimization of many component devices and subsystems, including (multi)processors, memory systems, hardware assists, interconnects, and I/O systems. Often, there are too many options to consider via detailed system simulation or prototyping alone.

System modeling can be an economical means of evaluating design alternatives; effective system models provide a fast and sufficiently accurate description of system performance. The modeling framework introduced here has been designed to help answer questions such as

+ Is a system S sufficiently provisioned to support application W at the target line rate and number of interfaces?

+ If not, where are the bottlenecks?

+ If yes, can S support application W (that is, application W plus some new task) under the same constraints?

+ Will a given hardware assist improve system performance relative to a software implementation of the same task?

+ How sensitive is system performance to input traffic?

The framework is composed of independent application, system, and traffic models that describe router functionality, system resources/organization, and packet traffic, respectively. The framework uses the Click Modular Router to describe router functionality. Click modules are mapped onto an object-based description of the system hardware and are profiled and simulated to determine maximum packet flow through the system and aggregate resource utilization for a given traffic model. This paper presents several modeling examples of uniprocessor and multiprocessor systems executing Internet protocol (IPv4) routing and IP security (IPSec) virtual private network (VPN) encryption/decryption. Model-based performance estimates are compared to the measured performance of the real systems being modeled; the estimates are found to be accurate within 10%. The framework emphasizes ease of use and utility, and permits users to begin full system analysis of existing or novel applications and systems very quickly. Framework users can include those writing router software, router system architects, or network processor architects.

The remainder of the paper is structured as follows. Section 8.1 introduces the modeling framework and describes its components, operation, and implementation. Examples of system models executing an IP router application are presented and analyzed in Section 8.2. Section 8.3 uses an IPSec VPN router extension to demonstrate application modeling within the framework. Likewise, Section 8.4 explores traffic modeling for the systems and applications from preceding sections. Section 8.5 considers future work.

8.1   FRAMEWORK DESCRIPTION

This section describes the framework component models, the Click Modular Router, and the overall operation of the framework. It begins with a high-level description of the models.

+ *Application.* A modular, executable specification of router functionality described in terms of program elements and the packet flow between them. Examples of program elements for an Ethernet IPv4 router include IP fragmentation, IP address lookup, and packet classification.

+ *System.* A description of the processing devices, memories, and interconnects in the system being modeled. For instance, one or more processors could be connected to SDRAM via a high-speed memory bus. All elements of the application model are mapped to system components.

◆ *Traffic.* A description of the type of traffic offered to the system. Traffic characteristics influence (1) which paths (sequences of elements) are followed in the application model, and (2) the resources used within each element along the path.

As previously mentioned, Click configurations are used to describe applications in terms of modular program elements and the possible packet flow between them. The traffic model dictates the packet flow between elements. The system model describes system resources in a manner compatible with the work description admitted by the application model. The general approach is to approximate application characteristics statistically, based on instruction profiling and program simulation when considering a software implementation of a task, and to use those approximations to form system resource usage and contention estimates.

In addition to these models, the user provides a *mapping* of the application elements onto the system; this mapping describes where each element gets executed in the system and how the packets flow between devices when they move from one program element to another.

8.1.1 The Click Modular Router

This section describes the Click Modular Router. A good introduction to Click is found in [8]; Kohler's thesis [7] describes the system in greater detail. Click is fully functioning software built to run on real systems (primarily x86 Linux systems). When run in the Linux kernel, Click handles all networking tasks; Linux networking code is avoided completely. This is of great benefit: Click can forward packets around five times faster than Linux on the same system due to careful management of I/O devices [8].

Click describes router functionality with a directed graph of modules called *elements*; such a graph is referred to as a Click *configuration*. A connection between two elements indicates packet flow. Upon startup, Click is given a configuration that describes router functionality. An example of a Click configuration implementing an Ethernet-based IPv4 router is shown in Figure 8.1. In this paper, configurations are often referred to as routers, even if they do more than route packets. The Click distribution comes with a fairly complete catalog of elements— enough to construct IP routers, firewalls, quality-of-service (QoS) routers, network address translation (NAT) routers, and IPSec VPNs. Click users can also build their own elements using the Click C++ API. Configurations are described in text files with a simple, intuitive configuration language.

We ported Click to the Compaq Alpha ISA [10] in order to profile and simulate the code with various processor parameters using the SimpleScalar toolkit [1].

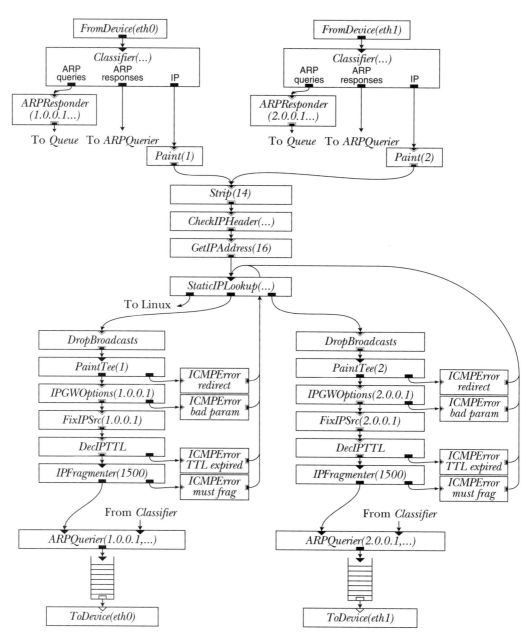

8.1   Sample Ethernet IP router Click configuration.

FIGURE

Within the framework, Click configurations function as application specifications and implementations. Using Click fulfills our goal to use real-world software rather than benchmark suites whenever possible; previous experience in evaluating network processor architectures [3] has shown the importance of considering complete system workloads.

In Click, the mechanism used to pass packets between elements depends on the type of output and input ports involved. Ports can use either *push* or *pull processing* to deliver packets. With push processing, the source element is the active agent and passes the packet to the receiver. In pull processing, the receiver is active and requests a packet from an element on its input port. Packet flow through a Click configuration has two phases corresponding to these two types of processing. When a *FromDevice* element is scheduled, it pulls a packet off the inbound packet queue for a specified network device and initiates push processing; push processing generally ends with the packet being placed in a *Queue* element near a *ToDevice* element; this can be seen by examining paths through Figure 8.1. When a *ToDevice* element gets scheduled, it initiates pull processing, generally by dequeueing a packet from a *Queue*. As a general rule, push processing paths are more time-consuming than pull processing paths.

Click maintains a worklist of schedulable elements and schedules them in round-robin fashion. *FromDevice*, *PollDevice* (the polling version of *FromDevice* used and described later in this paper), and *ToDevice* are the only schedulable elements. On a uniprocessor-based system, there is no need for synchronization between elements or for shared resources like free buffer lists since there is only one packet active at a time and packets are never preempted within an element. However, Click also includes support for shared memory multiprocessors [2] and thread-safe versions of elements with potentially shared state. Synchronized access and contention for shared resources will be of concern for shared memory multiprocessor (SMP) systems, as will be seen later.

8.1.2 Application Model

The application is modeled by profiling the Click configuration and simulating its execution on the target processor over the packet input described in the traffic model. This yields a tremendous amount of information, including instruction count and type information, cache behavior, branch behavior, ILP, and how each contributes to cycles per instruction (CPI). The specific information kept in the model depends on what aspects of the system are of interest.

Click code is profiled and simulated with the SimpleScalar toolkit [1], version 3.0, targeted for the Compaq Alpha ISA. In general, the application is simulated over the target traffic, on the target processor(s). This helps determine packet processing performance. However, execution time is only part of the overall packet forwarding time; even this time must later be adjusted to account for contention for shared resources and the cost of any synchronization overhead. If an element has no software implementation (i.e., a hardware assist) and cannot be simulated, the profile and external dependencies must be provided manually by the user.

The examples presented in this paper illustrate only a portion of the flexibility of application analysis provided by the framework. Click configurations, and individual elements, can be profiled in great detail. The studies found in later sections only use the number of instructions, CPI achieved, and number of system bus transactions (i.e., L2 misses) to estimate performance.

8.1.3   System Model

The system model consists of devices (e.g., processor cores and memories) and channels (e.g., memory and I/O buses) that connect devices. Each device component has internal operations (e.g., an add instruction), which are completely specified by the device, and external operations (e.g, a load that misses in caches), whose implementations are dependent on target devices (e.g., SDRAM) and the channels that connect them.

System resources and organization are described with two basic objects: devices and channels. Device and channel objects, once instantiated, are attached to one another to describe the system's organization. Once connected, the system can begin to deduce the cost of the external operations for each device; this is only a portion of the cost, however, since certain aspects of external operation cost such as locality and contention depend on the application and traffic models. A sample system model is shown in Figure 8.2.

The examples in this study involve only four device types: processors, memories, interfaces, and bridges. Other types are certainly possible within the framework, but only these are discussed here.

Many network processor designs include specialized instructions not present in the Alpha ISA. To explore the impact of a specialized instruction, the user can do the following: add a new op code and instruction class to the profiling tool, define a macro (e.g., compiler intrinsic) that uses the new instruction class, modify at least one Click element to use the macro rather than C/C++ statements, and update the system device to include the new instruction. Adding a new instruction to the profiler involves adding new instruction class and op code declarations, as well as adding a C function that implements the new instruction. Note that the application can no longer run natively, so this must be done after the element graph has been profiled with the traffic model to obtain path frequencies.

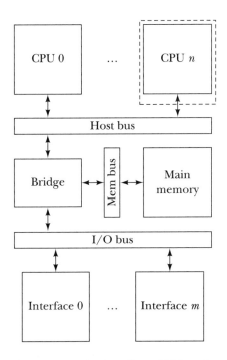

System organization for a PC-based router with n processors and m network interfaces.

8.1.4   Traffic Model

The traffic model is a statistical description of packet stream characteristics. These characteristics include packet size distribution, IP packet type distribution (e.g., UDP or TCP), interarrival time distribution, distribution of source addresses, and distribution of destination addresses. This description can be specified directly by the user or measured from a trace of packets.

8.1.5   Application-System Mapping

As mentioned previously, a complete model description also requires a mapping of Click elements onto system devices. Each element must be assigned to a processing device (usually a processor) for execution and one or more memory devices for data and packet storage. For example, if the system is a PC-based router, then all computation elements in the application are assigned to the host processor for execution and all packets and data are assigned to system RAM.

Given this mapping, the framework can find a packet's path through the system as it flows through the Click configuration. The mapping indicates where each element stores its packets, thus the packet must flow through the system, across channels from memory to memory, according to the elements visited along the packet's path through the Click configuration. Determining where packets must move is comparatively simple. However, accurately modeling the performance of such movements is difficult because, in general, it is no different from modeling a distributed shared memory system. The framework currently can model systems with a small number of shared memories with some accuracy; the multiprocessor examples presented later all use a single shared memory. This aspect of the framework is under active development.

While Click describes packet flow, it does not describe how packets are delivered to Click in the first place; the packet delivery mechanism is defined by the operating system (OS) and device drivers. Since OS code is not included in the application model, a manual analysis is required to model the packet arrival mechanism. The mapping must also indicate whether packet arrival is implemented with interrupts, polling, a hybrid interrupt/polling scheme [9], or special hardware supporting a scheme like active messages [4]. The Click system itself, when running in kernel mode on Linux, uses polling to examine DMA descriptors (a data structure shared by the CPU and the device for moving packets). This issue is of paramount importance in real systems, and is worthy of the attention it has received in the research literature. All examples presented in this paper will use polling, but any of the other schemes could be modeled within the framework.

8.1.6   Metrics and Performance Estimates

The primary goal is to find the forwarding rate, forwarding latency, and resource utilization for a given application, system, and traffic description. Intuitively, this means finding the time and resources needed to move the packet through the system, from input interface to output interface. This involves three phases:

1. Moving the packet from the input interface to memory (IM)

2. Processing the packet (PP)

3. Moving the packet from memory to the output interface (MI)

The principal metrics—latency, bandwidth, and resource utilization—for these three phases directly determine system performance.

Determining values for these metrics is complicated by the fact that the three phases generally rely on shared resources. For example, suppose the input and output interfaces both reside on the same I/O bus. Then, inbound and outbound packets will be forced to share the I/O bus's total bandwidth.

These phases have a further dependence. While each phase may have a different maximum throughput, the effective throughput of each is limited by that phase's arrival rate. A phase's arrival rate is determined by the throughput of the preceding phase since they act as stages in a pipeline: phase 3 is fed by phase 2, phase 2 by phase 1, and phase 1 by the traffic model.

8.1.7   Framework Operation

Overall forwarding rate (i.e., system throughput) will be limited to the lowest forwarding rate among the phases. Once the lowest of the three maximum forwarding rates is found, it can be used as the arrival rate for all phases to determine whether any resources are oversubscribed at that rate; if no shared resource is oversubscribed at this rate, then that rate is the maximum loss-free forwarding rate (MLFFR). System forwarding latency will be the sum of these individual latencies. Finally, resource utilization will be the aggregate utilization of all phases since they will generally operate in pipelined fashion.

The steps to determine MLFFR, as well as the latency and resource utilization seen at that rate, are summarized as follows:

1. Find the latency and throughput of each phase assuming no contention for shared resources.

2. Use the lowest resulting throughput as the arrival rate at each phase, and find the offered load on all shared resources.

3. If no shared resources are oversubscribed, then the MLFFR has been found. Otherwise, the current rate is too high and must be adjusted down to account for contention. The adjustment is made by iteratively charging arbitration cycles to the users of the congested channel until it is no longer oversubscribed.

The framework assumes that only shared channels can be oversubscribed; this is a reasonable assumption so long as the channels leading to a device saturate before the device itself does. For the buses presented here, oversubscription is said to occur when utilization reaches 80%. If no shared resources in the system are oversubscribed (i.e., if offered load is less than capacity), then the system is contention free. Any oversubscribed resources represent contention, and changes must be made to estimates of latency and throughput for any phases using those resources. To resolve contention, slowdown is applied equally to contributors. If capacity represents $x\%$ of offered load, then all users of the congested resource must reduce their offered load to $x\%$ of its initial value. Offered load is reduced

```
# Declare model objects
app = Application('npf_iprouter.click')
traffic = Traffic([[64], [1.0]], 'Uniform')
sys = System()

# Create channels
pci = bus('PCI',32, 33, 2, 8, 0, 0)
membus = bus('Membus',64, 100, 4, 4, 0, 1)
hostbus = bus('Hostbus',64, 100, 4, 4, 0, 1)

# Create & attach devices
brdge = bridge('Bridge', [pci, membus, hostbus])
cpu = proc('CPU', 700, 4, '16/4/32/1', '16/4/32/1','256/4/32/1', 1)
hostbus.attach(cpu)
ram = mem('Mem', 60, 64)
membus.attach(ram)
# 8 such interfaces
int0 = interface('Eth0', 'source')
pci.attach(int0)

# Add channels and bridge to system
sys.addbuses([pci, membus, hostbus])
sys.addbridges([brdge])
```

8.3

FIGURE

Framework code declaring traffic, application, and system models for the uniprocessor example.

by iteratively increasing the number of arbitration cycles needed for each user to master the bus until offered load on the channel drops below the saturation point. Initially, the model includes no arbitration cycles; they are only added to a device's bus usage latency once saturation is reached.

8.1.8   Implementation

The framework's object-based system description and modeling logic are implemented in the Python programming language. A sample set of model declarations using the Python object syntax is shown in Figure 8.3. Python is also used as a glue language to permit the modeling logic to interact with Click and SimpleScalar. As mentioned previously, Click provides the router specification and implementation, and SimpleScalar is used to profile and simulate Click's execution on a target processor.

The framework operates very quickly, in general: on the order of seconds when considering tens of thousands of packets. However, processor simulation can be time-consuming for experiments involving great amounts of traffic. Note that while an hour can be spent simulating system operation over a trace of tens of millions of packets, there are two reasons why this presents no problem: (1) most analyses can be conducted with far fewer packets (so this situation is unlikely to be useful), and (2) this is simulation time, not development time, and can, when needed, be tolerated.

8.2 SYSTEM MODELING

This section will now illustrate, by way of example, how the framework can be used to model network processing systems. The systems modeled here were chosen because they are the systems used by the Click designers to evaluate Click performance. Hence, the performance estimates yielded by the framework can be compared to the observed performance of the actual system.

8.2.1 Uniprocessor PC

The first example models the PC-based system used in [8] to measure the performance of the Click IP router configuration from Figure 8.1. The details of the system being modeled can be seen in Table 8.1 in row Uni-PC. The main features are a 700 MHz Pentium III Xeon processor and a 32-bit-wide 33 MHz PCI I/O bus. There are three channels in this system: the host, memory, and PCI buses. Of these, only the memory and PCI buses are shared.

The organization of the system model used here is shown in Figure 8.2. In addition to the single CPU, the system contains eight interfaces in total: four are used as packet sources and four as destinations. The code declaring models in this experiment is shown in Figure 8.3. The traffic used in the Click study was very simple. The packet stream consisted of 64-byte UDP packets generated by each of the sources; each source generated packets with uniformly chosen destinations (from among the four destination interfaces). Finally, since there is only one processing device, there are no mapping decisions to be made. The packet delivery mechanism, as mentioned, is polling.

Polling, with Click, involves checking the DMA descriptor for notice of a new packet, moving the new packet onto an incoming packet queue for processing, moving a packet from the outgoing packet queue into the DMA buffer, and

System	Processor						
	Number	Name	Clock	I.W.	Caches (L1s/L2)		Threads
Uni-PC	1	PIII	700	4	16/4/32	256/4/32	1
SMP-PC	1-4	PIII	500	4	16/4/32	512/2/32	1

System	Memory		Buses		Chipset
	Latency	Width	I/O	Memory	
Uni-PC	60	64	PCI/32/33/2-8/No	GTL/64/100/4-4/Yes	440GX
SMP-PC	50	64	PCI/64/33/1-4/No	GTL/64/100/4-4/Yes	440NX

8.1

TABLE

Parameters for the base systems used in this paper. (Clock units are MHz. Issue width is denoted I.W. Cache descriptions are size(KB)/associativity/line size(bytes). All caches are LRU. Memory units are ns and bits, for access latency and width, respectively. Bus descriptions are name/width(bits)/speed(MHz)/read-write burst size/separate address and data buses.)

updating the DMA descriptor to indicate the buffer modifications. Both the DMA descriptor and the DMA buffers are effectively noncached (since they are accessed by both the processor and the I/O devices), thus each of these steps involve L2 cache misses, for a total of five L2 misses per polling event.

These results are shown in Figure 8.4. The framework estimates an MLFFR of 322,000 packets per second. This is within 3% of the value of 333,000 reported in [8]. At this rate, system throughput is limited by the packet processing (PP) phase. Table 8.2 reports the per-phase details. Note that neither bus is oversubscribed at the MLFFR. With the PP phase, the Click configuration executes 2110 instructions at a CPI of 0.8467 for a total of 1787 cycles. With a cycle time of 1.43 ns (i.e., 700 MHz), those 2554 ns, plus the 550 ns spent on the five polling L2 misses per packet, become the bottleneck to system throughput.

In addition to the base system, the experiment presented here includes a number of speculative systems for which real performance numbers are not available. These speculative systems include faster processors and faster PCI buses. By increasing the CPU clock rate to 1 GHz, the MLFFR increases to 428,000 packets per second. Figure 8.4 also shows the performance for a simple configuration that performs no packet processing. This configuration is limited by PCI bandwidth. The PCI bus saturates (achieves 80% utilization) at 450,000 packets per second. This number also agrees well with the measured rate of 452,000 packets per second.

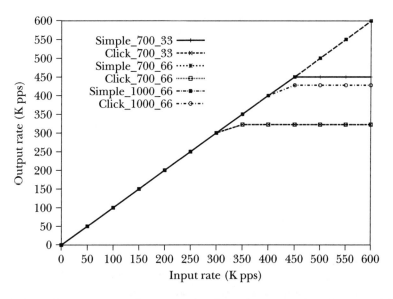

Forwarding rate versus input rate for the uniprocessor-based router with 64-byte packets. (Curves marked "Click" reflect modeling of full IP router performance; "Simple" indicates an empty configuration and reports maximum system forwarding rate. The two numbers at each label report CPU clock rate and PCI bus speed, both in MHz.)

While the thrust of this paper is to introduce the modeling framework, it is interesting to briefly discuss the bottleneck of this PC-based system. No matter how fast the processor, the forwarding rate will remain at 450K packets per second due to PCI saturation. This PCI saturation is due to Click's packet delivery mechanism; PCI could, in theory, deliver more throughput. The Click designers chose to implement polling to eliminate interrupt overheads. This means that the processor never initiates any DMA transactions; this fact has consequences for PCI performance. The reason is that most PCI bridge implementations (including the 440GX used here) only have good burst transfers when the source of the data initiates the burst. With Click, the network interface masters all transactions. This is desirable for packet delivery into memory; the interface is the source of the data, so the packet can be bursted into memory. For packet retrieval from memory, on the other hand, the interface is not the source and thus must use unbursted memory read transactions. This fact is reflected in the model's PCI bus characterization; PCI reads have a burst size of 2, while writes have a burst size of 4.

| | Latency | Max rate | Utilization at min rate | |
	(ns)	(Kpps)	Membus	PCI
Phase 1 (IM)	574	1442	0.04	0.18
Phase 2 (PP)	**3102**	**322**	0.03	0.00
Phase 3 (MI)	1212	825	0.07	0.39
Result	4888	322	0.14	0.58

8.2

TABLE

Per-phase details for Click IP routing on a uniprocessor. (The result entry for Max rate is a minimum of the column; other rate entries are sums.)

8.2.2   SMP PC

Click's operation on SMP-based systems is described and measured in [2]. As was the case for the uniprocessor-based PC, the system modeled here will be based on the system used in the study; model estimates will be compared to the observed results from the real system.

The system organization of the SMP-based PC is very similar to that of the single processor system; Figure 8.2 is still an accurate depiction. The only significant resource differences are additional processors on the host bus, slower clock rates on those processors (500 MHz versus 700 MHz), a wider PCI bus (64 b versus 32 b), and fewer interfaces (4 versus 8). System details can be found in Table 8.1.

Another difference of note is found in the packet handling mechanism. The network interfaces used in the uniprocessor system allowed the Click designers to implement polling and to make all host–device interaction indirect through DMA buffers. The interfaces on the systems used in the SMP study, however, do not have this flexibility. In fact, on every packet send, the host must write a pair of device registers on the interface; this requires an additional PCI transaction for every packet. In the uniprocessor case, the packet processing phase (PP—phase 2) involved no PCI bus traffic (the host just moved the packet into a DMA buffer and updated a descriptor); this is not the case for an SMP-based system.

Aside from system resources and organization, there are several other important differences between SMP and uniprocessor Click operation that need to be discussed. These include scheduling elements on CPUs, synchronizing access to shared data (e.g., mutable elements and the free buffer list), and cache misses due to shared data (e.g., *Queue* elements).

The four-interface version of Figure 8.1 has eight schedulable elements; a *PollDevice* and *ToDevice* element for each interface. Each of these must be assigned to a CPU. The Click designers considered both dynamic and static assignments and found static scheduling of elements to CPUs to be more effective than their own adaptive approach (the adaptive approach couldn't account for cache misses and therefore was capable of poor locality); static scheduling will be modeled here.

The experiments in this section will consider two and four CPU SMPs. In the two-CPU system, each CPU will be assigned two *PollDevice* and two *ToDevice* elements. To increase locality, each CPU is assigned *PollDevice* and *ToDevice* elements for different devices (incoming packets rarely depart on the same interface on which they arrived). Likewise, in the four CPU system, each CPU will host one *PollDevice* element and one *ToDevice* element, each element associated with a different interface.

Any sharing or synchronization between CPUs will involve accesses to memory. So, whenever possible, Click minimizes interactions between CPUs to keep all data cached. To this end, each CPU is given a private worklist from which to schedule elements; so, the static assignments of element to CPU are permanent. Each CPU is also given its own list of packet buffers to manage. Buffers are allocated and returned to this private list, so only when a CPU is overloaded will it incur cache misses to allocate a buffer from another CPU. Some elements have private state that must be protected via synchronized access. *Queue* elements are an especially important example. It is often the case that paths from multiple interfaces (and therefore multiple CPUs) lead to the same output *Queue*. As a result, enqueues must be synchronized. In many cases, however, multiple CPUs will not dequeue from the same *Queue* element, since *Queue* elements often feed *ToDevice* elements, which are CPU specific. Click recognizes when this common case holds and disables *Queue* dequeue synchronization.

While *ToDevice* elements are CPU specific, the *Queue* elements that feed them are not. In fact, *Queues* are the only way for packets to move between CPUs. Say a packet arrives at CPU A destined for interface N, which is assigned to CPU B. CPU A will initiate push processing, which culminates in an enqueue onto a *Queue* element. When the *ToDevice(N)* element gets scheduled on CPU B, it will initiate pull processing by dequeuing a packet from element *Queue* and send the packet on its way. Since the *Queue* element is used by both CPUs (and any other CPUs in the system), either of these accesses might have resulted in an L2 cache miss. Such cache misses will increase with the number of CPUs in the system. Note that in the uniprocessor case, there are no L2 misses of this sort.

Synchronization and L2 misses due to shared data are important because they represent the cost of having multiple CPUs. These costs tend to increase as CPUs are added to the system. The benefit, of course, is that multiple packets (ideally n, when there are n CPUs) can be processed in parallel. When the costs outweigh

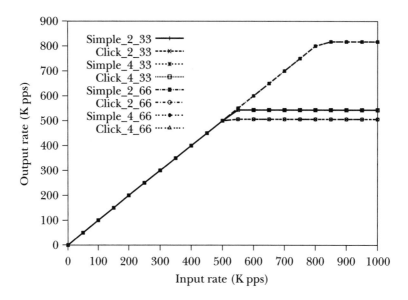

Forwarding rate versus input rate for the SMP-based router with 64-byte packets. (The two numbers at each label report number of CPUs and PCI bus speed in MHz.)

the benefits, increasing CPUs in an SMP system is wasteful. Similarly, when the benefits outweigh the costs, increasing CPUs is a design win.

For the situation modeled here, the cost is not very high. This is because, when processing a packet, the time spent outside of synchronization regions is much greater than the time spent within synchronized regions. Pushing packets onto *Queue* elements is the only significant synchronization event; enqueues, even when they involve L2 cache misses, are at least an order of magnitude faster than the rest of the IP routing processing path. So CPUs do not, for a moderate number of CPUs, back up at *Queue* elements. Furthermore, while the expectation of an L2 cache miss per enqueue goes up as CPUs are added to the system (more CPUs implies more remote users), the maximum is 1 L2 cache miss per enqueue. Again, this represents only a fraction of the total time needed to process the packet.

As in the previous section, the experiment presented here includes speculative systems for which no data has been published. The results of the IP routing experiments on SMT systems of two and four CPUs are shown in Figure 8.5. The results are once again within 10% of the original Click study's results. The two-CPU SMP model estimates the MLFFR at 506K packets per second, as compared

2 CPUs	Latency (ns)	Max rate (Kpps)	Utilization at min rate	
			Membus	PCI
Phase 1 (IM)	382	2612	0.05	0.19
Phase 2 (PP)	**3952**	**506**	0.06	0.03
Phase 3 (MI)	970	1031	0.10	0.49
Result	5304	506	0.21	0.71

4 CPUs	Latency (ns)	Max rate (Kpps)	Utilization at min rate	
			Membus	PCI
Phase 1 (IM)	382	2612	0.10	0.34
Phase 2 (PP)	**3952**	**1012**	0.11	0.12
Phase 3 (MI)	970	1031	0.20	0.98
Result	5304	1012	0.41	1.44

8.3

TABLE

Per-phase details for Click IP routing on SMPs (of two and four CPUs). (The Max rate result is a column minimum, not a sum. Note that the four-CPU case has an oversubscribed PCI bus at the minimum phase forwarding rate.)

to the observed rate of 492K packets per second. The four-CPU SMP model yields an MLFFR of 543K packets per second, as compared to a measured value of 500K packets per second.

The per-phase details are shown in Table 8.3. The two-CPU case is normal; the MLFFR is equal to the minimum phase forwarding rate. However, this is not the case for the four-CPU case since its PCI bus is oversubscribed at the minimum phase forwarding rate. The MLFFR, then, is the minimum forwarding rate beyond which the PCI bus becomes saturated; this rate is 543K packets per second. As described in Section 8.1.7, the framework finds the MLFFR by solving for the number of bus arbitration cycles needed per packet in order to keep the minimum phase forwarding rate beneath saturation.

While accurate to within 10%, the SMP models have not been as accurate as the uniprocessor models. This is because the SMP system is more complicated, and the model leaves out many details. For instance, the contention resolution method is only a coarse approximation. Also, the Pentium III processor modeled here uses a specific coherency protocol not captured by the model. Cache misses due to sharing are modeled, but the overhead due to coherency traffic is not.

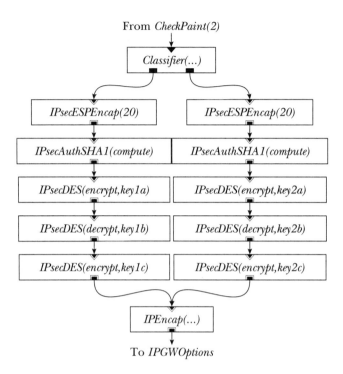

From *CheckPaint(2)*

Classifier(...)

IPsecESPEncap(20)   *IPsecESPEncap(20)*

IPsecAuthSHA1(compute)   *IPsecAuthSHA1(compute)*

IPsecDES(encrypt,key1a)   *IPsecDES(encrypt,key2a)*

IPsecDES(decrypt,key1b)   *IPsecDES(decrypt,key2b)*

IPsecDES(encrypt,key1c)   *IPsecDES(encrypt,key2c)*

IPEncap(...)

To *IPGWOptions*

8.6   Click VPN decryption configuration.

FIGURE

8.3   IPSEC VPN DECRYPTION

This section demonstrates how the framework can be used to explore application performance. The intent is to show that the framework can help determine the speed at which a given system can support a target application.

In this experiment, the IP router Click configuration is extended to include IPSec VPN [6] encryption and decryption. The VPN decryption and encryption blocks are shown in Figures 8.6 and 8.7, respectively. The figures indicate how simple it is to add significant functionality to an existing router; adding the same functionality to a Linux or FreeBSD router would be by no means trivial.

Note that in these experiments, only the packet processing phase is changed; packet receive and transmit will have the same characteristics for these systems as before. Simulation of the new Click configuration on the target processors shows that the processing of each packet requires 28,325 instructions, more than 13 times as many instructions compared to the baseline IP router model. Instruction

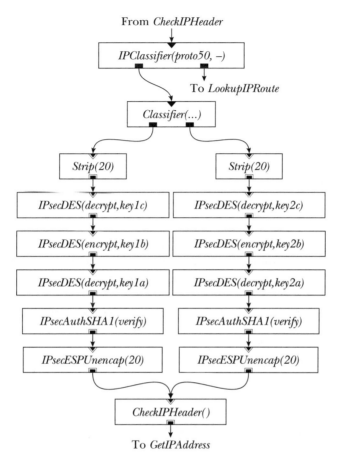

From *CheckIPHeader*

IPClassifier(proto50, –)

To *LookupIPRoute*

Classifier(...)

Strip(20)   *Strip(20)*

IPsecDES(decrypt,key1c)   *IPsecDES(decrypt,key2c)*

IPsecDES(encrypt,key1b)   *IPsecDES(encrypt,key2b)*

IPsecDES(decrypt,key1a)   *IPsecDES(decrypt,key2a)*

IPsecAuthSHA1(verify)   *IPsecAuthSHA1(verify)*

IPsecESPUnencap(20)   *IPsecESPUnencap(20)*

CheckIPHeader( )

To *GetIPAddress*

8.7   Click VPN encryption configuration.

FIGURE

processing, rather than packet traffic on the PCI bus, dominates performance in this case.

Hence, as the results indicate in Figure 8.8, the SMP system experiences linear speed up in the number of CPUs. Once again, the model's performance estimates match the observed values closely. Estimated MLFFRs for the uniprocessor, two-CPU SMP, and four-CPU SMP are 28K, 46K, and 92K, respectively. Observed values for the same systems are 24K, 47K, and 89K—all well within 10% of the model's estimate. The one speculative system included in the experiment, a 1 GHz uniprocessor, sees a performance increase in direct proportion to the increase in

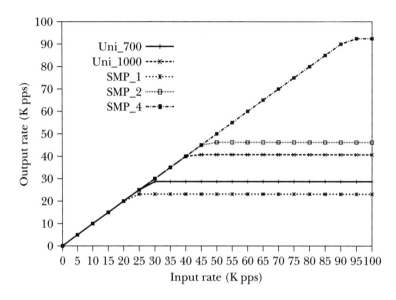

Forwarding rate versus input rate for the VPN router with 64-byte packets.

clock rate—an expected result on such a compute bound workload. Forwarding rate, it is noted, remains well below the system limit.

8.4   PACKET SIZE DISTRIBUTIONS

All of the previous experiments have used a simple traffic model: a stream of 64B packets at varying, uniformly distributed arrival rates. Changing the traffic model is a simple matter of specifying the distribution of packet sizes, distribution of packet arrival times, and the distribution of packet type (TCP, UDP, errors, etc.). Application profiling and system resource usage are both dependent on packet size. Thus, both steps must be carried out for relevant packet sizes and then weighted according to the distribution (and influence) of those sizes.

By using minimum-sized packets, these experiments tend to emphasize per-packet overhead. In the 700 MHz uniprocessor IP routing experiment, for instance, increasing packet size from 64B to 1000B reduces the MLFFR from 322K packets per second to 53K packets per second. While MLFFR decreases as packet size increases, the bit throughput of the system actually increases from 165 Mbps to 424 Mbps. This is, in fact, the expected result for two reasons: (1) the original system was limited by packet processing time (phase 2), and (2) that processing time is more or less independent of packet size (since only packet headers are involved).

8.5   CONCLUSION AND FUTURE WORK

This paper has presented a modeling framework for network processing systems. The framework is intended to enable quick analysis of systems that implement complete and detailed router functionality. To illustrate the modeling approach, a number of system, application, and traffic models were presented. The framework yielded performance estimates accurate to within 10%, as compared to the measured performance of the systems being modeled.

This modeling framework is very much a work in progress. The models presented in this paper have served a dual purpose: (1) they helped to introduce Click as Click was meant to be used, and (2) they helped to informally validate the modeling approach embodied in the framework. However, there are several other types of network processing systems that have organizations quite different from a PC. These systems tend to use a greater variety of devices, including switches and special-purpose hardware assists, as well as employ distributed memory and hardware queues and buffers. In future work, we plan to model these systems and devise ways to map Click configurations onto more heterogeneous systems.

To this end, the alpha release of the framework will include all the models presented here in addition to a model of a highly integrated network processor, such as the Intel IXP1200 [5] or one of its predecessors.

ACKNOWLEDGMENTS

This work was supported in part by NSF grant MIP-9700970.

REFERENCES

[1]   D. C. Burger, and T. M. Austin, "The simplescalar tool set, version 2.0," Technical Report CS-TR-1997-1342, University of Wisconsin, Madison, 1997.

[2]   B. Chen, and R. Morris, "Flexible control of parallelism in a multiprocessor PC router," in *Proceedings of the 2001 USENIX Annual Technical Conference (USENIX '01)*, pp. 333–346, Boston, June 2001.

[3]   P. Crowley, M. E. Fiuczynski, J.-L. Baer, and B. N. Bershad, "Characterizing processor architectures for programmable network interfaces," in *Proceedings of the 2000 International Conference on Supercomputing*, May 2000.

[4]   T. Eicken, D. Culler, S. Goldstein, and K. Schauser, "Active messages: A mechanism for integrating communication and computation," in *Proceedings of the 19th International Symposium on Computer Architecture*, pp. 256–266, Gold Coast, Australia, May 1992.

[5]   Intel Corp. Intel IXP1200 Network Processor Datasheet, *developer.intel.com*, 2001.

[6]   S. Kent, and R. Atkinson. "Security Architecture for the Internet Protocol," Internet Engineering Task Force, RFC 2401, *ftp://ftp.ietf.org/rfc/rfc2401.txt*, November 1998.

[7]   E. Kohler, *The Click modular router*. Ph.D. thesis, MIT, November 2000.

[8]   E. Kohler, R. Morris, B. Chen, J. Jannotti, and M. F. Kaashoek, "The Click modular router," *ACM Transactions on Computer Systems*, 18(3):263–297, August 2000.

[9]   J. C. Mogul, and K. K. Ramakrishnan. "Eliminating receive livelock in an interrupt-driven kernel," *ACM Transactions on Computer Systems*, 15(3):217–252, 1997.

[10]   R. L. Sites (editor), *Alpha Architecture Reference Manual*. Digital Press, 1992.

PRACTICES

9 **An Industry Analyst's Perspective on Network Processors**
John Freeman

10 **Agere Systems—Communications Optimized PayloadPlus Network Processor Architecture**
Bill Klein, Juan Garza

11 **Cisco Systems—Toaster2**
John Marshall

12 **IBM—PowerNP Network Processor**
Mohammad Peyravian, Jean Calvignac, Ravi Sabhikhi

13 **Intel Corporation—Intel IXP2400 Network Processor: A Second-Generation Intel NPU**
Prashant Chandra, Sridhar Lakshmanamurthy, Raj Yavatkar

14 **Motorola—C-5e Network Processor**
Eran Cohen Strod, Patricia Johnson

15 **PMC-Sierra, Inc.—ClassiPI**
Vineet Dujari, Remby Taas, Ajit Shelat

16 **TranSwitch—ASPEN: Flexible Network Processing for Access Solutions**
Subhash C. Roy

An Industry Analyst's Perspective on Network Processors

John Freeman
Industry Analyst

NPs possess the potential for being a disruptive force in the evolution of networking equipment. This chapter explores NPs from an industry perspective and looks at where they fit in the overall network silicon market. To understand this landscape, it is necessary to understand the history of packet processing. I begin by reviewing this history and examining the need for ever-increasing packet processing performance and flexibility. I then define what network processors are and where they fit in a system. Next, a criteria for evaluating NP solutions is presented. I conclude by examining trends that will drive future evolution of network processors.

9.1 HISTORY OF PACKET PROCESSING

9.1.1 The Classic Router

Early routers consisted of general-purpose computers running a specialized operating system to forward packets between two or more network interface cards (NICs). Even today, software-based routers are commonplace and provide an economical way for many smaller enterprises to add the functionality of a router to a server. In such systems, there is little difference, from a hardware perspective,

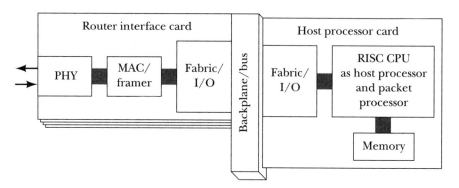

Centralized CPU router architecture.

between what is now termed "fast path" (e.g., routing decisions) and "slow path" (e.g., system management and alarm functions) packet processing functions, with both functions being handled by the same CPU. Figure 9.1 shows the architecture of a simple but typical computer-based router.

9.1.2   Emergence of Fast and Slow Path Processing

By the early 1990s, network equipment vendors realized that routers using central-ized off-the-shelf processors for both packet and host processing were reaching performance and scalability limits. They responded by pursuing two remedies. The first remedy focused on increasing overall router performance by distribut-ing the packet processing function to each interface card in the router. Figure 9.2 shows a distributed router architecture. The host CPU handles host process-ing functions (e.g., system control and the network management interface), and time-insensitive, slow path, packet processing functions (e.g., route calculation, unknown address resolution, and routing table). Distributed processors on line cards perform time-sensitive fast path functions (e.g., packet classification, mod-ification, and forwarding). The actual assignment of slow path and fast path functionality between distributed and centralized processors depends largely on specific vendor implementation. Nevertheless, distributing the packet processing function among multiple processors within a system has become a common way to accelerate the performance of processor-based routers.

The second remedy focused on the use of emerging Ethernet switches. An Ethernet switch is a high-performance, multiport version of earlier Ethernet

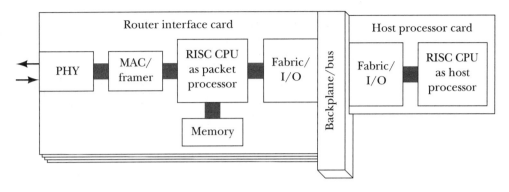

Distributed CPU router architecture.

bridges, which forward frames based on layer-2 MAC address information. They allow network managers to segment a LAN without creating additional subnets and, by doing so, have enjoyed almost immediate success in the enterprise market. The combination of Ethernet switches at the edges of a LAN and routers in the core results in the "route-once, switch-many" architecture, where traffic goes to a router only if the destination address is either unknown or outside the LAN environment. Local traffic is switched using layer-2 MAC addresses.

In eliminating the more complex processing required to route traffic, Ethernet switches can achieve a high degree of throughput by implementing the packet processing function in hardware. Specifically, these switches use Application-Specific Integrated Circuits (ASICs) for packet processing functions. By hardwiring these packet processing operations, ASICs eliminate the execution of software for fast path processing and thus perform better than corresponding processor-based implementations. Figure 9.3 depicts a layer-2 switch with distributed packet processing functions built into ASICs.

9.1.3 Hybridization of Routers and Switches

Predictably, system vendors have combined the two remedies described earlier in the same box, resulting in layer-2 switches that can perform routing or, alternately, routers with switching line cards. In this way, the distinction between layer-2 switches and routers has blurred. In hybrid switch/router systems, ASICs handle the layer-2 packet processing in the fast path for a majority of the network traffic,

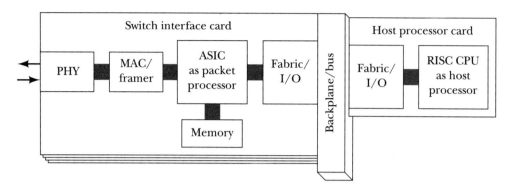

9.3

FIGURE

Layer-2 switch based on distributed packet processing using ASICs.

while off-the-shelf CPUs handle packet processing at layer 3 via more complex routing operations.

The advent of layer-3 switching further blurs the distinction between switches and routers, and even the distinction between the concepts of switching and routing. Layer-3 switching enables classification and forwarding of packets based on their layer-3 address—without implementation of more complex routing algorithms. This has been made possible largely by the de facto standardization of IP (Internet protocol) as the layer-3 protocol in LANs and WANs (wide-area networks). Since IP packets make up the vast majority of packets a switch/router processes, system vendors can hardwire IP packet classification and forwarding operations into ASICs. These operations represent a simpler subset of the longer and more complex routing code executed by off-the-shelf CPUs. In this way, both layer-3 (IP) and layer-2 protocols can be processed in the fast path, with the forwarding decision taking into account header information from the IP packet as well as its encapsulating layer-2 frame. Most layer-3 switches also feature off-the-shelf CPUs that can perform traditional routing in the slow path for "exception packets" (e.g., IP packets with unknown addresses).

9.1.4   Moving up the Stack

System vendors have not stopped at layer 3 in terms of the depth of packet classification. Standardization of IP enables layer-3 packet header classification to be implemented in ASICs. Likewise, the explosion of the World Wide Web and standardization of its associated protocols have enabled even deeper packet classification—at layers 4 and 5 (for the TCP or UDP protocols and the HTTP protocol, respectively).

The ability to capture information at layer 4 (e.g., TCP port number) and layer 5 (e.g., the URL) in the fast path is the basis for a number of ASIC-based systems generally categorized as "Web server switches." These products use this higher-layer information to provide intelligent load balancing and caching among Web servers and are being rapidly deployed in higher-end Web sites as a way to boost user response times and, increasingly, to provide other services based on higher-layer information.

9.1.5 The CPU versus Asic Tradeoff

Despite these gains, products performing higher-layer switching are now running into the limitations of their ASIC-based architectures. As packet processing functions move up the stack, a much greater degree of variability is encountered relative to more stable specifications found at layers 2 and 3. System vendors with ASIC-based products are having difficulty adding both recognition of additional protocol/application information and new forwarding and manipulation operations to the overall packet-processing function.

Certain elements of these ASIC-based systems can be updated, but many changes require the system vendor to redesign ASICs. Such a process requires at least 12 months and can significantly hurt a product's time to market. On the other hand, using completely programmable CPUs prevents these products from being competitive from a performance standpoint. This is the essence of the ASIC versus CPU tradeoff for packet processing.

Web server switches and IP service platforms are two examples of product categories beginning to meet the serious limitations imposed by both ASICs and general-purpose CPUs. NPs are poised to break this tradeoff by bringing both programmability and performance to the packet-processing function. NP vendors, especially the higher-end NP vendors that provide enough processing power to perform deep packet classification at gigabit-per-second speeds, are therefore targeting these two product categories. However, there are a number of other product categories of networking equipment that represent equally strong opportunities for NP adoption.

9.1.6 The Bandwidth Explosion

Using the fastest links in the Internet backbone as a yardstick, bandwidth increased 64-fold from OC-3 (155 Mbps) to OC-192 (10 Gbps) from 1994 to 2000. Since then, we have seen this dramatic rise in core network bandwidth flatten as capital spending has significantly slowed. However, even though the rise in aggregate bandwidth has slowed, and even though Moore's law has continued to provide increasing transistor densities with which to improve the CPU performance, CPU-based routers still fail to meet the performance requirements necessary for packet processing in the data plane at gigabit-per-second speeds.

There are numerous reasons to believe there will be a renewed demand for bandwidth. On the supply side, advances are being made in optical transmission technology, many of which have yet to be commercially deployed. These promise to increase the capacity of a single fiber strand into the hundreds of gigabit-per-second range. An even more compelling driver of overall bandwidth is the elimination of the bottleneck in the access space, the so-called last-mile problem.

While elimination of the access bottleneck has not occurred at the pace originally predicted, it is happening and is slowly unleashing latent demand for bandwidth in the consumer market. In step with the higher number of broadband subscribers, more and more Web sites are adding content and applications that can take advantage of these higher-speed connections. Furthermore, elimination of the access bottleneck is not simply a consumer-driven phenomenon. Businesses will be offered multi-Mbps services delivered over multiple DSL lines, broadband wireless connections, or a number of different fiber-optic technologies that are cost-optimized for the access domain. Fiber-optic access is also emerging as a viable option for businesses, especially those based on the Web. This increase, along with the demand for new bandwidth-consuming services, will prevent the CPU performance increases enabled by Moore's law from handling any data plane, packet processing applications aside from low-end access routers deployed at the customer premises.

9.1.7   Why CPUs Cannot Keep Up

There are two additional trends that make general-purpose CPU performance inadequate for packet processing in the data plane. The first is a greater implementation of QoS. The second is the introduction of a higher degree of intelligence in the network, especially at the service edge and within data centers.

It is likely that voice and video will make up an increasingly large component of traffic-over-IP networks, and that certain sessions within e-commerce applications will require higher priority than applications such as e-mail. An increasing variety of traffic types require different priority levels in the packet processing function at any given point in the network. Thus, routers are increasingly required to determine packet priority level and respond appropriately to that determination. To complicate matters further, the different QoS designations are often based on "policies." These policies are made up of a large number of parameters, including traffic type, application, a specific session within an application, user, time of day, and so on. The larger the number of parameters and associated QoS gradations, the more complex the algorithms needed to enforce QoS in the network. More complex algorithms require significantly more processing power. Thus, the bandwidth and processing requirements of modern QoS algorithms in general are beyond what most can deliver.

Another element of delay-sensitive traffic also increases the processing burden on CPUs used in the packet processing function. Unlike most data traffic, two-way voice and video traffic is transported over IP using small, 64-byte packets. Compared to processing large data packets, the processing of larger numbers of smaller packets that carry two-way voice/video imposes a substantial overhead on off-the-shelf CPUs. This explains the inability of CPUs to process larger numbers of smaller packets efficiently. It is also the reason that it is unusual to find high-performance ATM switches that use off-the-shelf CPUs to perform the packet processing in the data plane (i.e., ATM cells have a fixed 53-byte size).

9.1.8   Increasing Network Intelligence

Intelligence within networks refers to two capabilities. First is the ability of a device to use more information than a simple address header in making a forwarding decision. The second is the ability to perform a wider range of operations, most centered on transforming (e.g., protocol conversion, encapsulation, encryption) or copying (e.g., multicasting) packet data as it passes through a device. These capabilities, as well as the capacity for granular QoS enforcement discussed in the previous section, are based on the ability to "classify" a packet.

Classification entails matching information from an incoming packet to a table stored in the networking device. Even though this process may be simple, as the Internet has grown, routers at the service edge and in the core of the backbone must keep tables consisting of hundreds of thousands, if not millions, of entries. As tables get to this size, searching for an address match becomes a highly demanding task.

However, far more challenging is the task of matching longer patterns that correspond not only to an IP address but also to additional information in the packet header such as a TCP port number and URL. This higher-layer information found deeper in the packet is used to make more "intelligent" forwarding decisions—the type of intelligence that defines applications such as Web server load balancing and firewall filtering. Finally, the most challenging classification problem occurs when a device uses information in the packet payload.

The challenge is threefold: First, the patterns to be matched are longer, containing both header addresses and payload information, and longer patterns require larger table entries that require more processor cycles to search. A table entry for patterns that contain payload information may be as long as 512 bits, while a table containing only IPv4 addresses is only 32 bits. Second, patterns in the payload that correspond to application-layer information may have no fixed location in the payload. This requires the use of more cycles to parse the packet into pieces that will then be compared to patterns in the table. Third, as one moves up the protocol stack, the required pattern-matching algorithm itself may change and become more complex (e.g., exact match, longest prefix match, range match, and regular expression matching).

Three factors are presently driving the trend toward greater intelligence in the network and, therefore, deeper packet classification: SLM (service-level management), application/content–aware switching, and security. The most straight-forward use of higher-layer deep packet information is found in traffic reporting, or service-level management (SLM). Several SLM solutions have moved from being aware of only layers 2 and 3 and now capture and report detailed traffic statistics on a per-application (i.e., layer-7) basis. Enterprise network managers like application-aware SLM solutions because they relate network infrastructure requirements clearly to application requirements and their actual traffic patterns. SLM solutions thereby help eliminate much of the trial and error that network managers experience in troubleshooting and capacity planning. SLM applications also enable the creation of SLAs (service-level agreements) between service providers and subscribers. SLAs play a key role in making the migration to newer, packet-oriented services less risky for subscribers, especially for those with mission-critical applications. From the service provider's perspective, SLAs represent a critical way to differentiate services while maintaining profit margins.

Today, most SLAs are based on layer-2, or in some cases, layer-3 parameters. However, because SLAs are such an important differentiator, service providers are now trying to expand their SLA parameters to guarantee the performance of specific subscriber applications (i.e., layer-7 applications). Enforcing application-specific SLAs requires that SLM solutions recognize information contained in layer 7. In other words, they require SLM solutions to parse and classify not only information found in a packet's header, but information in its payload also.

However, both service providers and enterprise customers want not only reports about traffic flows on a per-application basis, but also network equipment that can actively use this higher-layer information to make real-time decisions regarding forwarding and data transformation. Therefore, in these applications, deep packet classification and associated operations must be accomplished in real time. Even multiple general-purpose CPUs operating in parallel have difficulty handling these real-time constraints. There are a number of emerging solutions being deployed in the enterprise and service provider networks that use higher-layer (through layer 7) information, to make forwarding and transformation decisions. Examples here include products in the content-aware and application-aware switching categories.

Finally, security applications are also dependent on deep packet classification—specifically, firewall filtering and intrusion detection. Firewall filtering and intrusion detection functions require more than just layer-2 and layer-3 information to determine the authorization status, authenticity, and "intent" of a packet. Presently, firewalls and intrusion detection solutions are usually implemented as stand-alone solutions similar to SLM probes. However, unlike SLM probes, these solutions are not passive; they execute quite complex operations that act directly on packets in the data path. Virtually all of these solutions are CPU based—many simply run as software on a standard PC server, and they presently represent a significant bandwidth bottleneck in the networks in which they are deployed.

Recent, well-publicized denial-of-service attacks are serving to magnify security issues as factors in the growth of e-commerce. To combat these types of attacks—and yet more serious and subtle ones sure to come—firewall filtering and intrusion detection operations need to become even more sophisticated, further increasing the processing burden on present CPU-based solutions. Moreover, they will need implementation at many more points in the network infrastructure, thereby threatening bandwidth bottlenecks throughout the network.

9.2   THE NEED FOR PROGRAMMABILITY

9.2.1   Why ASICs Are Not the Answer

Today's ASIC-based switches and ASIC-accelerated routers appear quite able to handle the processing challenges described in the previous section. By relying on the development of standards, ASIC designers can hardwire many elements of the packet processing function, leaving CPUs to handle only the least real-time operations and/or those functions that require complete programmability. However, the lack of programmability and associated flexibility in the exclusive use of hardwired ASIC-based architectures is a problem that will only become more acute as both private and public networks evolve. There are four factors preventing ASIC-centered designs in the long term from answering the performance challenges outlined in the previous section:

  ✦ IP-based protocols are still evolving.

  ✦ Layer-2 protocols are in a greater degree of flux than ever.

✦ As the packet processing function moves up the stack, the overall degree of variation increases.

✦ The long development cycles and inflexibility of ASICs are at odds with the requirement of system vendors to shorten their time to market.

9.2.2   IP Is Still Evolving

While the industry has settled on IP as the de facto layer-3 protocol, IP, as a protocol suite, is still in flux. The packet format is constantly being tweaked with both vendor-specific implementations and standards-based implementations. Additions such as DiffServe, IPSec encapsulation/tunneling, and L2TP tunneling-over-IP represent only the most recent developments that require adding more functionality to switches and routers. There will certainly be others to come, and they need to be implemented without redesigning ASICs and existing infrastructures. There is also the looming development of IPv6, which represents a fundamental change to the packet header structure. The speed with which IPv6 will become widely adopted is unclear, but it is clear that the protocols will continue to evolve.

Beyond the IP packet format itself, there are routing protocols used for IP that are also in a continuous state of evolution. In many cases, routing protocol changes can be made only in software code that runs only in the slow path on an off-the-shelf CPU used in tandem with ASICs. However, in the future, this may not be the case, and there are certainly situations where advanced routing/switching algorithms that are performed in the slow path may need to be performed in the fast path. Supporting truly scalable multicast routing is an example of a future requirement that may drive the blurring of fast and slow paths. At minimum, there is no doubt that the operations performed in fast path will become more complex, and this will increase the need for flexibility and programmability beyond what is possible using hardwired ASICs.

9.2.3   Layer 2 Is in Flux

De facto standardization of Ethernet as a layer-2 protocol in the LAN environment is one trend that has driven the success of ASIC-based Ethernet switches. Today, the creation of new MAC frame tags denoting VLAN membership (802.1Q) and priority (802.1p) is forcing vendors to redesign their LAN ASIC-based switches to support these new standards. Nonetheless, one can strongly argue that, for all intents and purposes, at layer 2 in the LAN, there is little risk in using an ASIC approach for the layer-2 portion of the packet processing function. The continued success of ASIC-based Ethernet switches in the LAN serves as strong testimony to this argument.

The same argument, however, does not hold in the case of WANs, where there are still many competing and co-existing layer-2 protocols and technologies. HDLC, Frame Relay, ATM, PPP, POS, L2TP frames, MAC frames (Ethernet), and several completely proprietary framing schemes optimized for wireless transmission will all continue to share the wide area at layer 2 for some time to come. Therefore, networking equipment can no longer support just a single layer-2 protocol. Networking vendors have realized this for some time now and, at least in terms of their marketing messages, rarely define their WAN networking products in terms of a specific layer-2 protocol. For example, one is hard-pressed to find a newly released networking product that is promoted as strictly "an ATM switch." New WAN-oriented networking products are typically referred to as "multiservice" and possess the ability to process multiple layer-2 protocol formats.

Beyond simply supporting multiple layer-2 protocols, many of the newest generation of WAN solutions are focused on providing interoperability between as many combinations of layer-2 protocols as possible. Whether they are called service selection gateways, broadband RASs, or tunnel switches, products that stack, unstack, and translate these layer-2 protocols in numerous combinations represent one of the hottest areas in networking—even given the recent downturn. Originally, service providers clearly expressed the need for products that can switch user traffic between different types of broadband networks without having to "route" at layer 3. To provide this flexibility, most "subscriber management systems" were forced to use off-the-shelf CPUs exclusively, although system scalability with these designs is limited for lack of processing horsepower.

Even within a specific layer-2 protocol, specifications are evolving and becoming more complex. ATM is the best example of a layer-2 protocol where the specification is both complex and continuously changing. The extremely large number of functions, protocols, and formats within the full ATM specification does, by itself, compel vendors to constantly update their ATM switch architectures—and this does not take into account proprietary features that a specific vendor may want to implement. Given that, for performance reasons, most ATM devices are ASIC based, most vendors shy away from actually implementing the full ATM forum specification.

In the next several years, there will likely be much greater change and variation at layer 2 before there is a consolidation. This change and variation calls for a maximizing of the programmability of the packet processing function, not for hardware optimization through the use of ASICs.

9.2.4   Increasing Packet Processing Complexity

I discussed earlier the increasing need to perform deep packet classification and perform more complex manipulation of packets based on information at layers 4 through 7. Moving the packet processing function up the stack and deeper into the packet requires greater processing power than simply dealing with layer-2 and layer-3 information in the packet header, but it also requires a greater degree of programmability.

There are only a handful of protocols and standardized formats found through layer 5, but there are thousands of off-the-shelf applications and tens of thousands of data formats found at layer 7. If customized applications are permitted, the number of possible patterns requiring classification grows significantly. Furthermore, these applications will change more frequently than corresponding changes at low levels. This will necessitate changing the data formats upon which classification is based and also potentially changing the application programs involved. Programmability of the parsing and classification elements is key in being able to design systems that can handle the sheer number and variability of data formats found at the application layer. However, as the classification function produces an increasingly large and complex set of results, there is a corresponding increase in the number and variability of operations that could be performed on a packet. Based on the results of classifying a packet through layer 7 and even injecting the results of a policy lookup into the manipulation and forwarding decisions, a very large number of potential operations could be performed on that packet. These operations could be any number of encryption or encapsulation schemes, compression algorithms, complex queuing/buffering schemes, and the like.

Finally, there will be a number of control path or even application-layer operations that will need to be performed on the fly at wire speed in order to provide increasingly compelling network-based services for which subscribers will be willing to pay a premium. Increasing the number and complexity of operations that can be performed on a packet makes hardwiring them more difficult. In summary, as intelligence moves up the stack, the rigidity of ASIC-based architectures will become more of a liability for system vendors.

9.2.5   Time-to-Market Pressures

One of the most compelling arguments against relying on ASICs to perform the packet processing functions comes from the system vendors themselves. Time to market has become a more critical factor in achieving success with network equipment. Note, however, that in this present period (since about 2001) of reduced capital spending on networking equipment, time to market is no longer quite as critical a factor for a system vendor as it was in 1999. At that time, a six-month delay in shipping could mean lost revenue in the hundreds of millions. Nevertheless, time to market is still important and will become increasingly important as soon as market conditions improve.

The bottom line is that the 12- to 18-month period necessary to design and build an ASIC-based system is too long in a robust growth environment. Furthermore, specifications cannot be altered on the fly since significant changes in ASIC functionality usually require a return to the drawing board. For this reason, ASIC development actually poses a substantial risk to the system vendor. One redesign of an ASIC can cause the system vendor to completely miss the window of opportunity for a particular product or for a feature addition to an existing product. In summary, the entire ASIC design process is an anathema to accelerating time to market and enabling the flexibility to react to customer demands. As one executive at one of the major networking vendors put it, "By the time you can build an ASIC that does something, you have built the wrong ASIC."

9.3   NETWORK PROCESSORS

As the problems associated with using either the general-purpose CPUs or custom ASICs have become more acute and more apparent, a number of companies began efforts to develop programmable devices optimized for processing packets in the data plane. An NP is a programmable microprocessor that is optimized for packet processing through three types of modification. The first type of modification occurs in the basic instruction set that defines the functions of the microprocessor. Most NP vendors use modified versions of standard RISC instruction sets, although they do differ in terms of the degree of modification. The added instructions provided to these processors are tailored to speed up operations that appear in time-critical portions of application code. Bit manipulation instructions, specialized data structure (e.g., tree) searching and addressing instructions, and CRC (cyclic redundancy code) calculation instructions are examples of instruction set extensions that are present. Naturally, the greater the change to the standard RISC instruction set, the more difficult it is for software developers to write packet processing code in industry-standard, higher-level languages such as C/C++.

The second type of modification involves the addition of hardwired function blocks designed to accelerate the performance of those functions that are common across packet processing applications. In some cases, where the use of these task-optimized function blocks is more prominent and function specific, they increase performance and/or reduce cost by incorporating functions that would normally be external to the NP. In other cases, the function can be viewed as another (more extensive) type of instruction and thus fits in the first type of modification discussed earlier. Note, however, that the use of task-specific function blocks comes at the cost of programmability and/or range of applicability. For example, there are a number of NPs on the market that incorporate Ethernet (MAC) framers on-die. These NPs would clearly hold a cost/performance advantage over NPs that rely on external framers or that rely on performing the MAC-layer framing function in software. However, these NP products are only applicable to line cards with Ethernet interfaces.

The third type of modification involves developing on-chip architectures that exploit parallelism and pipelining. Since different packet flows are independent, it is possible to route them to different on-chip processors, thus allowing for parallel operations across packets and providing for additional time to process a given packet. Additionally, since packet processing functions for a given packet normally proceed in a sequential manner (e.g., classification, QoS, routing), a pipeline architecture can be developed to provide for added parallelism (generally at the price of some latency). Most current NPs exploit either or both approaches in their architectures with the number of processors, for example, ranging from a few to a few dozen. This is likely to increase further in the near future.

We believe that NPs represent a disruptive technology and will alter not only how networking equipment is built but actually change the structure of the networking equipment industry. However, before that can occur, NPs must offer practical and irresistible advantages to system vendors in order to gain market share and catalyze the larger changes that NPs hold the potential to bring. NP vendors typically argue for one or more of the following value propositions to their system vendor customers:

✦ *Time to market (TTM)*. TTM is one of the central themes of the sales pitches of every NP vendor. Over the past five years, it has been well documented that the time required for a system vendor to bring a product from demand identification to commercial availability has increased tremendously as a factor that determines the success or failure of the product in the market.

✦ *Time in market (TIM)*. Several NP vendors are also emphasizing the time-in-market benefit that NP-based systems possess. That is, with a system that is based on a programmable packet processing engine (as opposed to a nonprogrammable ASIC), the system vendor's customers will not have to replace entire systems before they have been completely depreciated simply to add new and critical functions to the network (i.e., supporting a new protocol format or encapsulation scheme). The argument is that an NP-based system can be upgraded via a software download in order to add new features/protocol support. Given the financial pressure to extend the useful, revenue-bearing life of network equipment, TIM is a particularly important advantage for service providers. However, longer TIM is not necessarily an advantage for the system vendor, which is, after all, in the business of selling as many systems as possible over a given time period.

✦ *Expanded functionality.* A large percentage of the person-hours required to build a higher-end network equipment product is devoted to designing and debugging the ASIC that serves as the packet processing engine for the system. By using an NP, the system vendor can devote greater engineering resources to software development and build a broader set of features in the first version of the system than would be possible if the system vendor undertakes the silicon development themselves. Furthermore, many NP vendors supply common off-the-shelf packet processing applications, source code function blocks, and hardware/software simulators with their NP solutions. These enable customers to get a head start on building the suite of features that are needed.

✦ *Leverage third-party development of applications.* This is an extension of the preceding advantage, but it is applicable not only to third-party software vendors developing a particular NP but also to other network silicon vendors. Via partnerships with vendors of complementary components (PHYs, framers, switch fabrics, co-processors, host processors, and memory), NP vendors can offer system vendors a solution that has much of the integration work already finished, allowing the system vendor to focus on other issues that add greater value to their products. Far more powerful is the ability to support and/or be compatible with third-party software, including RTOS (real-time operating system) solutions, packet processing applications, and even higher-layer software. However, this advantage will take time to emerge and, given the resources required, will only be applicable for a handful of surviving NP vendors.

9.4 WHERE DO NPs FIT IN A SYSTEM?

At this point, we need to further define the NP category by looking at where the packet processing function fits in a networking device. A networking device can be broken down into four overall functions: PHY (physical) layer processing, host processing, packet processing, and switching.

✦ *Physical-layer processing.* On the egress side of a router, the PHY-layer processing function converts a digital bitstream into an analog or photonic signal and transmits that signal over a physical medium (copper wire pairs, co-axial cable, fiber, or air). On the ingress side of the router, it does the opposite. System vendors typically purchase PHY-layer processors from a number of vendors that specialize in particular types of media at particular speeds. In some cases, there is also a degree of functional specialization within the PHY layer. Examples of function specialization within the PHY layer include analog frontend processors used in conjunction with a discrete digital signal processor (DSP) and tunable lasers, and opto-electronic converters used in conjunction with serializing processors. In other cases, there is functional integration with some packet processing functions, usually Ethernet, TDM (time domain multiplexing), or SONET framing.

✦ *Host processing.* Host processing includes a number of higher-layer functions that lie outside the fast path. These functions range from slow path operations (e.g., routing algorithms, unknown address resolution, table updates, etc.) to purely control-related, nonreal-time operations that feed network management, service-level reporting, billing, and security applications. Host processors are usually off-the-shelf, RISC-based CPUs. Several NP vendors have incorporated a fully programmable, nonmodified RISC processor core on the NP die to handle host processing functions. However, most have opted to use a discrete processor external to the NP to handle host processing in their system designs.

✦ *Switching.* The switching function handles the transmission/receipt of data traffic between the ingress and egress port of the bus, backplane, or switching fabric of a router. Like the packet processing function, system vendors are increasingly moving from the use of fully customized ASIC switch fabrics to third-party, off-the-shelf switch fabrics that are available from various vendors. Typically, higher-performance switching requires the use of special-purpose chip sets that are composed together to form a switching fabric.

✦ *Packet processing.* Packet processing performs all of the necessary manipulations of network traffic as it passes through the device and, therefore, is usually the core function of the networking device in terms of that device's value in the network. In terms of the classic model, packet processing includes the following five functions: framing, parsing/classification, modification, and queuing.

✦ *Framing.* Framing can be thought of as packet processing at layer 2 only. Essentially, this function revolves around inserting and deleting layer-2 frame tags. For many synchronous layer-2 protocols, it is necessary to keep the layer-

2 framing function separate from higher-layer packet processing, where the time required to process each packet is far less deterministic. By keeping the layer-2 framing function separate from packet processing at the upper layers, systems can enforce the stricter timing constraints associated with synchronous protocols. HDLC and SONET framing are two common examples of synchronous framing functions that are typically executed by separate "framer" processors. For cost-performance reasons, layer-2 processing for asynchronous layer-2 protocols such as ATM and Ethernet may also be done on separate dedicated processors rather than within the NP.

+ *Parsing/classification.* Before a system knows what actions to take on a packet (e.g., whether or not it should be dropped, how it should be modified, where it should be placed in a buffer queue relative to other packets, etc.), the system needs to be able to extract and read the relevant information within the packet. The information extracted from a packet may be used not only to determine how the packet should be treated by the system but also to feed applications for performance management, service-level reporting, billing, and so on. As indicated earlier, there has been a clear trend toward deeper packet inspection in order to extract information at higher layers (i.e., application layer 7). Parsing entails dividing and buffering discrete elements of the packet header and payload, while classification entails matching these elements to patterns preloaded in memory. In general, deeper packet classification requires greater processing.

The growing importance of deeper packet inspection and associated processing requirements has lead to the development of specialized parsing/-classification co-processors. These co-processors are best described as optimized content addressable memories (CAMs) or programmable state machines (PSMs). Furthermore, it is important to distinguish these co-processor products from NPs even though much of the marketing language used by vendors of both of these product types is similar. Parsing/classification co-processors are not competitive with NPs and are in fact complementary.

+ *Modification.* Modification entails a number of operations, including replacing incoming packet headers with new packet headers that correspond to the next-hop destination address (e.g., the classic routing function), encapsulating a packet within a new data format (e.g., encapsulating an IP packet into an L2TP frame for tunneling), segmenting/reassembling variable length packets (e.g., IP) into fixed-length cells (e.g., ATM), and insertion of tags into a packet in order to communicate how that packet should be treated downstream in the network (e.g., QoS priority).

+ *Encryption/compression.* Execution of these two functions is optional in many situations, but it nonetheless represents a discrete functional stage in packet

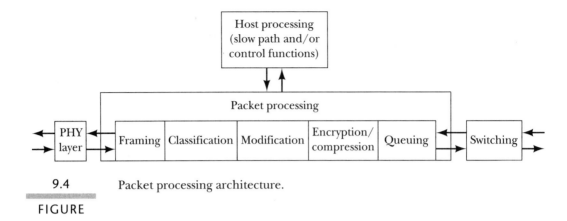

9.4

FIGURE
Packet processing architecture.

processing. Encryption is the scrambling of data in a packet for secure transport over an "open" network such as the Internet. Compression is used to reduce the size of a packet payload for more bandwidth-efficient transport. Both encryption and compression utilize mathematical algorithms that are fairly specific to their respective tasks and, as such, are often executed by discrete processors that are optimized for running these algorithms. This is especially the case in situations where the networking device must encrypt/compress hundreds of megabits per second. However, in some cases where either the total throughput of the device is relatively low or the instances of encryption/compression are infrequent (relative to the total volume of traffic processed), NPs can be used to execute these functions.

✦ *Queuing.* This function performs reordering (based on priority) and buffering of packets and the transmission of those packets to the switch fabric. For highly granular QoS enforcement (i.e., multiple QoS levels applied to hundreds of thousands of packet flows) at high line speeds, a dedicated processor may be necessary. Many NP vendors that are developing NPs capable of 10 Gbps+ throughput are also developing dedicated traffic management co-processors for this purpose.

Figure 9.4 depicts the primary elements of a networking device, including the five functions that make up packet processing.

Software functions of a system can be generally categorized as residing in the data plane or the control plane. Data plane functions are applied on packets moving through the system and, therefore, face real-time performance constraints. Most NPs handle only data plane functions. Control plane functions are very broad and include management functions that are required for internal coordination among components of a system and between the system and external systems. Control plane software also handles a number of other operations dealing with traffic passing through the system that are less time sensitive. These operations include routing algorithms, operations for resolving unknown addresses, policy/access list lookups, address/route updates, session setup/tear down, and any number of other "out-of-band" signaling/messaging functions. In general, control plane software is much larger, more complex, and far more varied in terms of functionality than data plane software.

9.5   EVALUATING NP SOLUTIONS

Companies developing NPs differ significantly in their approaches. Different NP vendors have targeted different points along the performance–programmability continuum, disparaging the competitive NP solutions in one of two ways depending on where their own solution stands on the continuum. Vendors emphasizing "true programmability" pass off many competitive solutions as "a configurable ASIC" and, therefore, not offering the degree of programmability necessary in today's environment. Vendors emphasizing "deterministic performance for wire-speed forwarding" call many competitive solutions nothing more than "RISC-based CPUs with a few changes to their instruction set," implying that such solutions are fundamentally ill-disposed to solving the problem of transmission speed increases.

However, where an NP solution sits on the performance–programmability continuum is only one of many criteria upon which that solution should be evaluated. It is still true that NP solutions and the criteria by which they are measured must be viewed with a strong dose of "it depends on the application." This high degree of application dependency with regard to performance tends to obfuscate direct comparisons among NP solutions—the system vendor must practically build the system in order to get a true understanding of how the NP will perform.

One of the most effective ways NP vendors can differentiate their solution for a particular type of system is to make available reference code for packet processing applications commonly used by that type of system. With the strong "silicon orientation" of most NP vendors, developing such code to the point where it is usable and valuable to the system vendor is not as easy as it may seem. It requires a great deal of experience in writing packet processing software for full-fledged systems, experience that is typically not found in an NP vendor; it is usually found in the NP vendor's customers. This situation is beginning to change as the larger NP vendors realize the need to hire such system software experts and as more platform-oriented NP solutions reduce the technological and operational barriers to entry for third-party software vendors to develop such off-the-shelf packet processing applications for use by system vendors.

There are a number of other features that make certain NP solutions more appropriate than others for particular applications. For example, the addition of particular hardware-assist engines for specific functions is one clear way NP vendors can differentiate their products. However, in general, we have not seen the implementation of narrowly targeted hardware elements in the leading NP solutions. One of the primary reasons the large NP vendors have resisted the temptation to capture a specific market segment through hardware-based acceleration or integration of a function that is specific only to certain types of systems (e.g., an ATM SAR) is that the emerging NP market is platform oriented. That is, it is critical to gain relatively broad third-party support, a difficult thing to do if your chip is too niche oriented by virtue of specific hardware acceleration or functional integration. It is much more effective to let a larger number of third parties build multiple applications targeted at a wide range of specific markets—even if the platform, in this case an NP solution, is not itself optimized for any of these specific markets. In effect, the narrower market optimization is the value added by the third party. In most cases, these third parties are software vendors although a number of co-processor vendors would also fit into this category.

The survivability of a particular platform, regardless of whether that platform is marketed by a startup or a more established company, is a real issue that system vendors need to consider when selecting the NP that will drive the packet processing function of their system. The following are some of major criteria that system vendors use in evaluating NP solutions. I have divided these criteria into those that pertain to the product itself and those that pertain to the NP vendor as a whole.

9.5.1   Degree of Programmability/Applicability

The degree of programmability/applicability refers to the range of tasks, functions, system types, and protocols that the NP can handle. For example, there are NPs that have task-specific function blocks directed at processing certain protocols (i.e., ATM or Ethernet frames), and there are NPs that can handle packet classification above layer 4, whereas others cannot. Furthermore, some NPs are better described as being "configurable" rather than programmable, meaning that they are restricted to a certain subset of packet processing applications. All of these factors should be taken into consideration in this rating, which essentially measures the total number of applications for which an NP solution can be reasonably programmed to deal with.

This category is difficult to measure since, while a particular NP solution can be theoretically programmed to handle a particular task, in practice, programming such a task may be extremely difficult. In some cases, the NP can be programmed to handle a particular task but performance degrades so precipitously when this task is executed that, for practical purposes, performing the task on this NP is not reasonable. In other cases, the task can be programmed, but the implementation of additional co-processors or other silicon components is necessary to achieve acceptable performance. In these cases, the importance of that particular application must be weighed against the cost of the additional components necessary to execute the application acceptably.

The problem is that often the measurement of "acceptable performance" for a particular application remains an unknown factor until well into the development of the system. Therefore, system vendors have to take their best guess as to whether they believe an NP can be programmed to handle a particular application. The system vendor's decision can be greatly aided by the availability of a commercial-grade hardware development environment. The environment should be sophisticated and "real" enough that it can be taken "as is" and used in a real system with only minor modifications.

9.5.2   Ease of Programmability

Ease of programmability is one of the most important NP attributes, especially when time to market is a critical success factor for the system vendor's product. The criterion is related to the availability of special instructions that have been added to the NP's processor cores. It is also somewhat of a subjective rating because of the differing preferences on the part of software engineers. Many NP vendors have created a considerably "thick" layer of software abstractions and APIs that hide the complexity of the underlying hardware from the software engineer. However, if this abstraction layer prevents the software engineer from accessing the underlying hardware completely, it may, in the end, be counterproductive and increase the difficulty associated with low-level programming when that is necessary. However, for other software engineers, NPs with highly abstracted software architecture make coding common packet processing applications almost a matter of "dragging and dropping." Naturally, the software engineer must be satisfied with the generally unoptimized performance delivered by such wizard-driven creations.

9.5.3   Choice of Programming Language

This criterion is related to ease of programmability, but with some distinctions. The level of abstraction provided by the development language does not necessarily equate to programming "ease." Nevertheless, for strategic reasons relating to future migration of NP solutions and systems, the programming language that an NP vendor has chosen is an important consideration in the NP selection process.

Some NP vendors support only low-level assembler languages and/or microcode for writing data plane applications, making the programming task both time-consuming and very difficult for those developers with little experience in packet processing applications. However, because packet processing applications are much more performance sensitive than applications in the general computing environment, with efficient use of every processor cycle being a critical consideration, many software engineers actually prefer to code in assembler/microcode in order to have complete control over how the application executes even on a cycle-by-cycle basis.

Despite the control advantages of lower-level code, most NP vendors now provide a compiler that allows routines to be programmed using a higher-level language. In most cases, the language is C/C++; however, because the architectures and instruction sets of most NPs differ from standard RISC machines, complied C/C++ code does not always execute the way the programmer envisions. Therefore, some NP vendors have developed proprietary "C-like" scripting languages that have a syntax and vocabulary similar to that of C/C++. The downside of this approach is that it is not conducive to broad third-party application development.

In addition to the controversy over the use of C/C++ for data plane applications, there is substantial disagreement regarding the use of 4GLs (fourth-generation languages) to handle the classification function. 4GLs used for classification are designed such that the bit patterns of a packet, both header and payload, can be easily and intuitively described and loaded into memory. The syntax of these 4GLs allows for new patterns to be described and loaded by the user of the system. 4GL proponents cite the use of SQL in the database domain as an analogous development. The problem with 4GLs presently (and unlike SQL) is that they are vendor specific and proprietary. While there is a movement to establish a standard 4GL, little concrete progress has been made to date.

9.5.4 Off-the-Shelf Applications and Reference Code Library

Using off-the-shelf applications and function blocks enables a system vendor to accelerate a product's development and expands the degree of system functionality. While there are many cases where a system vendor may want to write these function blocks itself, it is generally easier and faster to modify the source code of a given function block than to write it from scratch. In evaluating NP solutions regarding this category, one should take into account both the breadth of such code (i.e., how many types of packet processing applications are covered in an NP vendor's library?) and the quality of that code (i.e., is it sample reference code used for testing purposes or can it be used pretty much "as is" in a system being developed for commercial availability?).

In addition, availability of function blocks from third parties is important. With time, the amount of packet processing code from third parties will exceed that available from the leading NP vendors—but only for the market-leading solutions. The de facto expansion of the code libraries of the leading NP vendors by third-party developers is an inevitable result of the "winner-take-all" phenomenon that is characteristic of platform-type products such as NPs.

9.5.5   Performance

Given the large number of variables involved in applications, gaining an understanding of the true performance of an NP is, perhaps, the trickiest area of evaluation. For NPs, performance measurement is so heavily dependent on application and the use of external components that it is virtually impossible to pinpoint a processor's performance numbers beyond putting that processor into a general performance "bucket." In other words, one can group NPs into certain broad categories based on performance, but it is close to impossible to differentiate between NPs within a category based on performance.

An additional performance category concerns architectural scalability of the NP. In many cases, utilizing more advanced fabrication processes can increase NP performance. As fabrication processes improve, NP performance improves both in terms of the speed associated with a given design and the ability to improve performance by increasing the level of parallelism associated with a design (e.g., place more embedded processors on the same die). These improvements often can be achieved without fundamentally changing the architecture. Comparison of competitors should account for the fabrication process employed, recognizing that products usually go through successive cycles where improvements in both design and fabrication process occur.

This is particularly important when comparing NP solutions from startup competitors with those from the incumbent NP players. In some cases, the faster performance of startup NP solutions is due more to the fact that they are using a fabrication process that produces greater die density than to any fundamentally superior architecture for processing packets. Clearly, this is not a sustainable competitive advantage since all network vendors essentially have access to the same density of fabrication process.

9.5.6   NP Cost

Although chip pricing matters much more at the lower end of the performance spectrum in the NP market, it is still an important consideration when designing any system. In addition, larger established network equipment vendors have a price negotiation strategy that is especially effective when dealing with startup NP suppliers. The ability to publicize an early design is of great value to startups since it validates the solution approach taken and aids greatly in obtaining additional customers. Therefore, a system vendor should be able to receive a substantial additional discount in exchange for allowing the NP startup (or even in some cases a more established NP vendor) to publicize the design win and even imply that additional design wins for other systems may be in the pipeline.

9.5.7   Total System Cost

Per-chip pricing is a clear and important cost component, but it is not the whole story. System vendors need to be able to give a reasonably accurate estimate of the other components that will be necessary to accompany each of the NP solutions they are considering before they make their final decision. For example, if a particular NP has integrated Ethernet MACs and the system requires Ethernet interfaces, then the cost of external MACs must be added to the cost of a competing NP solution that does not have MACs integrated on-die. In some situations, such as determining whether an NP's on-board classifier is sufficient for higher-layer classification or whether an external classification co-processor is required, the determination of total cost becomes more difficult without having already made some progress in designing the system.

Factors such as per-chip pricing and the degree of functional integration affect the COGS (cost of goods sold) for a particular system product. However, the fixed development cost of that system can also be affected by NP selection. Development schedules, for example, can be severely impacted by poorly conceived development tools, especially debuggers and simulators that are either inaccurate or nonautomated. While evaluating the development tools and software elements of an NP solution, a system vendor should also give weight to the financial cost in terms of development time and resources that a deficiency in these areas will cause.

9.5.8   Vendor Solutions

One-stop, single-vendor shopping is generally an advantage in complex high-tech markets. One of the benefits of using a single network silicon supplier is the additional price discount that an equipment vendor can receive. Beyond pricing, there are often additional benefits when the complexities of intercomponent compatibility are an issue. For example, by using an NP and a switch fabric from the same supplier, the use of FPGAs and associated "glue-logic" for NP-to-fabric interconnect can be eliminated, saving time and money. However, the integration benefit of using a single supplier for multiple components is not automatic. Many network silicon vendors have built their product line, ranging from PHY-layer chips to NPs, through acquisition. It may require a long time to eliminate the interoperability problems among the components in their product line that were obtained as part of an acquisition process.

9.5.9 Multivendor Integration

Even the largest network silicon vendors cannot satisfy all the needs of their customers. In most cases, major components (i.e., PHY-layer chip, framer, NP, host processor, memory, switch fabric) are supplied by different vendors. Therefore, to maximize system time-to-market value, it is critical for NP vendors to form partnerships and cooperate with other network silicon providers. Thus, for this category, system vendors should try, at least subjectively, to measure the quantity and quality of the partnerships that an NP vendor has formed with other network silicon vendors having complementary products. Along with this, the system vendor should take into consideration the use of emerging standardized interfaces (e.g., CSIX, SPI-4), which can provide at least a baseline of compatibility among multiple vendors. However, standards compliance is not as valuable as having two network silicon vendors with a track record of working together to make the integration effort as seamless as possible.

9.6 TRENDS

9.6.1 Operational at OC-192

For many vendors, first-generation NPs have performed below expectations. Nevertheless, they are currently pursuing a strategy of developing higher-performance NPs prior to finishing up on their first-generation products. These second-generation components are moving ahead toward higher-performance OC-192+ speeds in anticipation of optical requirements, before the lower-performance rollout has hit the steepest part of the growth curve. This development could result in higher upfront R&D costs without commensurate ROI (return on investment) on initial products. At this time, however, virtually every startup NP vendor has focused on achieving the 10GE/OC-192 performance rather than improving and differentiating the performance of first-generation NPs through lower power, deeper classification, software functionality, development environment innovations, and the like.

9.6.2   Control Plane and Data Plane Integration

Control plane software often executes on a general-purpose CPU while the time-constrained data plane operations are accelerated for maximum performance by executing on an NP. The differences between control and data plane requirements are reflected in a number of ways. Data plane software often consists of fewer than 1500 lines of code and is typically written in languages for creating ASIC logic (i.e., Verilog or VHDL) or low-level microcode. Control plane software often consists of millions of lines of code and is usually written in C/C++.

Several first-generation NPs featured embedded on-chip control processors, thus providing a hardware platform to run software for both the data and control planes. The initial benefit of these embedded control processors is to save the cost and board space of an external control processor. However, a number of vendors did not supply the necessary integration between runtime software for the control plane and the data plane, and did not offer appropriate development tools for control plane software. Without sophisticated software integration between the control and data planes, the embedded control processor was often left unused. Software engineers favored the use of an external control processor with which they were familiar, and on which system vendor's legacy control plane applications could be executed.

Going forward, the strict line between the control and data plane software, functionality and programming tools, and development processes will become blurred. More intelligent networking devices will execute a much larger number of operations per packet related to control applications, and these applications will apply to much higher percentage packets. Policy-based networking schemes, security-related, application-layer QoS designations, and application-layer network services are emerging applications that will require greater integration between control and data plane operations.

9.6.3   Linux-Based Applications

One of the most common alliances between NP vendors and third parties has been in the area of using Linux as a control plane operating system and providing integration between Linux-based software and the NP vendor's own low-level software running in the data plane. For example, Intel has formed a number of alliances with vendors of Linux-based RTOSs and higher-layer Linux-based switching/routing applications. In fact, they are offering a third party (LynuxWorks)

Linux-based RTOS, runtime applications, and a development environment for use with their IXP12xx line of NPs.

Meanwhile, with the continued rapid adoption of NPs by network equipment vendors, third-party Linux developers will have an increasingly large market for packet processing applications. Furthermore, new software functions and features could be added much more rapidly in response to market demands since there will be a large number of developers willing to write and support such open source code. Lower-cost, "manufacturing-oriented" network equipment manufacturers can then build equipment that leverages the "market-leading NP" and the large base of Linux-based software written for that NP.

9.6.4 On-the-Fly Application-Layer Processing

Network service providers have a well-recognized problem: provision of connectivity over increasingly wider pipes is, by itself, no longer a very profitable business. Over the past five years, service providers have been struggling to move up the stack and provide higher-margin, so-called value-added services. These service providers have moved aggressively into highly tiered offerings that provide a mix of QoS parameters backed by SLAs. In this way, they have increased their ability to offer services with highly granular prioritization parameters that match the subscribers' multiple applications and traffic types, while gaining the statistical multiplexing advantage that packet-based networks hold over circuit switched networks. Yet these services, while providing a higher margin than straight bandwidth services, are still essentially providing only connectivity. Services based primarily on connectivity are vulnerable to commoditization and an inability to profitably serve smaller enterprise organizations. Thus, network service providers are seeking an element to truly differentiate them in the marketplace and attract a larger customer base.

In the last several years, network equipment vendors have offered IP service delivery platforms and closely related "high-touch" router products in answer to this demand. For the most part, the value-added services that these platforms can offer fall into the area of security, enabling the subscriber to outsource VPN authentication and termination/origination, firewall filtering, and to a limited degree, intrusion detection. Security-related services are potentially very high margin and lend themselves well to NP-based equipment.

However, the expansion of security-related services has been rather disappointing. While there are a number of reasons for this, the most important has simply been reluctance on the part of many subscribers to outsource any security-related function to a network service provider. While security-related system integration, auditing, and consulting services are growing very rapidly, these are not the types of services that most network service providers possess the core competency to provide.

Despite the low-level reception of outsourced VPNs (as distinct from roll-your-own VPNs, which are far more common) and firewalls, service providers need to develop and offer services that operate at higher layers, performing on-the-fly transformation of network traffic at the application layer. This must be done in a way that provides an attractive value to the customer. These services will be differentiated from many of the application-layer services provided today (i.e., Web-based services or outsourced applications) by the fact that the operations that constitute "the service" must be executed in real time, on the fly as the network traffic passes through the device. The highly latency-sensitive nature of these applications prevents the data from being written or read to or from a hard disk and, therefore, cannot be server based.

Beyond security-related services, two types of application-layer network services are expected to emerge over the next several years. The first will be existing applications that will benefit from the performance acceleration generated by on-the-fly processing within the network infrastructure. One example would be the automatic conversion of HTML documents to a format that would be more efficient for transmission over a mobile wireless access network and appropriate for display on a smaller handheld screen (e.g., WAP).

The second type of application-layer network service does not exist today because the current infrastructure is incapable of handling its processing requirements. To date, these services are universally considered too futuristic for practical deployment. One example is real-time language translation for text-based chat or, even more challenging, a scheduled conference call. Clearly, the availability of a real-time language translation service is years away. However, in many ways, the trend toward true application-layer network services has already begun, and a number of less complex application-layer services can be delivered in a shorter time frame.

Continued rapid growth of this trend will require a much larger universe of stakeholders to conceive, create, and promote this next generation of application-layer network services. Many of these stakeholders will come not from the world of network services, network equipment, and packet processing but from fields such as finance, content publishing, entertainment, supply-chain management solutions, e-commerce, and database software. Given the broad range of companies that will be required to participate in the creation, deployment, and promotion of compelling application-layer services, I believe that the leverage provided by a platform-oriented NP and an extensive, open-ended value-chain creation strategy is critical for long-term success.

10

CHAPTER

Agere Systems— Communications Optimized PayloadPlus Network Processor Architecture

Bill Klein, Juan Garza
Agere Systems

PayloadPlus is a complete OC-48c network processing solution. The three-chip solution performs all of the classification, policing, traffic management, quality-of-service (QoS)/class-of-service (CoS), traffic-shaping, and packet modification functions needed for a carrier-class networking platform. With its communications-focused architecture, the PayloadPlus product family represents a technological advance in the construction of intelligent communication equipment capable of layer 2–7 processing.

The PayloadPlus network processor family includes the Fast Pattern Processor (FPP), the Routing Switch Processor (RSP), and the Agere System Interface (ASI). The programmable FPP performs wire-speed classification and analysis for multiple protocols at layers 2 through 7. The FPP is programmed with a simple protocol processing language, the functional programming language (FPL), to recognize and classify incoming packets based on millions of data packet patterns—without the use of expensive content-addressable memory (CAM) or segmentation and reassembly (SAR) devices. The RSP performs various queuing, traffic management, traffic-shaping, and packet modification functions on traffic flows on a fully programmable basis. The ASI provides an industry-standard peripheral component interconnect (PCI) interface between a host processor and Agere's high-speed processors for control and management functions, including routing table and virtual circuit updates, hardware configuration, and exception handling. The ASI also assists the FPP in policing both cell and packet-based traffic at up to OC-48c rates, maintaining state information on data flows and capturing statistics.

10.1   TARGET APPLICATIONS

Applications for the PayloadPlus solution include

- ✦ Layer-2 and layer-3 switching and routing
- ✦ Upper-layer service creation
- ✦ VPNs
- ✦ Protocol interworking
- ✦ Access control list processing
- ✦ Access system packet processing and line services
- ✦ Programmable fine-grained QoS
- ✦ Rapid bandwidth provisioning
- ✦ Voice and data processing (IP, AAL5, or AAL2 based)

Since the FPP, RSP, and ASI are programmable processors, not fixed-function ASICs, they can handle new protocols or applications as they are developed or as new network functions are required, thereby giving systems a longer life in the field. Agere's approach also avoids the use of expensive support components like CAM or SAR devices.

10.2   PAYLOADPLUS OPTIMIZED PIPELINE-BASED HARDWARE ARCHITECTURE

Agere's PayloadPlus solution is specifically designed to handle the data flow associated with the preceding applications by using a unique pipeline-based, communications-focused architecture. Most network equipment built to address these types of applications handles traffic as shown in Figure 10.1. Agere Systems offers all major components shown, including optics, framers, network processors, and fabrics needed to build scalable solutions.

The PayloadPlus architecture uses a technology called *pattern-matching optimization* to achieve greater than 5× performance improvement over RISC processors. This performance reaches the level of fixed-function ASICs while allowing

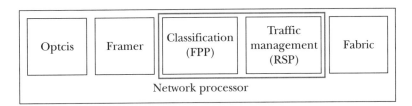

10.1

FIGURE

Line card configuration with Agere's NPU solution.

equivalent flexibility and superior programmability when compared with RISC-based solutions. The PayloadPlus architecture is able to realize both dramatic performance gains and simplified programming by using a pattern-matching engine and a pipelined architecture. This combination leads to lower overhead, fewer necessary clock cycles, and more data processing per transistor than other available solutions.

Figure 10.2 shows how PayloadPlus breaks down this networking problem into a functional solution using dedicated, programmable engines to address specific tasks. The FPP accepts a data stream through standard interfaces: UTOPIA level 3, UTOPIA level 2, and POS-PHY level 3. The FPP can classify traffic based on information contained *anywhere* in the packet, thus allowing for processing at layers 2 through 7. The FPP analyzes and classifies these frames and cells, reassembles them into protocol data units (PDUs), then transmits the PDUs and their classification conclusions to the RSP over a POS-PHY level-3 interface. The RSP handles queuing, packet modification, traffic shaping, QoS tagging, and segmentation. The FPP, RSP, and ASI combine interfaces to a control processor via the ASI's PCI-compliant interface bus.

By partitioning the solution based on the pipelined approach shown in Figure 10.2, the FPP utilizes its pattern-matching abilities on incoming traffic and performs the lookups necessary to determine a "transmit command" decision,

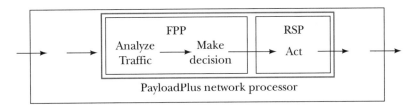

10.2

FIGURE

PayloadPlus pipeline breakdown.

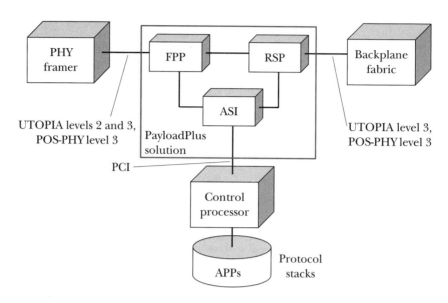

Agere's OC-48c PayloadPlus solution.

which is then tagged to each PDU. The RSP uses the transmit command and its programmable, very large instruction word (VLIW) engines to perform the traffic management and packet modification functions. With this approach, no changes or modifications are needed during the classification or decision-making process. Hence, the PayloadPlus solution breaks down very complex network traffic-handling problems into defined, programmable blocks. In addition, each functional block can work simultaneously on the different stages of the pipeline, thereby allowing for much more aggregate processing to be done on a per-packet basis.

In PayloadPlus systems, processing tasks occur in one of two domains, called the *fast (wire-speed)* and the *slow path*. The fast path includes all tasks necessary for normal data stream processing. The slow path includes tasks such as exception handling, management, configuration, and updates. Figure 10.3 shows how PayloadPlus devices and buses are divided between the fast path and the slow path. Key attributes of the FPP include

+ *High-level/full-performance programmability.* The FPP's programmability combines the flexibility and performance needed to address a wide variety of applications and protocols via the FPL. Protocols can be implemented in hundreds of lines of code rather than thousands, and even code optimization is done at this high level rather than through microcode manipulation.

+ *Fast, deterministic searches.* The FPP's search algorithm allows the creation of lists that can be searched quickly, within deterministic time limits. Data patterns of any size are supported, and search time is independent of the number of entries in the search table; it depends only on the size of the portion of the data pattern to be analyzed. Even robust access control lists (ACLs) can easily be supported.

+ *Use of standard memory.* The FPP stores pattern-matching data in standard off-the-shelf RAM instead of expensive CAM devices.

+ *High performance at lower clock speeds.* The FPP's efficient design lets it support OC-48c speeds at a minimal 133 MHz clock speed, saving on hardware costs and allowing for greater scalability.

+ *SAR.* The FPP and RSP combination provides ATM SARing capabilities for multiservice applications, eliminating the need for separate SARing ICs.

The RSP has four major capabilities: queuing, traffic management, traffic shaping, and packet modification, all of which are handled in a programmable fashion. Key attributes include

+ Transmit data queuing, including QoS and CoS

+ Support for up to 65,535 queues for per-flow queuing even for large numbers of connections

+ Programmable QoS and CoS parameters for each queue

+ Fully programmable discard policies, including RED, EPD, and WRED

+ Fully programmable outgoing data modifications

+ Support for multicasting

+ Support for real-time traffic, such as VBR-rt

+ Support for independent scheduling up to 256 logical ports

+ Segmentation capabilities for interfacing to cell-based fabrics or ATM line interfaces

+ Generation of required checksums and CRCs

+ Industry-standard interfaces for input and output

The ASI seamlessly integrates the FPP and RSP with the host processor. The wire-speed data stream operations are performed by the FPP, RSP, and ASI. The ASI provides

✦ An industry-standard interface to the FPP and RSP for a host microprocessor that allows

  • Centralized initialization and configuration of the FPP, RSP, and physical interfaces
  • Classification table updates to the FPP
  • Queue processing updates to the RSP
  • Implementation of routing and management protocols
  • Exception handling

✦ High-speed, flow-oriented state maintenance for the FPP, including

  • RMON statistics gathering
  • Packet sequence checking
  • Packet time stamping
  • Cell- or packet-based policing at up to OC-48c rates

Another example of the PayloadPlus pipelined building block approach is the Voice Packet Processor (VPP). The VPP is an additional IC designed to fit on the data path between the FPP and the RSP to handle ATM adaptation layer-2 (AAL2) traffic. The VPP architecture is designed to generate and terminate AAL2 traffic or perform CPS switching. The VPP accepts AAL2 cells, CPS packets, and other PDUs from the FPP. It processes the AAL2 cells and CPS packets, and passes the other traffic to the RSP transparently. The VPP parses AAL2 cells into CPS packets and assembles CPS packets into AAL2 cells. It also keeps global, virtual connection, and channel statistics. VPP capabilities include

✦ Parsing AAL2 cells to CPS packets. At OC-12, supports a total of 32,767 unique conversations.

✦ Assembly of AAL2 cells from CPS packets. At OC-12, supports a total of 32,767 unique conversations.

✦ Carrying up to 16,383 conversations on AAL2 VCs

✦ Supporting up to 248 active voice channels per VC

✦ CPS packet switching between VCs. Up to 16,383 conversations can be switched on up to 8191 VCs in each direction.

✦ Bypassing other traffic with remaining bandwidth available for IP/AAL5, MPLS, and other data traffic

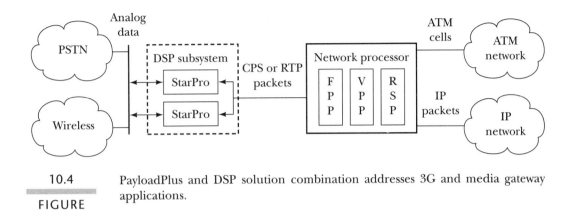

10.4

FIGURE

PayloadPlus and DSP solution combination addresses 3G and media gateway applications.

10.3   3G/MEDIA GATEWAY APPLICATION EXAMPLE

A media gateway or 3G network application example of the PayloadPlus solution is shown in Figure 10.4. In both cases, analog traffic is digitized by a DSP subsystem, then sent to the network processor for processing and interfacing the traffic to ATM or IP networks. In this case, PayloadPlus would work in conjunction with a DSP subsystem. Traffic from the DSP subsystem would be classified, then routed to the appropriate connection. The VPP would be used to handle AAL2 traffic since that protocol is used in both applications.

With this configuration, the various packets, cells, and voice samples, once classified in the FPP, would be queued and scheduled (with the required QoS) to the appropriate network using the RSP's programmable traffic management options. In addition, the programmable bitstream processing nature of PayloadPlus allows the system to adapt to new standards, protocols, and networking environments to handle a wide array of network traffic, including AAL2, AAL5, CPS, VoIP, IPv4, IPv6, MPLS, frame relay, and more.

10.4   FPP DETAILS

The FPP performs programmable, high-performance data classification. Its highly pipelined, multithreaded architecture processes 64 PDUs simultaneously. This parallel processing is transparent to the developer, who programs the application as a single thread and does not need to utilize any complex programming techniques. The internal architecture of the FPP is shown in Figure 10.5.

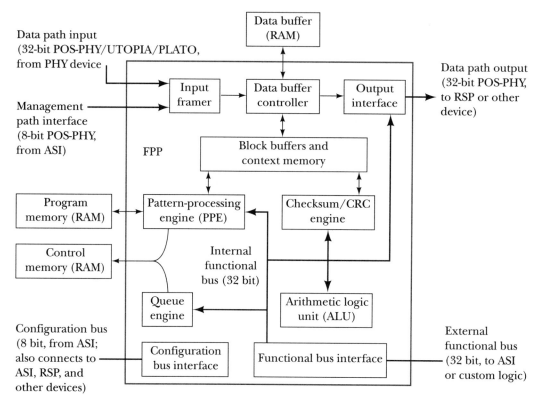

10.5 FPP internal architecture.

FIGURE

The FPP's pattern-processing engine (PPE) uses an algorithm to perform pattern matching at a consistent speed, regardless of the number of patterns that it must match against. The PPE can match any part of the data stream—header, payload, or trailer—against a defined set of patterns. The FPP's pattern-matching behavior is specified by a control program written in FPL, then is compiled and loaded into the FPP. FPL is a classification-specific language that lets you intuitively specify both the patterns to match against PDU data and the processing to perform based on those pattern matches.

As a descriptive language, FPL merely requires the user to have a knowledge of the protocol to be processed to efficiently develop an application. The FPP makes classification conclusions for each input PDU based on the FPL program. The FPP passes those conclusions, along with the PDU, to downstream logic, which, in turn, uses the conclusions to modify the PDU, perform traffic management, maintain QoS and CoS for connections, and route the PDU.

Each PDU is processed by a separate processing thread, called a *context*, that keeps track of the blocks that compose the PDU. The FPP does not use speculative execution and does not suffer the pipeline stalls or context-switching overhead that are usually associated with sequential processing architectures. The FPP processes data in two passes, enabling the FPP to first reassemble PDUs, then classify the complete PDU, all at wire speeds. The two passes are typically used as follows:

+ The first pass stores data as 64-byte blocks and computes data offsets for each block, creating a linked-list data structure that defines the reassembled PDU.

+ The second pass processes the whole PDU, simultaneously performing pattern matching and transmitting the reassembled PDU. The last step of the second pass is transmitting the conclusions of the pattern-matching process for that PDU.

The FPP's 64 contexts are allocated between first- and second-pass processing during initial configuration. Both first and second pass can be programmed to use 1 to 63 contexts. The exact processing that occurs in the first and second passes is specified by the FPL program.

10.4.1 FPP Functional Blocks

+ *Input framer.* The 32-bit input path is configurable into any combination of 8-, 16-, or 32-bit UTOPIA level-3, UTOPIA level-2, or POS-PHY level-3 input.

+ *Data buffer controller.* The data buffer controller manages movement of data blocks between the data buffer, input framer, block buffers, and output interface.

+ *Output interface.* The output interface transmits PDUs and their classification conclusions to the RSP or other downstream logic.

+ *Block buffers and context memory.* Each context has a block buffer, which stores the block currently being processed, and context memory, which stores configuration information for the context.

+ *Pattern-processing engine (PPE).* The PPE matches data from blocks against a set of patterns specified by the FPL program and informs the program of its results.

+ *Checksum/CRC engine.* The checksum/CRC engine performs four types of checksum and cyclic redundancy check (CRC) calculations, as requested by the FPL program. Supported checksums include generic checksum, IPv4 checksum, CRC-10, and CRC-32.

+ *Arithmetic logic unit.* The ALU performs arithmetic functions such as addition, subtraction, shifting, and Boolean operations.

+ *Configuration bus interface.* The configuration bus interface enables the ASI to configure the FPP, RSP, physical input interface, and other system modules. In the FPP, the CBI is used to initialize memory and registers, load the FPL program into the program memory, and dynamically update routing tables and access control lists in the program memory.

+ *Functional bus interface.* The FBI is the external portion of the bus used to service functions called by the FPL program. Predefined functions are processed by functional blocks connected to the internal portion of the FBI. The external FBI passes external function calls to devices outside the FPP, enabling external function processing at wire-speed rates. For example, the ASI provides additional functions such as policing and statistics generation. You can also attach custom logic modules to the external FBI to provide additional functionality.

+ *External memories.*

  • *Data buffer.* The data buffer stores PDU blocks received from the input framer.
  • *Program memory.* The program memory stores the FPL program and pattern-matching lists such as routing tables and access control lists.
  • *Control memory.* The control memory stores control data structures such as the link lists that logically join blocks into PDUs.

10.5　RSP DETAILS

The RSP architecture is designed to provide a high level of PDU processing capabilities at wire speed. The RSP accepts PDUs and their classification information on up to 128 logical input ports. It queues them on up to 64K programmable queues, then outputs the modified PDUs on up to 256 logical output ports. The RSP uses programmable VLIW compute engines to process PDUs while maintaining a high throughput. Each compute engine is dedicated to a processing function:

+ *Traffic management compute engine.* Enforces discard policies and keeps queue statistics.

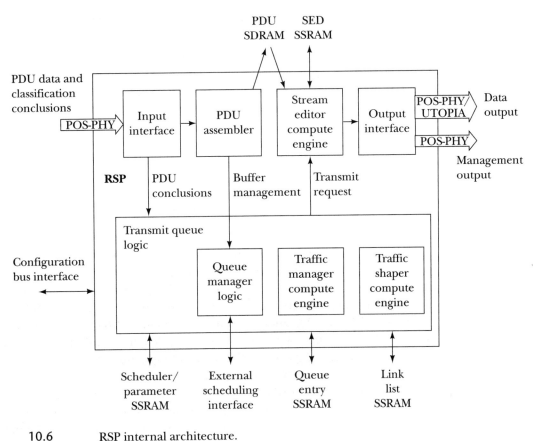

10.6   RSP internal architecture.

FIGURE

+ *Traffic shaper compute engine.* Ensures QoS and CoS for each queue.

+ *Stream editor compute engine.* Performs any necessary PDU modifications.

As shown in Figure 10.6, the RSP architecture consists of the following major components:

+ *Input interface.* Connects the RSP to the 32-bit POS-PHY from the FPP. It accepts up to 64-byte blocks and sends the incoming PDU blocks to the PDU assembler, and the FPP classification conclusions for PDUs to the transmit queue logic. Although the RSP can accept blocks smaller than 64 bytes, 64-byte blocks provide maximum efficiency.

+ *PDU assembler.* Assembles received blocks into PDUs.

+ *Transmit queue logic.* Provides the overall control of RSP operations.
    • *Queue manager logic.* Allocates queues.
    • *Traffic manager compute engine.* Based on the queue, determines if a PDU should be queued or discarded, and keeps per-queue statistics.
    • *Traffic shaper compute engine.* Maintains the QoS and CoS for each queue, performing dynamic scheduling.
+ *Stream editor compute engine.* Modifies the PDU.
+ *Output interface.* Accepts blocks from the stream editor and sends them to the appropriate port manager and output port. The output interface connects the RSP to the 32-bit POS-PHY/UTOPIA interface that links to the backplane or physical ports, and the 8-bit POS-PHY management interface that links to the ASI and host processor.

The stream editor compute engine allows PDU modifications to be programmed for each queue. The PDU modifications for a queue can be defined at system initialization or dynamically assigned during operation. The modification instructions and parameters are part of the programmable queue definition. Typical uses for PDU modifications include encapsulating PDUs into AAL5, segmenting to ATM cells with appropriate headers, implementing MPLS operations (swapping labels or pushing tags), and implementing IP operations (e.g., decrementing time-to-live counts and updating checksums). The stream editor can be programmed to pad or remove data both at the block and the PDU level. The data that is added to the head or tail can also be modified. The RSP internal scheduler provides support for common traffic shaping or rate strategies, including constant bit rate (CBR) traffic, variable bit rate (VBR) traffic, unspecified bit rate (UBR) traffic, and two-level traffic shaping for virtual paths. Traffic scheduling and shaping are defined by the RSP's scheduling logic and the programmable queue definitions.

10.6   SOFTWARE ARCHITECTURE AND OVERVIEW

PayloadPlus NPs are programmed in high-level application-oriented languages. The resulting software is focused almost entirely on performing the application and does not contain underlying details of the microarchitecture. FPL is used for packet classification. Fewer lines of code are required in FPL than in a language such as C, which offers benefits such as reduced development time and cost, improved defect rates, and maintainability. FPL is also efficiently mapped directly into the instruction set that drives the underlying pattern-processing engines that embody Agere's classification technology. Agere Scripting Language (ASL) is used for packet modification, policing, and statistics. Effectively a subset of C (with typical scripts requiring fewer than 50 lines of executable code), ASL can be efficiently mapped into the underlying VLIW engines that provide the associated functionality on the PayloadPlus devices.

FPL is a high-level functional protocol processing language. It instructs the FPP to perform complex layer-2 through layer-7 classification and analysis on the wire-speed data path traffic. FPL, and the FPP engine that processes it, is implemented using algorithms that allow it to function far faster and more efficiently than conventional processing approaches. As a functional rather than a procedural programming language (such as C), FPL requires far fewer lines of code to program a function. Once the basic constructs and syntax of FPL are understood, writing code is highly intuitive. And with fewer lines of code, it is easier to debug, reuse, and modify. An additional benefit of FPL and ASL programming is that programs are usually small, and there is no need to optimize performance in assembly or lower-level languages.

To provide a fast and flexible way to program the processors, Agere provides a set of software development tools. The PayloadPlus software development environment (SDE), shown in Figure 10.7, provides high-level languages for faster programming, as well as API-level access for configuration when necessary. The SDE consists of the following components:

+ *FPL compiler.* Used to program the FPP for reassembling and classifying incoming PDUs.

+ *ASL compiler.* Used to program the RSP and the ASI compute engines for processing and policing traffic.

+ *Traffic generator utility.* Utility for generating files of simulated traffic for use with the simulator.

+ *Agere application programming interface (API).* API calls that provide low-level access to the PayloadPlus chip set. The API runs in Linux and VxWorks environments.

+ *System performance analyzer.* Graphical interface used to configure application parameters and run compilers, simulators, and utilities. Configurable simulators, of the chip set allow evaluation and debugging of PayloadPlus application programs.

+ *Support for WindowsNT, Solaris, and Linux platforms.*

+ *FPL debugger.*

+ *Advanced system configuration for simulation of multiple Agere or custom components.*

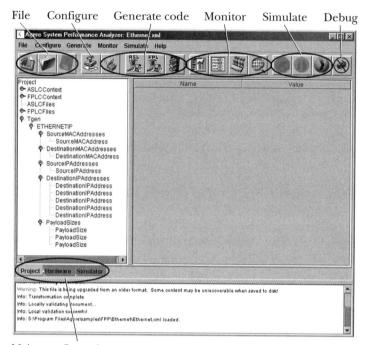

File   Configure   Generate code   Monitor   Simulate   Debug

Major configuration panes

10.7

FIGURE

PayloadPlus SDE 3.0 application-enabling environment.

In addition to software tools, multiple third-party engagements have been announced for the PayloadPlus network processor. These partnerships preinte-grate third-party software products with the PayloadPlus software and hardware environment. This allows customers faster time to market by saving them valuable engineering resources from doing this integration work. Announcements made to date include WindRiver Systems, DCL, Intoto, and Hifn. Please consult the Agere Web site for specifics on these announcements.

10.7   AGERE PERFORMANCE BENEFITS AT OC-48C

Performance benefits of the PayloadPlus solution include

✦ OC-48c programmable, multiprotocol capability
✦ ATM SAR capability @ OC-48c

+ 64K queues

+ 500K routing table entry support

+ Low clock speed of 133 MHz

+ Programmable packet- or cell-based traffic scheduling

A technology summary of the PayloadPlus solution is shown in Table 10.1.

Price	OC-48c 3 IC solution in 10 k unit quantities: $650
Package	FPP/RSP in 665-pin PBGA, ASI in 456-pin PBGA, VPP in 560-pin EBGA
Required voltages	1.8 V core / 3.3 V or 2.5 V I/O for FPP, RSP, and ASI
Power	12 W max power for all three components of FPP, RSP, and ASI chip set solution

10.1

TABLE

Technology summary.

REFERENCES

[1]   Agere Web site, *www.agere.com.*

[2]   PayloadPlus Web site, *www.agere.com/metro_regional_transport/network_processors.html.*

[3]   PayloadPlus news Web site, *www.agere.com/support/enterprise_metro_access/nps_news.html.*

Cisco Systems—Toaster2

John Marshall
Cisco Systems

Cisco's Toaster2 ASIC is a high-performance network processor capable of forwarding millions of packets per second. The ASIC is internally organized as a pipelined, multiprocessor, parallel processing engine. Toaster's multiprocessor matrix consists of 16 uniform processors arranged as 4 rows by 4 columns. One Toaster microcontroller, TMC, performs processing within each element of the matrix. Each TMC has a local instruction RAM and a local memory controller used to access a number of internal and external memory devices.

11.1   TARGET APPLICATION(S)

Toaster is marketed under the name Parallel eXpress Forwarding (PXF). PXF technology is currently available in a number of Cisco products, including the 7200 NSE-1, 7300, 7400, 7600, 10000, and 10720 series platforms. The ASIC is intended to provide fast packet forwarding based on packet header processing. A typical Toaster-based system will consist of one or more Toaster ASICs, a packet buffer ASIC, media-specific interfaces, and a route processor. The route processor is a traditional processor that is used to run routing protocols, collect network management statistics, and maintain Toaster forwarding tables. Because the network processor is primarily designed to operate on packet headers, a packet buffer ASIC is used to store the packet body while the packet header is being processed.

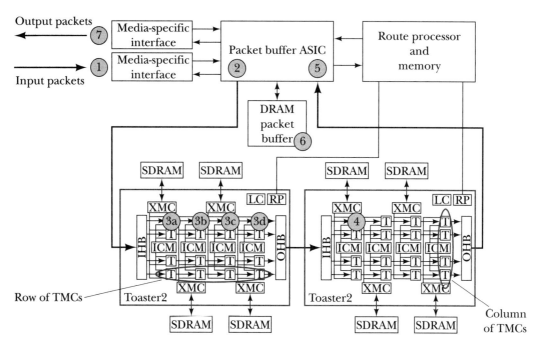

11.1

FIGURE

Example of a system using Toaster2 in centralized configuration.

Media-specific interfaces are required to adapt multiple physical interfaces to a common packet format used by the packet buffer and network processor(s). Toaster-based systems provide the capability to support a diverse set of interfaces ranging from ATM to Ethernet.

Toaster2 has been designed to support multiple configurations. These configurations generally fall into one of two categories that are referred to as being either centralized or distributed. The choice of configuration is based on the target platform's forwarding requirement. A centralized configuration is used for systems whose aggregate throughput is less than OC-48. Within a centralized system, all packets are forwarded by a single Toaster or pipelined array of Toaster ASICS (see Figure 11.1). Each Toaster has a maximum forwarding rate that is in excess of seven million packets per second; however, the processor's packet processing time usually restricts forwarding throughput. A distributed configuration can be used to increase the system's forwarding capability by allowing multiple Toasters to operate in parallel. In a distributed system, each media interface could have a dedicated buffer ASIC and network processor. A switch fabric is then used to interconnect each group of ASICs to increase system through-

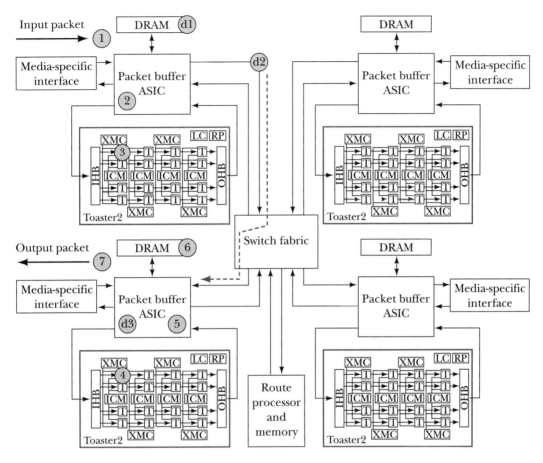

11.2

FIGURE

Example of a system using Toaster2 in distributed configuration. *Note:* Toaster memory is not shown.

put (see Figure 11.2). A distributed configuration theoretically increases packet forwarding throughput based on the amount of parallelism and the number of nonblocking paths through the switch fabric. For example, an eight-port switch fabric could increase the system's aggregate capacity by a factor of eight given that all eight ports could be attached to a different Toaster group.

The example in Figure 11.1 illustrates the pipelining of multiple Toasters. This configuration allows a forwarding task to be divided into eight software pipeline stages. Optimal software pipelining is achieved when all pipeline stages require the same execution time. The term *phase length* is used to describe the length in clock cycles of a software pipeline stage. This configuration also allows four-way parallelism across processor rows. Toaster provides for staggered parallel execution across processor rows. The term *phaselet* is used to measure the number of cycles that a given row lags behind the previous row.

11.2   PACKET FLOW EXAMPLE FOR A CENTRALIZED SYSTEM

The following operations are applied to a packet as the packet flows through a centralized forwarding engine consisting of two Toasters and a packet buffer ASIC. Note that media-specific interfaces are not considered part of the forwarding engine.

1. Packet arrives at media interface. The media-specific interface provides for physical and link-layer processing. Valid packets are then forwarded to the packet buffer.

2. The packet buffer receives the entire packet and then forwards the first n bytes of the packet and a packet descriptor to the Toaster ASIC. The descriptor contains the length of the received packet and a handle that will be used to associate the forwarding result with the body of the packet stored in the packet buffer. The term *toaster context* is used to describe the packet descriptor and packet header sent to the Toaster ASIC. To maintain full utilization, all rows must receive a new context every phase. A typical context size is 128 bytes.

3. The packet is processed by four stages of Toaster microcode within a row of the processing matrix. During on-chip processing, the packet remains in the same row. Typical operations performed by Toaster are packet classification, input/output access control lists (ACLs), accounting, Cisco express forwarding (CEF), netflow, and header rewrite. Within each row, four packet headers are simultaneously processed. The total packet processing time available to a packet within each row is four phases. Each step—3a, 3b, 3c, and 3d—has one phase time allocated for processing.

4. Packet is processed by four more stages of Toaster microcode.

5. The Toaster context is transferred to the packet buffer ASIC. The packet buffer merges the rewritten packet header with the packet body and then moves the packet to the queue designated by the modified packet descriptor. The packet buffer ASIC may provide the ability to process header reassembly commands from Toaster. While Toaster has the capability to perform all

necessary header manipulation, adding multifield insert capability to the packet buffer ASIC saves Toaster processing cycles.

6. Packet copied to external DRAM address indicated by queue management logic. The packet buffer memory size is application dependent and could provide hundreds of milliseconds of buffering.

7. Dequeue packet from buffer memory and transmit to egress media-specific interface. Depending on the packet buffer's capability, a dequeue request can be initiated by a traffic-shaper function provided by the packet buffer or by a Toaster dequeue request. In the latter case, traffic management is provided by microcode.

11.3   PACKET FLOW EXAMPLE FOR A DISTRIBUTED SYSTEM

The following operations are applied to a packet as the packet flows through distributed forwarding engines. In this example, there are four distributed forwarding engines, each of which consists of a single Toaster and distributed packet buffer ASIC. Operations 1 through 7 are the same as the centralized forwarding example. Toaster tasks are divided between the ingress and egress forwarding engine. Additional operations d1, d2, and d3 are necessary to support distributed forwarding.

d1 The distributed packet buffer requires more than twice as much memory bandwidth as a central packet buffer supporting the same media type. The extra bandwidth is necessary because the packet buffer performs queuing at two locations in the data path. Depending on the fabric type, a speedup factor associated with the switch fabric may be necessary to reduce output buffer contention. For example, virtual output queuing is a technique used to reduce the necessary speedup factor. Step d1 represents the additional queuing operation associated with transmitting the packet through the switch fabric. Prior to step d1, Toaster microcode is responsible for choosing the switch fabric queue that will direct the packet to the selected egress engine.

d2 The packet is copied from the external packet memory and transmitted through the switch fabric to the egress packet buffer.

d3 The egress packet buffer receives the entire packet and then forwards the first *m* bytes of the packet and a descriptor to the Toaster ASIC. The descriptor contains the length of the packet, an input interface identifier, and a handle that is necessary to associate the result with the body of the packet stored in the packet buffer.

Output processing is then performed in a similar manner as compared to steps 4 through 7 from the centralized example although (not shown in this example) multicast packets require replication. A simple multicast implementation could be achieved by causing the ingress Toaster to produce multiple enqueue requests to the ingress packet buffer ASIC. The ingress packet buffer would then create multiple copies of the packet, each addressed to a different media interface.

11.4   TOASTER2 HARDWARE ARCHITECTURE

The Toaster2 ASIC of consists of six functional blocks. The external column memory controller (XMC) is replicated four times to support each column in the processor matrix. Similarly, there are four instances of the internal column memory (ICM). The Toaster microcontroller (TMC) is replicated 16 times within the chip. The packet interface consists of two subblocks called the *input header buffer* (IHB), which is used to receive Toaster contexts, and *output header buffer* (OHB), which is used to transmit contexts. The route processor interface (RPI) allows the route processor to access all Toaster resources. The lock controller is used to provide semaphore support.

External interfaces are provided to support context transfer, external memory devices, and RP connectivity. Toaster2 contains the following I/O:

+ The packet interfaces associated with the IHB and OHB blocks are each unidirectional 64-bit buses that operate at a speed greater than 100 MHz. These interfaces are capable of sustaining in excess of 7M Toaster contexts per second.

+ Each XMC interface consists of a bidirectional 36-bit data bus and a 24-bit address bus. The interface can be configured to support a single 32-bit SRAM device or two channels of 16-bit-wide SDRAMs. The additional data bits are used for ECC protection on SDRAM devices. For SDRAM configurations, single-bit errors are automatically corrected for data being returned to the TMC or RPI. Parity protection is provided for SRAM devices.

+ The RPI consists of a bidirectional 32-bit bus that operates by multiplexing of address and data.

11.5   EXTERNAL MEMORY CONTROLLER

The external column memory controller (XMC) provides access to the external column memory from the RPI, and the four processors in that column. There is one instance of the memory controller per column. The controller performs arbitration between five possible request sources, handles the timing for reads and writes to the memory, and provides ECC/parity protection.

To offload the TMC processors, the memory controller provides atomic memory operation capability. By performing atomic operations within the controller, memory bandwidth is more efficiently utilized as compared to a semaphore-based traditional multiprocessor implementation. An atomic memory operation does not require a semaphore to guard a memory region during an update.

Physical addresses are aligned on a 32-bit boundary. Byte masking is provided to support 16- and 8-bit writes. The memory subsystem also provides multiword read capability. A multiword memory fetch is typically used to provide packet rewrite data.

11.6   INTERNAL COLUMN MEMORY

The internal column memory (ICM) subsystem provides an internal RAM accessible from the RPI and any of the four processor complexes in that column. This memory is replicated for each column. The memory is organized as $n \times 64$ bits. If no contention occurs, this memory can be accessed in three clock cycles from the column processors. The internal column memory controller performs arbitration between the five request sources for access to the memory. The internal column memory provides atomic memory operations.

11.7   INPUT AND OUTPUT HEADER BUFFERS

The input header buffer (IHB) is the data interface to each of the four rows of processors and is the synchronization block for the entire chip. Data is given to each row in succession. A new phase for each row is started by the input header buffer when all of the processors in the row are finished processing their current context.

The output header buffer (OHB) receives data from each of the four rows of processors in a synchronous manner. When the selected row indicates that its current data is completely processed and placed in the OHB's buffer, the OHB may transmit the buffer off the chip through the output data interface, it may feed the data back to the IHB to be sent to the next row, or it may do both simultaneously. When the current row's data is completely transmitted, the OHB moves to the next row in a round robin fashion.

11.8   TOASTER MICROCONTROLLER

The Toaster microcontroller (TMC) is intended for integrated packet processing applications that require high performance. A block diagram of the TMC is shown in Figure 11.3. A 64-bit instruction word is decoded to operate on multiple 32-bit data values. The TMC introduces several modifications over traditional RISC processors:

+ Support for fast task context switching enables efficient software pipelining across multiple controller cores.

+ The TMC is capable of performing logical operations on indirect memory operands. This improves the overall code density by merging arithmetic instructions with load/store instructions into one instruction. Accessing an indirect operand does not incur a performance penalty, thus, there is no inherent performance difference between register operands and indirect operands.

+ Each instruction word contains two major opcodes and up to three minor opcodes (or micro-ops) that execute in parallel. Instruction-level parallelism is scheduled by software as opposed to hardware. This eliminates the need for hardware-based schedulers currently found in superscalar RISC implementations while enabling completion of multiple instructions per cycle.

+ The TMC provides a high-performance memory subsystem. The TMC is intended for hierarchical memory configurations. The TMC local bus attaches to local memory, context memory, and a tag buffer. The local bus can sustain one 64-bit read and one 64-bit write per cycle for aligned accesses. The maximum sustainable rate for nonaligned accesses is one 32-bit read and one 32-bit write.

+ TMC and memory subsystem clocks are synchronized to reduce memory latency.

Both the context and local memory support zero wait state, nonaligned accesses. For accesses to the internal column memory and external memory, prefetches must be issued to avoid wait states. The TMC provides a performance-monitoring

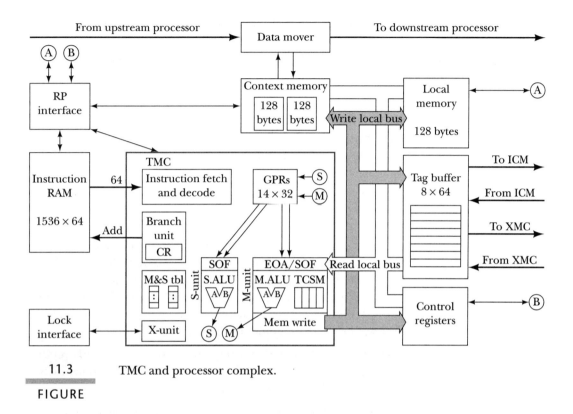

From upstream processor

Data mover

To downstream processor

(A) (B)

RP interface

Context memory

128 bytes | 128 bytes

Write local bus

Local memory

128 bytes

(A)

Instruction RAM

1536 × 64

64

Add

TMC

Instruction fetch and decode

Branch unit

CR

M&S tbl

S-unit

SOF

S.ALU

A\B

GPRs 14 × 32

(S)
(M)

M-unit

EOA/SOF

M.ALU TCSM

A\B

Read local bus

Tag buffer 8 × 64

To ICM

From ICM

To XMC

From XMC

Control registers

(B)

Lock interface

X-unit

(S) (M)

Mem write

11.3

FIGURE

TMC and processor complex.

mechanism to enable software optimization of shared memory accesses. The TMC's performance monitor can be enabled to maintain statistics regarding the magnitude and frequency of bus wait states.

The tag buffer can operate as an eight-entry cache that provides caching and a read/write buffering function. The deferred store through cache allows multiple outstanding write requests without stalling the TMC. Several opcodes are provided for cache control. The TMC prefetch interface provides a mechanism for software to specify the amount of data needed by the prefetch and attributes relating the cache entry's aging policy, coherency requirement, and suggested cache index.

◆ *Instruction fetch and decode unit (IFID).* This unit receives 64 bits of instruction data from the instruction RAM, IRAM, each cycle. If the IRAM interface is not ready, the IFID unit will suspend operation. The IFID logic will issue decoded instructions to two of the four functional units each cycle.

◆ *Branch unit.* The branch unit controls the flow of a program's execution. Control of a program's executions can be changed by a branch, jump, or exception branch instruction. The TMC core provides an external indication signal that allows external logic to control the program's flow. This capability should not be confused with an interrupt. The branch unit literally interprets a branch indication as a branch instruction.

+ *M-unit.* The multifunction unit (M-unit) is a pipelined execution unit that performs arithmetic, logical, and shift operations. The M-unit supports multiple operand types. Source operands may originate from memory, register, or immediate data. For arithmetic and logical operations, the source operand presented to the B side of the ALU is first masked, then shifted based on data from the mask and shift table. Destination operands can write either to memory or to the register file.

  • *Effective operand address (EOA).* This logic performs effective address calculation for displacement memory operands. An effective address calculation is performed for either the source or destination operand. The effective source memory address is presented to the local bus interface to initiate a memory fetch request. If the calculation is for a destination operand, the address is saved until the memory write back stage.

  • *Source operand fetch (SOF).* This unit receives data from the IFID unit, register file, pipeline feedback, or local bus during the instruction decode pipeline stage. The SOF performs the function of a data multiplexer.

  • *Arithmetic logic unit (M.ALU).* This unit performs 32-bit logical and arithmetic operations as defined by the multifunctional opcode. Prior to the ALU operation, a mask and shift is applied to the B-side source operand.

  • *Mem write.* Mem write writes result value to memory. Data alignment is performed between result register and the local bus write data.

  • *Tightly coupled state machines (TCSMs).* TCSMs are used to accelerate networking-specific operations.

+ *S-unit.* This unit provides 32-bit arithmetic, logical, and shift operations on register and immediate operands. The S-unit operates in parallel with the M-unit and X-unit.

+ *X-unit.* The extended instruction (X) unit is a nonpipelined execution unit that is used for all nonbranch and nonarithmetic instructions. It implements the instructions for tightly coupled state machine (TCSM) initialization, tag buffer control, and hardware semaphore instructions.

11.9 TAG BUFFER

The tag buffer provides access to the internal and external column memories from the TMC core. It contains eight tags that can be assigned to either prefetch, posted-write, or primitive operators. Returned data from accesses is returned to the tag buffer on completion. In addition, data-dependent reads can be issued that wait for the read results from a previous request before proceeding. The status of each tag buffer is maintained and is accessible from the TMC core.

Read operations can perform an address compare to determine if a hit has occurred. Accesses that test for address compares operate in "address compare mode"; accesses that do not use "nonaddress compare mode." When in address compare mode, accesses that miss in the tag buffer will request data from the memory controller. For nonaddress compare mode, attempts to read invalid locations will result in a bus exception.

11.10 ROUTE PROCESSOR INTERFACE

The route processor interface (RPI) provides access to all resources internal to the Toaster ASIC as well as the external column memory. The interface provides read and write access to the processor's instruction RAM, context memory, and local memory. In addition to resource access, the RPI block also maintains a set of synchronized timers that are accessed via individual processors.

Toaster's debug capability is also accessed through the RPI. Individual block state can be read via the interface. A single-step capability is provided for each processor as well as IHB and OHB blocks.

11.11 LOCK CONTROLLER

To support efficient multiprocessor synchronization, hardware semaphore operations are provided for each column of processors. This capability allows software to manage shared resources (internal and external column memory) among the four processors in the same column and the RPI.

There are multiple binary semaphores per column. To request a lock, the processor must execute a *get_lock* instruction. The lock mechanism for the RPI is based on accessing the lock controller's memory map. Each processor or the RPI can request 1 to n semaphores. If multiple locks are requested, the controller will only grant the lock(s) when all of the requested lock(s) are available.

11.12   SOFTWARE ARCHITECTURE

There are two components associated with the software architecture. Parallel Express Forwarding is used to describe the microcoded portion of the software architecture that executes on the network processor. In addition to microcode, the route processor must be able to communicate with the network processor. A network processor driver must be able to configure and manage Toaster memory based on the varying configurations, handle packet forwarding cases that are not supported in microcode, and periodically collect forwarding statistics. While the Toaster device driver is conceptually similar to a hardware-based device driver, the interface should be designed in a flexible manner so as to accommodate future functional changes.

11.13   TOASTER DEVELOPMENT METHODOLOGY AND ENVIRONMENT

Because Toaster requires software-based pipelining, each microcode function has to be partitioned in a manner such that it fits into one or more pipeline stages. Within Toaster, each column of processors represents a pipeline stage. The maximum processing rate is defined by the longest pipeline stage. The following equation describes the maximum forwarding rate based on the pipeline's phase length:

Maximum forwarding rate = (processor frequency ∗ number of rows) / phase length

Toaster's column-based resource sharing implies that the number of competing processors reduces the number of available memory accesses available to a given processor. The size of the memory operation also affects the number of available accesses. Since the memory controller supports a variety of different request types, a simple equation is not sufficient to represent the number of memory operations available to any given processor.

A microcoding technique called *memory scheduling* can be used to improve memory efficiency. Memory scheduling takes into account physical aspects of each memory such as interface turnaround time, as well as bank access restrictions associated with DRAM devices. Memory scheduling is not functionally required; however, the memory subsystem efficiency can be substantially improved.

When the microcode function has been partitioned to fit into a software stage, there are a number of tools available to simulate microcode behavior. All microcode written to execute on the Toaster2 part must be written in TMC assembler. A macroassembler is provided to generate machine code and to perform assembler-based lint checking.

A cycle accurate simulator has been developed to execute microcode. The simulator can emulate a single Toaster2 or an entire chip set. The chip set simulation environment includes C-based models for multiple Toaster ASICs, as well as packet buffer and media interface devices.

The simulation environment provides the capability to

+ Insert test packets from a file or based on random packet generation

+ Trace Toaster memory usage to identify possible memory corruption or memory leaks

+ Provide a user interface to utilize the TMC's break point, debug, and single step capability

+ Provide formatted debugging information

+ Preload memories for specialized tests

+ Capture simulation traces so that information can be fed to hardware simulation environment

A memory scheduling tool is also available for applications that require increased performance associated with memory scheduling.

11.14   PERFORMANCE CLAIMS

Toaster2-based systems provide feature-rich OC-48 rate forwarding. See product documentation for specific performance and feature capabilities.

Cisco 7200 NSE-1: *www.cisco.com/warp/public/cc/pd/ifaa/prossor/nse1/*

Cisco 7300: *www.cisco.com/warp/public/cc/pd/rt/7300rts/prodlit/7300q_ov.htm*

Cisco 7400: *www.cisco.com/warp/public/cc/pd/rt/7400rt/index.shtml*

Cisco 7600: *newsroom.cisco.com/dlls/Cisco-7600-OSR-overview.pdf*

Cisco 10000: *www.cisco.com/warp/public/cc/pd/rt/10000/index.shtml*

Cisco 10720: *www.cisco.com/univercd/cc/td/doc/pcat/10720.htm*

11.15   FAMILY OF TOASTER NETWORK PROCESSORS

There are multiple ASICs in the Toaster network processor family. The Toaster2 ASIC is currently the most widely used part. There is a low-performance version of the Toaster2 that contains a 4 × 2 processing matrix. Cisco has also developed a performance-enhanced ASIC for OC-192 applications called Toaster3.

11.16   CONCLUSION

The Toaster2 ASIC has provided the system infrastructure necessary to deliver a variety of products that provide flexibility and high performance. Toaster2 has been successful in bridging the performance gap between microprocessor-based forwarding engines and hardwired ASIC implementations. While network processors have successfully enabled feature development more quickly than nonprogrammable ASIC implementations, there are still opportunities for improvement. Evolutions in network processor programming methods will continue to abstract the underlying multiprocessor environment so as to ease the transition from traditional software design to network processor–based software design.

12

IBM—PowerNP Network Processor

Mohammad Peyravian, Jean Calvignac, Ravi Sabhikhi
IBM Corporation

Network processors have emerged to support the ever-changing and complex packet processing functions at media speed [3]. In this paper, we present the IBM PowerNP NP4GS3[1] network processor. PowerNP provides wire-speed packet processing and forwarding capability through a set of programmable embedded processors and co-processors with a multiplicity of high-bandwidth embedded and external memories [1, 2]. Co-processors operate in parallel with processors and perform functions that are computationally intensive to perform in software such as classification, checksum calculation, tree search (for table lookup), statistic gathering, and traffic policing. With an integrated switch interface, PowerNP provides the basis for a wide range of solutions from a low-end stand-alone system to a large multirack system through an external switching fabric. PowerNP supports multiple network interfaces through integrated MACs: up to 40 10/100 Ethernet, 4 Gigabit Ethernet, and 1 OC-48 packet-over-SONET (POS). It has an embedded IBM PowerPC processor that can function as the control point (CP) for the system. For an externally attached CP option, it provides a PCI bus interface that can be used to communicate with the internal PowerPC as well as other processors within PowerNP.

---

1. In this paper, we use the abbreviated term *PowerNP* for the IBM PowerNP NP4GS3, which is a high-end member of the IBM network processor family.

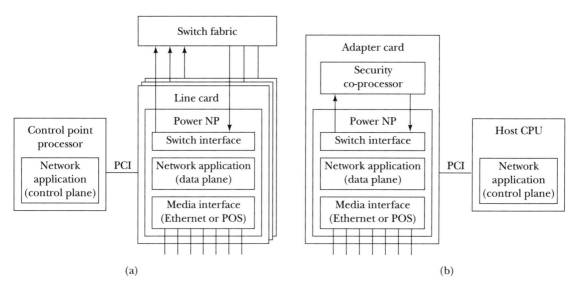

PowerNP application examples: switch-based model (a) and server-based mode (b).

PowerNP can be used in the traditional switch/router equipment as well as in the emerging applications for the server and storage equipment (see Figure 12.1). For example, in a switch-based model, multiple PowerNP line cards are interconnected using a switch fabric, with each PowerNP supporting a number of external network interface ports such as Ethernet or POS. PowerNPs provide data plane packet processing functions. A separate, external general-purpose processor (GPP) such as an IBM PowerPC provides control plane and system management functions and acts as the CP for the whole system. The CP can be attached through the PCI interface, as shown in Figure 12.1, or through an Ethernet link.

In the emerging application space for the network edge, PowerNP can be used to support scalable traffic engineering functions (e.g., load balancing and Web caching) or security features (e.g., firewalling, intrusion detection, and virus detection). For example, in a server-based model as shown in Figure 12.1, PowerNP may be used in conjunction with an external security co-processor to provide IPSec or SSL offload. In this configuration, the switch interface can be used as a high-speed interface for attaching the security co-processor. The PCI interface can be used to attach the PowerNP adapter card to the host CPU subsystem. The host CPU executes the control plane functions, and the PowerNP along with the co-processor performs the data plane packet processing functions.

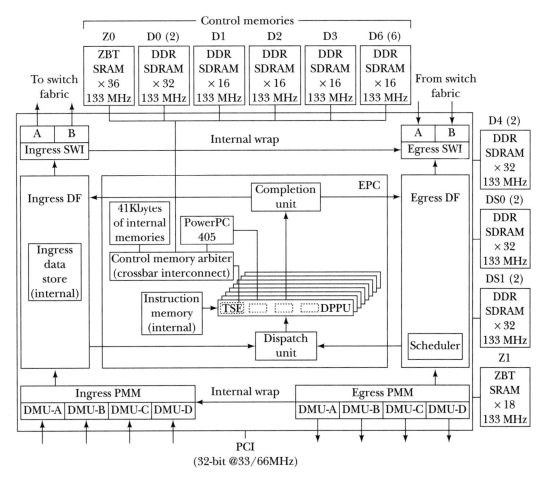

12.2   PowerNP hardware architecture.

FIGURE

12.1   HARDWARE ARCHITECTURE

Figure 12.2 shows the overall hardware architecture of the PowerNP network processor. PowerNP is fabricated with 0.18 μm IBM SA-27E technology and is implemented in a single 1088-pin BSM-CCGA package with 795 signal I/Os. It has a power dissipation of 9 W nominal and 12.5 W worst case with a core voltage of 1.8 V. In the remainder of this section, we describe the major blocks within PowerNP.

The embedded processor complex (EPC), under software control and with hardware co-processors, performs the packet processing functions for PowerNP. The EPC receives packets for processing from both the ingress and egress data flows (DFs). The EPC contains 16 programmable processing engines, known as *picoprocessors*. The picoprocessors are grouped into sets of two, known as *dyadic protocol processor units* (DPPUs), and each set shares a number of co-processors that can operate in parallel with the picoprocessors. Each picoprocessor supports two threads. The picoprocessor is a 32-bit scaled-down RISC, consisting of sixteen 32-bit or thirty-two 16-bit general-purpose registers per thread and a one-cycle ALU. The picoprocessor instruction set is specifically designed for packet processing operations. Each DPPU contains 4 Kbytes of shared memory pool—1 Kbyte per thread. The picoprocessors run at 133 MHz, providing 2128 MIPS of aggregate processing capability.

Each DPPU co-processor is a specialized hardware-assist engine that runs in parallel with the two picoprocessors and performs functions that would otherwise require a large amount of serialized picocode. The DPPU coprocessors are tree search engine, data store, control access bus, enqueue, checksum, string copy, policy, counter, co-processor response bus, and semaphore. Each co-processor maintains resources for four threads.

Within the EPC, there is an internal instruction memory consisting of eight embedded RAMs. The instruction memory is loaded during initialization and holds the "picocode"[2] for packet processing and system management. The instruction memory provides 128 Kbytes (i.e., 32K words) of internal picocode instruction store.

The dispatch unit is a hardware function that dequeues packet information from the ingress DF and egress DF queues. After dequeue, the dispatch unit reads part of the packet from the ingress or egress DS and places it in an internal RAM inside the dispatch unit. As soon as a thread becomes idle, the dispatch unit places the packet into the shared memory pool and passes the packet control information to the thread for processing.

Table lookup is performed using a specialized co-processor known as the *tree search engine* (TSE). The TSE co-processor provides hardware search operations for full match (FM) trees, longest prefix match (LPM) trees, and software-managed trees (SMTs). Software initializes and maintains trees. Leaves can be inserted into and removed from FM and LPM trees without a CP intervention. The TSE co-processor uses both internal and external memories to achieve high-speed lookups. An internal table structure defines 128 trees that indicate in which

---

2. Picocode is the picoprocessor assembly language program.

memory (i.e., internal or external) trees exist, whether caching is enabled, key and leaf sizes, and the search type to be performed. Large external memories are used to store leaves and tables. Specifically, D0, D1, and D2 are used for storing leaves, and Z0 and D3 for direct tables.

The control memory arbiter controls access to control memory among the threads of all the DPPUs. The control memory is shared among the TSE co-processors, and the picocode can directly access the control memory through commands to the TSE co-processor. The TSE co-processor also accesses the control memory during tree searches.

The completion unit, which is a hardware function, provides the interfaces between the EPC and the ingress and egress DFs. It also guarantees packet sequence. Since multiple threads can process packets belonging to the same flow, the completion unit ensures that all packets are enqueued in the ingress or egress transmission queues in the proper order.

PowerNP provides two options for the CP. The embedded 405 PowerPC can function as the CP processor for the system, or an external processor can be attached to PowerNP via the PCI bus. The internal PowerPC has 16 Kbytes of I-cache and 16 Kbytes of D-cache and runs at 133 MHz. The embedded PowerPC has a six-slice dedicated external memory, labeled D6 in Figure 12.2. The CP is responsible for initialization, configuration, and executing the control plane protocol functions.

The physical MAC multiplexer (PMM) moves data between external physical-layer devices and PowerNP. The PMM interfaces with the network processor's external ports in the ingress PMM and egress PMM directions. The PMM includes four data mover units (DMUs), labeled A, B, C, and D. The four DMUs can each be independently configured as an Ethernet medium access control (MAC) or a packet-over-SONET (POS) interface. Each DMU moves data at 1 Gbps, in both the ingress and the egress directions. There is also an "internal wrap" link that enables traffic generated by the PowerNP egress side to move to the ingress side without going out of the chip. The PMM can be configured to support up to four ports of 1 Gigabit Ethernet or 40 ports of fast Ethernet (10/100 Mbps). It can also be configured to support the following POS modes: 16 OC-3c, 4 OC-12c, or 1 OC-48c.

The switch interface (SWI) acts as the interface between the packet-based DF and the cell-based switch fabric. The ingress SWI segments the packets into 64-byte switch cells and passes the cells to the switch fabric. The egress SWI reassembles the switch fabric cells back into packets. It uses an external memory (i.e., D4) for storing reassembly information. There is also an internal wrap link that enables traffic generated by the PowerNP ingress side to move to the egress side without going out of the chip. The SWI supports two high-speed data-aligned synchronous link (DASL)[3] interfaces, labeled A and B. Each DASL link provides up to 4 Gbps of bandwidth. The DASL links A and B can be used in parallel with one acting as the primary switch interface and the other as an alternate switch interface for increased system availability.

The ingress data flow (DF) interfaces with the ingress PMM, the EPC, and the SWI. Packets that have been received on the ingress PMM are passed to the ingress DF. The ingress DF collects the packet data in its internal data store (DS) memory—a 131 Kbyte SRAM. When it has received sufficient data (i.e., the packet header), the ingress DF enqueues the data to the EPC for processing. Once the EPC processes the packet, it provides forwarding information to the ingress DF. The ingress DF then invokes a hardware-configured flow control mechanism and then either discards the packet or places it into a queue to await transmission. After it selects a packet, the ingress DF passes the packet to the ingress SWI.

The egress DF interfaces with the egress SWI, the EPC, and the egress PMM. Packets that have been received on the egress SWI are passed to the egress DF. The egress DF collects the packet data in its external DS memory (i.e., DS0 and DS1). The egress DF enqueues the packet to the EPC for processing. Once the EPC processes the packet, it provides forwarding information to the egress DF. The egress DF then enqueues the packet to either the scheduler, when enabled, or to a target port queue for transmission to the egress PMM. The egress DF invokes a hardware-assisted flow control mechanism, like the ingress DF, when packet data enters the network processor. When the egress DS is sufficiently congested, the flow control actions discard packets.

The scheduler provides traffic-shaping functions for the network processor on the egress side. It addresses functions that enable QoS mechanisms required by applications like IP DiffServ, MPLS traffic engineering, and virtual private networks (VPNs). The scheduler manages bandwidth on a per-packet basis by determining the bandwidth a packet requires (i.e., the number of bytes to be transmitted) and comparing this against the bandwidth permitted by the configuration of the packet's flow queue. The bandwidth used by a first packet determines when the scheduler permits the transmission of a subsequent packet of a flow queue. The scheduler supports guaranteed rate, peak rate, and best-effort traffic shaping for 2K flow queues and uses an external memory (i.e., Z1) for storing calendar information.

---

3. Currently, other switch interfaces, such as CSIX, can be supported via an interposer chip. On-chip support for CSIX will be provided in a future version of the network processor.

12.2   SOFTWARE

PowerNP offers a parallel "run-to-completion" programming model that allows the programmer to see a single image that processes packets from arrival to departure. This simple programming model appears as a single thread to the programmer and allows him or her to access the entire instruction memory space and all the shared resources (tables, counters, etc.). In this model, the picoprocessors are used as a pool of processing resources, all executing simultaneously, either processing packets or in idle mode waiting for work. In the following sections, we discuss the PowerNP software architecture and development tools.

12.2.1   Software Architecture

The PowerNP system software architecture is divided into two main components: control plane and data plane (see Figure 12.3). Typical control plane protocols (e.g., RSVP, OSPF, SNMP) are not performance critical and have few performance requirements. Control plane protocols are best suited for GPPs since they have long code paths and exhibit little data parallelism. The control plane processor can be the embedded PowerPC or an external processor. The control plane processor is in charge of the system initialization and overall system management.

The control plane software communicates with the data plane software using a set of application programming interfaces (APIs) and a message-based protocol. Two types of APIs are defined. One type, known as *protocol services APIs*, handles hardware-independent protocol objects such as IP and MPLS. These APIs can be used to support generic control plane protocol stacks. The other type, known as *management services APIs*, manages PowerNP hardware resources and is used for services such as PowerNP initialization and debug.

The data plane protocols (e.g., IPv4/v6) are responsible for packet forwarding. Data plane processing is performance-critical since it must be performed at wire speed to avoid dropping packets and to meet QoS requirements. Data plane protocols are best suited for parallel processors since they have short code paths and exhibit large data parallelism due to independency between packets. PowerNP is optimized for data plane packet processing functions. That is, many threads execute the same protocol processing code in parallel, as shown in Figure 12.3.

The data plane software has two main components: system library and forwarding software. The system library provides basic functions such as memory management, debugging, and tree services. These functions provide a hardware

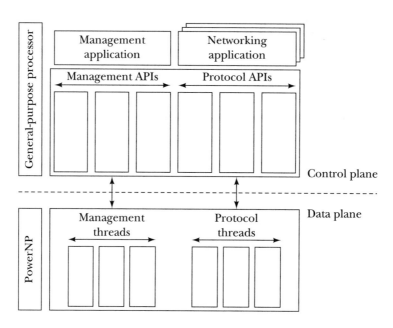

PowerNP software architecture.

abstraction layer that can be used either from the control plane, using a message-passing interface, or from the data plane software using API calls. The forwarding software is responsible for performing high-speed packet processing that handles the data plane steady-state portion of networking applications (e.g., the IP packet forwarding protocols). These components help a programmer develop PowerNP applications rapidly.

12.2.2   Software Development Toolkit

The PowerNP software development toolkit provides a set of integrated tools that address each phase of the software development process. The tools are designed to run on top of either the actual hardware or the chip-level simulation model. The toolkit is supported on several operating systems, including Windows, Sun Solaris, and Linux. The toolkit includes the following components: assembler, simulator, debugger, test case generator, and performance profiler.

The assembler generates images from picocode that execute on a chip-level simulation model or PowerNP. The simulator provides a TCL interpreter that allows a programmer to execute picocode in a simulated environment. The debugger generates files that programmers can use to debug picocode. The test case generator provides a TCL interface for the initial testing of picocode and for test case regression. The performance profiler generates picocode execution performance data using an event-driven simulation model.

12.3   PERFORMANCE

The PowerNP picoprocessors provide 2128 MIPS of aggregate processing capability. However, this figure alone does not represent the total processing capability of PowerNP since it encompasses a large number of specialized co-processors that are used in conjunction with picoprocessors for packet processing. This makes providing a single performance figure for PowerNP a challenging problem. Given this, we discuss two performance measures: (1) raw cycle budget per packet for POS and Ethernet, and (2) available headroom over typical IP packet forwarding.

For an OC-48 POS application with a minimum packet size of 48 bytes (i.e., PPP POS) and a 1-byte flag between packets, there are about 6.1 million packets arriving per second. This results in a maximum code cycles per packet of about 350 and a maximum TSE cycles per packet of about 700. The large TSE cycles provided by PowerNP are important since lookup operations are quite computationally intensive if performed in software. For a 4 Gbps Ethernet application with a minimum packet size of 64 bytes and a 20-byte preamble between packets, there are about 5.95 million packets arriving per second. This provides a maximum code cycles per packet of about 360 and a maximum TSE cycles per packet of about 720.

The cycle budgets per packet do not directly quantify the number of cycles required to execute a particular code path since factors such as memory access, co-processor use, data structure, and branch instructions have a major impact on the performance. An event-driven simulation model is used to project performance for the IP forwarding paths provided in the PowerNP software package. The following code paths achieve OC-48 line speed at minimum packet size:

+ IGP layer-3 routing
+ BGP layer-3 routing
+ BGP layer-3 routing with behavior aggregate (BA) lookup for QoS
+ MPLS forwarding

A significant performance aspect of PowerNP is that it provides additional headroom over the basic IP forwarding that can be used for enhanced features. For example, for the BGP layer-3 routing with behavior aggregate (BA) lookup for QoS with the "Internet mix," which has an average packet size of 476 bytes, PowerNP provides about 3000 cycles of additional headroom for the OC-48 POS application.

12.4   CONCLUSION

As deep packet processing functions migrate to the edges of service provider networks, network edge equipment will require a great degree of flexibility to support evolving high-level services at media speed. GPPs are highly flexible but do not achieve the level of performance required at high packet rates. Traditional ASICs are not flexible enough to support complex operations and ever-evolving protocols. The key advantage of the PowerNP network processor is that hardware-level performance is complemented by flexible software. The power and flexibility of PowerNP make it suitable for supporting a wide range of existing and emerging applications. With a simple run-to-completion programming model and a scalable architecture, it provides lots of functionality and headroom at extraordinary performance.

ACKNOWLEDGMENTS

We gratefully acknowledge the significant contributions of a large number of our colleagues at IBM who, through years of research, design, and development, helped create and document PowerNP, which we have built upon to write this paper. The PowerNP project would not have been possible without the tremendous efforts and contributions put forth by many of our peers.

REFERENCES

[1]   IBM Corporation, "NP4GS3 Datasheet," *www.chips.ibm.com/techlib*, February 2002.

[2]   IBM Corporation, "NP4GS3 Network Processor Solutions," *www.chips.ibm.com/techlib*, April 2001.

[3]   L. Gwennap and B. Wheeler, *A Guide to Network Processors*, The Linley Group, November 2001.

Intel Corporation—Intel IXP2400 Network Processor: A Second-Generation Intel NPU

Prashant Chandra, Sridhar Lakshmanamurthy, Raj Yavatkar
Intel Corporation

Many trends are driving the need for intelligence and flexibility in network systems. Intel has developed next-generation network processors optimized for applications from the customer premises to the core of the network. The Intel IXP2400 network processor delivers a new level of intelligence and performance for access and edge applications, enabling the realization of quality of service (QoS), enforcement of service-level agreements (SLAs), and traffic engineering at OC-48/2.5 Gbps and 4 Gbps data rates. These capabilities allow OEMs and service providers to offer differentiated and tiered services to their customers while efficiently managing their network resources and bandwidth.

13.1   TARGET APPLICATIONS

Increasingly, packet processing requirements vary significantly by market segment. For example, access networking equipment must support multiple interfaces and protocols. At the same time, this equipment needs to meet tight power and real estate requirements dictated by space constraints in wiring closets. Equipment deployed at the edge of the network must support rapid provisioning of services, scalable performance to provide support for emerging services at wire rate, and smooth migration to emerging standards. For all applications, minimizing costs and maximizing time in market are also critical concerns.

The IXP2400 has the ideal set of features to support these access and edge requirements at line rates up to OC-48/2.5 Gbps and 4×1 GbE. The performance and flexibility of the IXP2400 make it desirable for a wide variety of high-performance applications such as multiservice switches, DSLAMs (DSL access multiplexers), CMTS (cable modem termination system) equipment, 2.5G and 3G wireless infrastructure and layer 4–7 switches, including content-based load balancers and firewalls. The programmability of the IXP2400 also makes it well suited for VoIP gateways, multiservice access platforms, edge routers, remote access concentrators, and VPN gateways.

Usage models for the IXP2400 network processor in the target markets listed are as follows:

+ Aggregation, QoS, ATM SAR functions, traffic shaping, policing, forwarding, and protocol conversion in DSLAM equipment

+ Aggregation, QoS, forwarding, and protocol conversion in CMTS equipment

+ ATM SAR, encryption, and forwarding in base station controller/radio network controllers (BSC/RNC)

+ General packet radio services (GPRS) tunneling protocol, tunneling, and IPv6 in wireless infrastructure

+ ATM SAR, multiprotocol label switching (MPLS), QoS, traffic shaping, policing, protocol conversion, and aggregation for multiservice switches

+ Content-aware load balancing, forwarding, and policing for edge server offload

Figure 13.1 shows the system configuration for a full duplex OC-48 line card implemented using the IXP2400 network processor, while Figure 13.2 shows a single chip IXP2400-based line card that supports a 4 Gbps data rate.

13.2   HARDWARE ARCHITECTURE

This section provides a brief overview of the IXP2400 external interfaces and the internal hardware architecture. Figure 13.3 illustrates the external interfaces supported by the IXP2400 network processor.

The external interfaces supported by the IXP2400 include

+ 32-bit RX and TX interface that supports UTOPIA 1,2,3, POS-PHY-L2, SPI3 and CSIX protocols. This interface can be independently configured to be 1×32, 2×16, 4×8, or $2 \times 8 + 1 \times 16$ and can be clocked at 25 MHz to 125

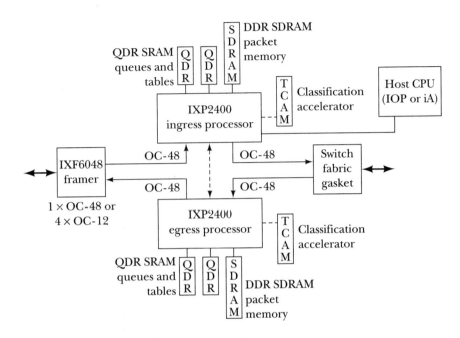

13.1   IXP2400-based line card solution.

FIGURE

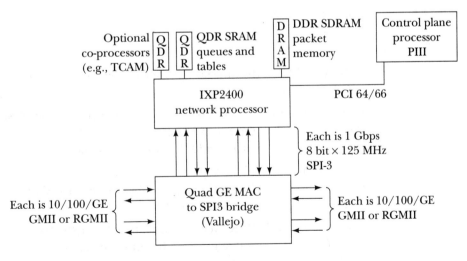

13.2   Single IXP2400-based solution.

FIGURE

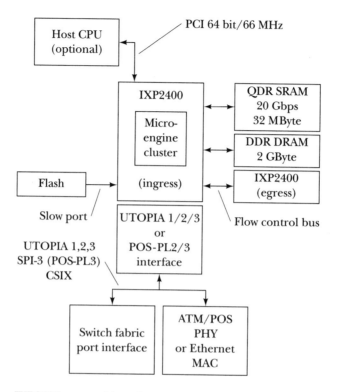

13.3
FIGURE

IXP2400 external interfaces.

MHz. At 125 MHz, the interface provides a peak bandwidth of 4 Gbps in and out of the chip.

✦ 4-bit/8-bit CSIX flow control bus that is used to communicate fabric flow control information to the egress IXP2400. At 125 MHz, this interface provides up to 1 Gbps of peak bandwidth for flow control messages.

✦ One 64-bit (72-bit with ECC protection) channel of DDR DRAM running at 150 MHz or 300 MHz, providing 19.2 Gbps of peak DRAM bandwidth. The channel can support up to 2 GB of DRAM.

✦ Two channels of QDR SRAM running at 200 MHz or 400 MHz, providing 12.8 Gbps of read bandwidth and 12.8 Gbps of write bandwidth. Up to 32 MB of SRAM can be populated on the two channels.

✦ 64-bit PCI running at 66 MHz, providing a peak bandwidth of 4.2 Gbps.

Figure 13.4 shows the internal architecture of the IXP2400.

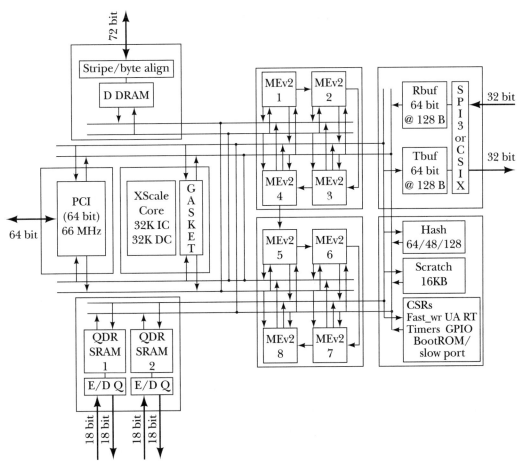

13.4 IXP2400 internal architecture.

FIGURE

13.2.1 Intel XScale Core Features

The Intel XScale core is a general-purpose 32-bit RISC processor (ARM Version 5 Architecture compliant) used to initialize and manage the network processor, to handle exceptions, and to perform slow path processing and other control plane tasks. The Intel XScale core runs at the same frequency as the IXP2400 microengines (i.e., 600 MHz). The microarchitecture incorporates an extensive list of architecture features that allows it to achieve high performance. These include

- ✦ 32 KB, 32-way set associative instruction cache

- ✦ 128-entry branch target buffer

- ✦ 32 KB, 32-way set associative data cache and a 2 KB, 2-way set associative minidata cache

Additional information about the Intel XScale core is available in [3].

13.2.2   Microengine (ME)

The microengines (MEs) do most of the programmable per-packet processing in the IXP2400. There are eight microengines, connected in two clusters of four, as shown in Figure 13.4. The microengines have access to all shared resources (SRAM, DRAM, etc.) and have private connections between adjacent microengines (referred to as *next neighbors*).

The microengine provides support for software-controlled multithreaded operation. Given the disparity between processor cycle times and external memory times, a single thread of execution will often block waiting-for-memory operations to complete. Having multiple threads allows for threads to interleave operation—there is often at least one thread ready to run while others are blocked.

Control Store

The control store is a parity protected RAM, which holds the program that the microengine executes. It holds 4096 instructions, each of which is 40 bits wide. It is initialized by the Intel XScale core.

Contexts

There are eight hardware contexts (or threads) available in the microengine. To allow for efficient context swapping, each context has its own register set, program counter, and context-specific local registers. Fast context swapping allows a context to do computation while other contexts wait for IO (typically, external memory accesses) to complete or for a signal from another context or hardware unit.

Data Path Registers

Each microengine contains four types of 32-bit data path registers:

1. 256 general-purpose registers (GPRs), used for general programming

2. 512 transfer registers, used for transferring data to and from the microengine and locations external to the microengine (DRAM, SRAM, etc.)

3. 128 next neighbor registers, used for communication between adjacent microengines

4. 640 32-bit words of local memory is addressable storage located in the microengine

Special Hardware Blocks in the ME

The ME also provides the following special hardware blocks to assist in various packet processing tasks:

+ *CRC unit.* Computes 16-bit and 32-bit CRC. This accelerates the performance of applications such as ATM AAL5 SAR.

+ *Pseudo random number generator.* Assists in supporting QoS algorithms for congestion avoidance (e.g. WRED, RED).

+ *Timestamp, timer.* Assist in supporting metering, policing, rate-shaping functionality required in IP DiffServ and ATM traffic-management services.

+ *Multiply unit.* Assists in QoS blocks such as policing and congestion avoidance.

+ *16-entry CAM.* Assists in caching and software pipeline implementation.

13.2.3 SRAM

The IXP2400 network processor has two independent SRAM controllers, which each support pipelined QDR synchronous static RAM (SRAM) and/or a co-processor that adheres to QDR signaling.

Queue Data Structure Commands

The ability to enqueue and dequeue data buffers at a fast rate is key to meeting line rate performance. This is a difficult problem since it involves dependent memory references that must be turned around very quickly. The SRAM controller includes a data structure (called the *Q_array*) and associated control logic in order to perform efficient enqueue and dequeue operations. The Q_array has 64 entries, each of which can be used in one of the following ways:

+ Linked list queue descriptor

+ Cache of recently used, linked list queue descriptors (the backing store for the cache is in SRAM)

+ Ring descriptor

The ME provides read_Q_descriptor, write_Q_descriptor, enqueue, and de-queue commands to read, write, and manage queue descriptor data between QDR SRAM memory and the Q_array.

13.2.4   Scratchpad and Hash Unit

The scratchpad unit provides 16 KB of on-chip SRAM memory that can be used for general-purpose operations by the Intel XScale core and the ME. The scratch also provides 16 hardware rings that can be used for communication between MEs and the core.

The hash unit provides a polynomial hash accelerator. The Intel XScale core and microengines can use it to offload hash calculations in applications such as ATM VC/VP lookup and IP 5-tuple classification.

13.2.5   PCI, Intel XScale Peripherals and Performance Monitors

IXP2400 supports one 64-bit PCI Rev 2.2–compliant IO bus. PCI can be used either to connect to a host processor or to attach PCI-compliant peripheral devices. The PCI bus is clocked at 66 MHz.

Intel XScale technology peripherals interface (XPI) is used to connect the IXP2400 to interrupt controller, timers, UART, general-purpose IO (GPIO), and flash ROM.

The performance monitor unit provides counters that can be programmed to count selected internal chip hardware events. These counters are used to analyze and tune performance of the software running on the chip.

13.3   SOFTWARE DEVELOPMENT ENVIRONMENT

As network processors become widely used, the quality and completeness of the associated software development environment takes on greater importance. To benefit from the programmability of the network processor, developers need software tools in several key areas. These include data plane code development, control plane code development, and system development tools.

The Intel Internet Exchange Architecture SDK 3.0 enables hardware and software development to proceed in parallel. The SDK provides an easy-to-use graphical development environment that can be used to develop, debug, op-timize, and simulate code. By using the development tools, network building

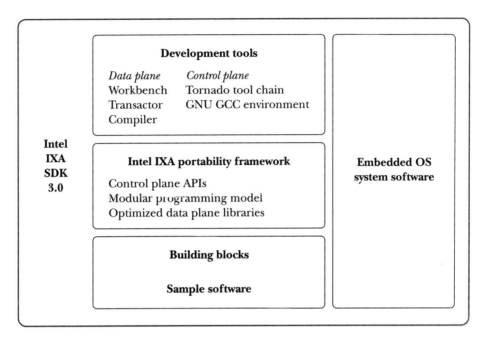

Development tools

Data plane   *Control plane*
Workbench   Tornado tool chain
Transactor   GNU GCC environment
Compiler

Intel
IXA
SDK
3.0

Intel IXA portability framework

Control plane APIs
Modular programming model
Optimized data plane libraries

**Embedded OS
system software**

Building blocks

Sample software

13.5   Intel IXA SDK 3.0 components.

FIGURE

blocks and the modular development framework, a customer can achieve a time-to-market advantage. Figure 13.5 shows the various components of the Intel IXA SDK 3.0, which we next explain in greater detail.

13.3.1 Development Tools

The microengine development environment (MDE) consists of the developer workbench, compiler, and transactor. The developer workbench provides an integrated development environment for the development, debugging, profiling, and simulation of microengine code. The transactor is a cycle-accurate simulator of the network processor and can be used to identify opportunities for code optimization by capturing history and statistics that show cycle-by-cycle interactions among the microengines and memory units.

The MDE provides developers with a choice of two programming languages to develop microengine code. The microengine C compiler offers faster time to market, optimum code portability, and the benefits of a familiar high-level programming language that provides isolation from specific hardware. Microengine

C extensions to the ANSI C standard allow direct access to specialized hardware functions available on the microengines. The second option is to work in microcode to maximize application performance and minimize space utilization. Microcode can also be used within microengine C programs for optimum results.

SDK 3.0 supports WindRiver VxWorks 5.4 (big-endian) and Linux (big-endian) operating systems on the XScale core of the IXP2400 processor. The Intel Xscale microarchitecture is widely supported by a large ecosystem of tools from leading third-party vendors. This includes cross-development tools such as Wind River Tornado and Linux-hosted or Windows-hosted GNU GCC environment.

13.3.2   Programming Model

The microengines employ a software pipeline model in the fast path processing of the packets. Typically, there are two software pipelines: the first is the receive pipeline that receives packets from the POS-PHY L3 (SPI-3) or CSIX interfaces and places them onto transmit queues; the second is the transmit pipeline that removes packets from the queues and transmits them out the SPI-3 or CSIX interfaces.

Each pipeline is composed of smaller elements called *pipeline stages*. Some typical examples of pipeline stages include packet reception, L3 forwarding, metering, and weighted random early detection (WRED). The developer will combine each of these stages to build the full pipeline.

There are two types of pipelines: context pipeline and functional pipeline.

Context Pipeline

In a context pipeline, the pipeline stages are mapped to different MEs. Each ME constitutes a context pipe stage, and cascading two or more context pipe stages constitutes a context pipeline. The context pipeline, shown in Figure 13.6, gets its name from the fact that it is the context that moves through the pipeline.

Each thread in an ME is assigned a packet, and each performs the same function but on different packets. As packets arrive, they are assigned to the ME threads in strict order so that if there were n threads executing on an ME, the first thread, A must complete processing on its first packet before the next n packets arrive so that it can begin processing the $n + 1^{st}$ packet.

The advantage of the context pipeline is that the entire ME program memory space can be dedicated to a single function. This is important when a function supports many variations that result in a large program memory footprint. The context pipeline is also desirable when a pipe stage needs to maintain state (bit

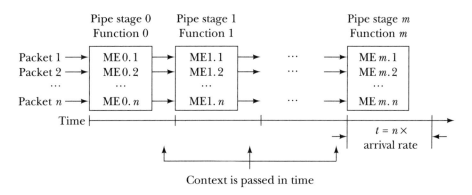

Pipe stage 0   Pipe stage 1   Pipe stage m
Function 0   Function 1   Function m

13.6   Context pipeline.

FIGURE

vectors or tables) to perform its work. The context pipe stage can use the local memory to store this state, eliminating the latency of accessing external memory.

Cases where the context pipeline is not desirable are ones in which the amount of context passed to and from the pipe stage is so large that it affects system performance. Another disadvantage of the context pipe stage is that all pipe stages must execute at minimum packet arrival rates. This may make partitioning the application into stages more difficult.

Functional Pipeline

In a functional pipeline, the context remains with an ME while different functions are performed on the packet as time progresses. The ME execution time is divided into n pipe stages, and each pipe stage performs a different function. A single ME can constitute a functional pipeline. The functional pipeline gets its name from the fact that it is the function that moves through the pipeline.

Packets are assigned to the ME threads in strict order so that if there were n threads executing on an ME, the first thread, A, must complete processing its first packet before the $n + 1^{st}$ packet arrives so that it can begin processing the $n + 1^{st}$ packet. Figure 13.7 shows a functional pipeline implementation.

There is little benefit to dividing a single ME's execution time into functional pipe stages. The real benefits come from having more than one ME execute the same functional pipeline in parallel. These benefits include the following:

+ A packet remains with a thread for a longer period of time as more MEs are added to the functional pipe stage. For example, with four MEs in the functional pipeline, the packet remains with a thread 32 packet arrival times

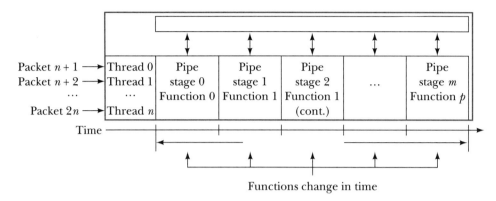

Packet $n+1$ →	Thread 0	Pipe stage 0 Function 0	Pipe stage 1 Function 1	Pipe stage 2 Function 1 (cont.)	...	Pipe stage m Function p
Packet $n+2$ →	Thread 1					
...	...					
Packet $2n$ →	Thread n					

Functions change in time

13.7

FIGURE

Functional pipeline.

(8 threads × 4 MEs) because thread 0 in ME0 is not required to accept another packet until all the other threads get their packets.

✦ The number of pipe stages is equal to the number of MEs in the pipeline. This ensures that a particular pipe stage only executes in one ME at any one time. This is required to provide a pipeline model that supports critical sections, a section in which an ME thread is provided exclusive access to a resource (e.g., CRC residue, reassembly context, or a statistic) in external memory. Critical sections are described in more detail later.

✦ Functions can be distributed across one or more pipe stages. However, the exclusive access to resources as described cannot be supported in these pipe stages.

When designing a functional pipeline, the goal is to identify critical sections and place them into their own pipeline stage. The noncritical section code then naturally falls into pipe stages that become interleaved with the critical sections. Noncritical code that takes longer than a pipe stage time to execute can be allocated more than one pipe stage.

The advantages of functional pipelines are as follows:

✦ Unlike the context pipeline, there is no need to pass the context between each pipe stage since it remains locally within the ME.

✦ They support a longer execution period than context pipe stages.

✦ If one pipe stage does not consume its allocated time budget, this time can be used by another pipe stage (if the longer pipe stage is not a critical section).

The disadvantages of functional pipelines are as follows:

+ The entire ME program memory space must support multiple functions.

+ Function control must be passed between stages; therefore it should be minimized.

+ Mutual exclusion may be more difficult because you have multiple MEs accessing the same data structures.

Elasticity Buffers

When a pipe stage transition occurs between two MEs, it is beneficial if the two stages do not need to run in lock-step. Instead, an elasticity buffer (implemented as a ring) is used and this has an advantage over executing in lockstep. Each pipe stage must be designed to execute in the time allocated to the pipe stage. However, elasticity buffers accommodate jitter in a pipe stage execution. So if a pipe stage falls behind in execution due to a system anomaly such as an unusually high utilization of a memory unit over a short time period, the elasticity buffer will allow the pipe stage context to be buffered so that the previous pipe stages are not stalled waiting for the next stage to complete. Statistically, the pipe stage that falls behind will be able to catch up with its processing and the system will normalize. Elasticity buffers also allow different pipe stage latencies to be used in each pipeline.

The IXP2400 processor supports multiple methods for implementing elasticity buffers for communication between the pipe stages.

+ *SRAM/Scratch rings*. These are multiproducer, multiconsumer, message-passing queues maintained by hardware.

+ *Next neighbor rings*. These are single-producer, single-consumer, optimized message-passing queues between adjacent microengines.

Critical Sections

A critical section is a section of code where it is assured that only one ME thread has exclusive modification privileges for a global resource (e.g., a location in memory) at any one time.

Exclusive modification privileges between MEs To ensure exclusive modification privileges between MEs, the following requirements must be met:

1. Only one function modifies the critical section resource.

2. The function that modifies the critical section resource executes in a single pipe stage.

3. The pipeline is designed so that only one ME executes a pipe stage at any one time.

In a context pipeline, each ME is assigned exclusive modification privileges to the critical data, satisfying requirement 1. Requirements 2 and 3 are satisfied because each pipe stage is partitioned into different functions and only one ME executes a specific function.

In a functional pipeline, an ME should not transition into a critical section pipe stage unless it can be assured that its "next" ME has transitioned out of the critical section. This can be accomplished by placing a fence around the critical section using interthread signaling.

Exclusive modification privileges between threads in an ME   A critical section involves three steps: reading a resource, modifying a resource, and writing back the results. If more than one thread in a pipe stage is required to modify the same critical data, a latency penalty will be incurred if each thread reads the data from external memory, modifies it, and writes the data back. To reduce the latency penalty associated with the read and write, the ME threads can use the ME CAM to assist in caching the data in local memory and to fold these operations into a single read, multiple modifications, and, depending on the cache eviction policy, either one or more write operations. In this case, the ME thread is assured exclusive access to the data by performing the modification and write operations on the critical data without swapping out.

13.3.3   Portability Framework

The Intel IXA portability framework is one of the foundations of the Intel Internet exchange architecture. It enables fast and cost-effective code development, while protecting software investments through software portability and the reuse of code for the microengines and the Intel XScale core across current and future generations of IXA NPUs.

The portability framework enables the development of modular, portable code blocks and integration of third-party software products for longer product life and easier maintenance, while eliminating the time-consuming development of crucial infrastructure software. The Intel IXA portability framework includes

+ Optimized data plane libraries for hardware abstraction, protocol processing, and utility functions
+ A modular programming model for software pipelining

✦ A library of standards-based network processor forum (NPF) APIs for communication with control plane protocol stacks. The APIs will adhere to the NPF standards as they evolve.

The microengine modular programming model allows partitioning of functional blocks across microengines and threads, as well as combining independent modular building blocks into a single managed pipeline. This model facilitates the retargeting of code between Intel IXA NPUs with a differing number of microengines and threads.

13.4 IXP2400 SYSTEM CONFIGURATIONS AND PERFORMANCE ANALYSIS

IPv4 and IPv6 forwarding, IP DiffServ and QoS, ATM AAL5 and AAL2 SAR function, ATM policing and traffic shaping, IP/UDP/RTP header compression, encap/decap, and tunneling are examples of key functions performed by equipment in the target market space for the IXP2400. This section presents the IXP2400 performance for some of the key applications. Table 13.1 summarizes performance of the IXP2400 running applications representative of the target market segments.

Application	Media interface	Minimum packet size	IXP2400 performance
IPv4 forwarding + IP DiffServ	SPI3	46B	OC-48, 2.5 Gbps
IPv4 forwarding + IP DiffServ	Ethernet	64B	4 Gbps
ATM AAL5 SAR + TM4.1 compliant traffic shapers	UTOPIA	53B	OC-48, 2.5 Gbps
IPv6 forwarding + IP DiffServ	SPI3	66B	OC-48, 2.5 Gbps
VoAAL2	UTOPIA/SPI3	40B	16K voice channels
AAL2/AAL5 in wireless (node-B/RNC)	UTOPIA/SPI3	53B	Full-duplex OC12

13.1 IXP2400 performance summary.

TABLE

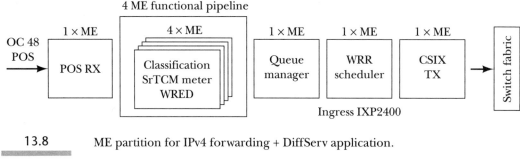

13.8 ME partition for IPv4 forwarding + DiffServ application.

FIGURE

- ✦ For the VoAAL2 application, IXP2400 supports 16K voice channels ($2 \times OC12$ each direction) and provides AAL2 SAR (ITU-T I.363.2) and audio services processing such as jitter buffering (as specified in ITU-T I.366.2).

- ✦ IXP2400 supports full-duplex OC12 data rate for AAL2 CPS SAR and SSSAR (ITU-T 363.2 and ITU-T I.366.1), IP/UDP processing, and AAL5 SAR processing applications in the wireless RNC and node-B.

13.4.1   IPv4 Forwarding + IP DiffServ Application

The configuration shown in Figure 13.8 is used for analyzing the performance for this application. At OC48 line rate, the interarrival time for a minimum-size POS packet of 46B is 88 ME cycles (assuming ME frequency is 600 MHz). In order to achieve line rate, the ME must execute each pipeline stage within this budget of 88 cycles. The blocks of this application running on the ingress and egress IXP2400 are specified next. Figure 13.8 shows the ME partition for this application.

- ✦ *Ingress processor blocks.* POS frame receive, IP header classification using 5-tuple lookup, route lookup, SrTCM meter, WRED, queuing, WRR scheduler, and CSIX segmentation and transmit

- ✦ *Egress processor blocks.* CSIX cell reassembly, further IP classification, SrTCM meter, WRED, queuing, DRR scheduler, and POS transmit

13.5   CONCLUSION

Next-generation access and edge equipment require flexible programming, high performance, low power consumption, and small real estate. These applications require support for a wide range of functions such as IP forwarding with QoS,

Technology	Manufactured in 0.18 micron Intel process
Package	1356 Ball FCBGA 37.5 mm × 37.5 mm, 1 mm solder ball pitch
Required voltages	1.3 V core, 1.5 V QDR, 2.5 V DDR, and 3.3 V I/O
Power	10 W typical and 12.4 W max

13.2

TABLE

IXP2400 technology summary.

ATM AAL5 and AAL2 segmentation and reassembly and ATM traffic shaping, and header compression, among others. The IXP2400 network processor has been optimized to meet these requirements. The eight microengines supporting 5.4 Giga ops per sec provide fully flexible programming and processing power to meet 2.5 Gbps and 4 Gbps wire-rate performances. The flexible media interface allows a variety of media devices, ranging from OC3 to OC48 speeds to be connected without glue logic to the IXP2400 for easier design and lower system cost. Performance analysis demonstrates that the Intel IXP2400 network processor is an ideal product for meeting these requirements at OC-48 wire rate.

Table 13.2 provides the technology summary for the IXP2400 network processor.

REFERENCES

[1]   www.intel.com/design/network/products/npfamily/index.htm

[2]   www.intel.com/design/network/devnet/

[3]   www.intel.com/design/pca/applicationsprocessors/index.htm

Motorola—C-5e Network Processor

Eran Cohen Strod, Patricia Johnson
Motorola, Inc.

The C-5e network processor (NP), the second generation of Motorola's C-Port family of network processors, is a highly integrated, flexible, and functionally rich processor for developing and deploying advanced services for next-generation networks. With its 5 Gbps of line bandwidth and more than 4500 MIPs of computing power, the C-5e architecture is targeted at the demanding communications requirements of next-generation network systems. The C-5e NP includes several on-chip subsystems: programmable VLIW engines that can support a variety of layer-2 interfaces, a bank of RISC engines for services processing, a high-performance classifier/table lookup engine, a traffic manager, a fabric interface, a host CPU manager, and a payload buffer manager.

The C-5e architecture flexibly supports external devices to provide extensions in processing and bandwidth as needed. The C-5e NP can be connected to PCI-enabled external host processors (e.g., Motorola's family of 32-bit processors based on the PowerPC instruction set architecture) for running the control plane software. As quality-of-service requirements increase, the C-5e NP can also be connected to Motorola's powerful Q-5 traffic management co-processor (TMC). To support channelized applications or OC-48c full-duplex data rates, the C-5e NP can be combined with Motorola's M-5 channel adapter. In addition, alliances with Motorola support connections to third-party fabric chip sets, security co-processors, and external classification co-processors as warranted by the application.

The C-Port NP family is protocol agnostic, supporting IP, ATM, and custom interfaces/protocols. Further, Motorola has defined a robust API that provides customers with a stable interface that may easily scale to future chip architectures. The C-Port NP family makes an ideal platform architecture with cost-effective T1/E1 through OC-48c performance and a roadmap that scales to 10 Gbps and beyond.

14.1   TARGET APPLICATIONS

The C-Port NP family is targeted for access and edge networking applications—products typically distinguished by the range and sophistication of services that they support. The characteristics of these applications include

- Interface requirements ranging from multi-T1 through OC-48c, such as GbE, 10/100 Ethernet, FiberChannel, OC-3c, OC-12, OC-12c, OC-48, OC-48c, and T/E-x

- Technology discontinuity and protocol diversity driven by new and developing technologies such as advanced quality of service (QoS), protocol interworking, encapsulation, and tunneling

- Risk and uncertainty resulting from unclear market requirements or evolving standards

- "Platform" approach to product design in which multiple products and line cards can be developed from a single platform, maximizing design reuse and enabling faster time to market

Key access/edge areas that reflect these requirements and are thus a focal point for C-Port NP family designs include

- Multiservice access/edge platforms

- Wireless infrastructure

- Broadband access

- Media gateway

- High-function routing

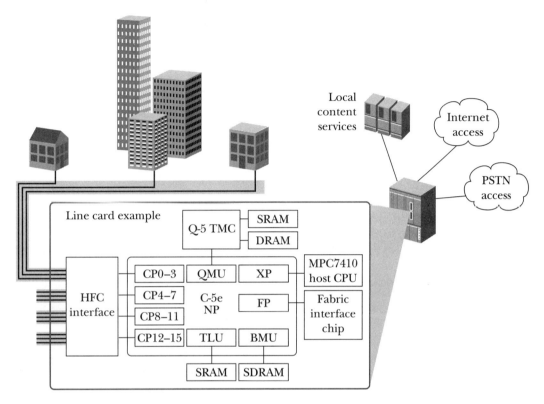

Cable modem termination system (CMTS) using the C-5e network processor.

14.1.1   Application Example: Cable Modem Termination System (CMTS)

CMTS equipment design can be challenging because of the combination of protocol evolution and diversity, higher performance, and advanced QoS requirements occurring in the broadband cable space. With a trend toward more distributed implementations, a platform approach to the design, where the same software can be leveraged everywhere from the distribution points to the cable head-end, offers significant benefits. The C-Port NP family brings the high-service, high-functionality requirements together in an integrated silicon solution. Further, the programmability of the C-Port line interfaces allows the processor to be flexibly adapted to market-specific layer-2 requirements. An example of a line card in a CMTS is shown in Figure 14.1.

14.2   HARDWARE ARCHITECTURE

The C-5e NP supports a total of 16 line interfaces that are managed by channel processors (CPs). The CPs are made up of three processing elements each. The first two are microprogrammable, dedicated receive (Rx) and transmit (Tx) serial data processors (SDPs) that allow the C-5e NP to be programmed to connect to virtually any layer-2 interface. C-Port provides SDP microcode for many standard interfaces, including DS1, DS3, OC-3, OC-12, RMII, GMII, and TBI. The programmability of the SDPs also allows users to create custom layer-2 implementations or to customize standard interfaces. The third element of a CP is its own dedicated channel processor RISC core (CPRC) running at 266 MHz that can be used for any application-specific purpose.

The control plane is accessed via an integrated PCI bus (66 MHz, 32-bit) block that is managed by the executive processor (XP): the 17th RISC core. The XP may be used for overall chip management as well.

The C-5e NP also has several specialized co-processors that support the CPs and the XP:

+ *Table lookup unit (TLU).* The C-5e NP's classification engine provides access to application-defined topology, control, and statistics tables in external SRAM.

+ *Buffer management unit (BMU).* Responsible for managing the external SDRAM for the C-5e NP. The payload of a packet is typically stored in an SDRAM buffer while the packet waits to be processed and/or forwarded.

+ *Queue management unit (QMU).* A global queuing resource serving all processors on the C-5e NP. The QMU provides up to 512 queues that provide quality-of-service (QoS) features.

+ *Fabric processor (FP).* An on-chip processing unit that behaves like a high-speed network interface port, allowing the C-5e NP to interface to other C-Port network processors or directly to a switching fabric.

Internal buses offer 60 Gbps of aggregate bandwidth to connect the internal subsystems of the C-5e NP. The subsystems and buses of the C-5e NP are shown in Figure 14.2, and all elements are further described in the following section. Table 14.1 summarizes the performance of the C-5e NP.

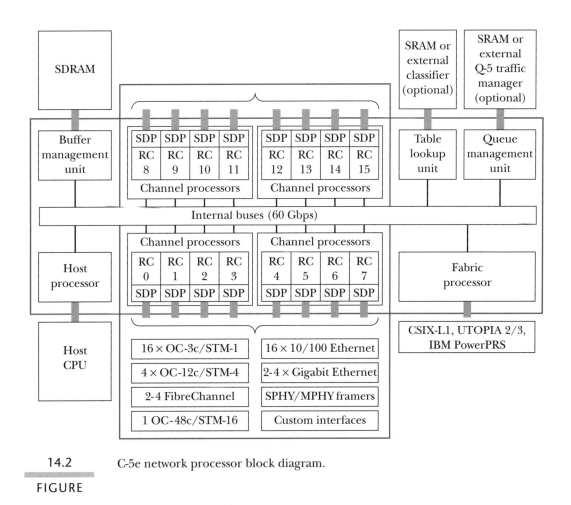

14.2 C-5e network processor block diagram.

FIGURE

14.2.1 Channel Processors

Because of the flexible combination of SDPs and CPRCs, the CPs can be programmed to take on different personalities to support ATM, Ethernet/IP, PPP/IP, frame relay, SONET/SDH, or even proprietary protocols.

Bit- and byte-oriented manipulations are typically done by the SDPs. The SDPs control programmable external pin logic, allowing them to implement virtually any layer-2 interface, including connection to T/E-carrier framers, 10/100 Ethernet PHY (RMII), Gigabit Ethernet PHY (GMII or TBI), OC-3/STM-1 PHY, OC-12/STM-4 PHY, and OC-48/STM-16. There are seven physical I/O pins associated with each CP that are either capable of receiving/driving data or may be

Processing	4500 RISC MIPS and 22,000 SDP MIPS
CPRC context switch time	Two clock cycles typical
Classification	133M table lookups per second (index)
	46M IPv4 lookups per sec (typical) for MAE-West database
Traffic management	Fine-grain traffic management at OC-48 rates
Memory bandwith	16 Gbps
Interconnect bandwidth	60 Gbps

14.1   Performance summary.

TABLE

configured as input clocks, output clocks, or PHY status/control signals. The functionality of these signals is determined by SDP microcode, which allows the user to implement a layer-2 state machine that provides Ethernet MAC functionality. The SDP also contains OC-3/OC-12 SONET framers. This architecture reduces system cost by eliminating the need for external MACs and SONET framers in many implementations. It also allows board designers to quickly add layer-2 support for a new interface to an existing hardware design.

The SDPs also handle data encoding/decoding, framing, formatting, parsing, and error checking (CRCs), and they may launch lookups to the TLU. They are also responsible for sending payload to the BMU for storage. Because the SDPs are programmable, they can support proprietary and custom interfaces as needed, which provides extensive layer-2 flexibility. Figure 14.3 depicts the internal blocks of both the receive SDP and the transmit SDP.

The CPRC is a 266 MHz RISC processor that can execute 32-bit instructions quickly. The RISC cores, programmed in C language, are dedicated to the advanced services that benefit the most from high-level language implementations. For example, the RISC core focuses on higher-level forwarding tasks such as final forwarding decision making, scheduling, and statistics gathering. Each RISC core has dedicated, internal 8 Kb of private instruction memory (IMEM) and 12 Kb of private data memory (DMEM). Under program control, the CPRC switches among four contexts, which may be used in any way that the application designer chooses. Applications often use one context for the receive path, another for transmit, a third for debug/supervisory tasks/event handlers, and the last for an application-specific purpose.

Channel processors can be used individually to manage a single line interface that is less than 156 Mbps. However, four channel processors can be coordinated in a *cluster* to support a single higher-speed interface per cluster. For example, a C-5e NP can support up to four ports of Gigabit Ethernet (GMII and TBI), OC-12/OC-12c/STM-4, or FiberChannel. All 16 CPs can be used in unison to

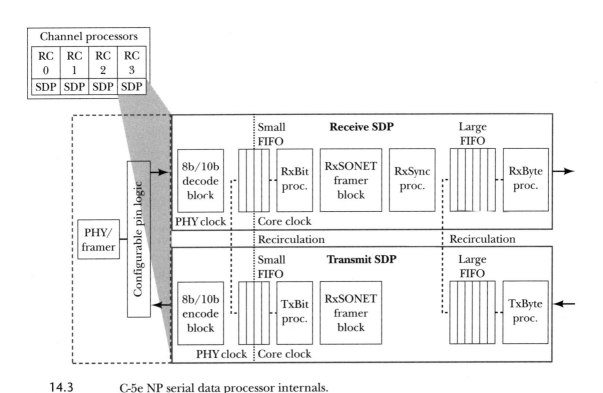

14.3   C-5e NP serial data processor internals.

FIGURE

support OC-48/OC-48c full-duplex with the help of the M-5 channel adapter, which interfaces the 16 CPs or the fabric interface to an OC-48/OC-48c framer.

When IMEM and DMEM are shared among a cluster of four CPs, the cluster has 32 Kb and 48 Kb of IMEM and DMEM, respectively. When used in a cluster of four, the CPs use a hardware semaphore to coordinate processing. Channel processors may also be linked programmatically in a cascading fashion to provide additional processing power as needed—this is achieved through a process called *recirculation*. In recirculation, the transmit path of a CP is connected to the receive path of another CP. The output from the second CP can similarly be connected to a third CP. A packet might enter at CP0, be passed to CP1, and finally progress to CP2. CP2 could then transmit the packet out to the PHY. An example of this type of application is a SAR: CP0 receives and transmits Ethernet packets, CP1 acts as a SAR, segmenting and reassembling the packets or cells, and CP2 could be an OC-3 port transmitting and receiving cells. It is possible to cascade all 16 CPs together to have a very deep pipeline with 16× the processing power of a single CP. The benefit of this highly flexible architecture is that it allows the designer to trade off bandwidth for processing power, which allows the C-5e NP to adapt to a variety of different applications with diverse requirements. There are no restrictions on the order or manner in which CPs are combined to work on a particular problem.

14.2.2   Executive Processor

The executive processor (XP) is responsible for overall chip management. At boot time, the XP loads executable code. It can download code from PCI memory or from across a PCI bus. It can also load a program from a PROM. Once the XP has loaded an executable image, it configures all the co-processors and then loads code into each CP's IMEM. Finally, the XP releases the CPs from reset. The CPs are released last during chip initialization so that when they start receiving data from the line interface, all the co-processors will be ready to assist.

During runtime, the XP manages the chip's shared resources and may also be used to assist the application. The XP is also responsible for communicating with an external host processor during runtime when control plane interaction is required. The control place is attached via a 66 MHz, 32-bit PCI interface. The C-5e NP is capable of being both a PCI initiator and target. If required by the application, the external control plane CPU is capable of accessing many on-chip resources, such as CP registers and data memory, and can participate in chip initialization.

The XP runs the same instruction set as the channel processor RISC cores. It has dedicated, internal 48 Kbytes of private instruction memory (IMEM) and 32 Kbytes of private data memory (DMEM).

14.2.3   Table Lookup Unit

The table lookup unit (TLU) provides powerful and flexible on-chip classification and table lookup capabilities supporting performance metrics such as 133M index lookups per second and 46M IPv4 lookups per second. The CP receives a PDU and identifies the sequence of bytes (up to 112 bits) that the application wants to use as a lookup key. The CP can send this bit sequence (or key) to the TLU. The TLU uses the key to locate a table entry in external SRAM. The result of the table lookup is then returned to the CP. The TLU is often used to find the egress port for a given packet.

The TLU is designed for layer-2, layer-3, and layer-4 types of lookups. It can implement longest prefix match algorithms for IP routing tables and exact match algorithms for bridging tables. It also supports simple data tables that are indexed rather than searched. These different algorithms are implemented by various combinations of subtables. There are five varieties of subtables: PFX (longest prefix match), hash, trie, index, and data. One can combine the subtables to implement different lookup algorithms. For example, an exact match algorithm is implemented with a hash–trie–key combination. Each of 16 possible tables can be up to 16 million entries long. Table entry size is 8–1024 bytes. Table memory is implemented with four physical banks of 64-bit ZBT SRAM.

In most cases, system designers find the TLU capabilities sufficient to accomplish all but the most complex classification tasks. However, for systems requiring very deep packet classification, it is possible to remove one of the four banks of SRAM and replace it with a co-processor. Motorola is currently working with multiple co-processor vendors for deep packet classification of very long, variable length, or variable location keys.

14.2.4 Queue Management Unit and External Traffic Management

When a protocol data unit (PDU) enters the C-Port network processor, it is separated into two parts: payload and control information. The payload information is stored off-chip in an SDRAM buffer. Application-specific control information is stored in a short data structure called a *descriptor*. The descriptor usually contains a buffer handle, which points to the PDU payload, classification keys, and quality-of-service (QoS) information. This method of abstracting the PDU allows the C-5e NP to achieve a deterministic level of efficiency whether PDUs are fixed or variable, long or short. Also, the descriptor may be circulated around the various on-chip resources without moving the full payload around. This improves determinism, shortens latency, and allows the application designer to recirculate the descriptor without stressing the chip's internal data pathways. Descriptors are passed between chip resources via the queue management unit (QMU), which in a generic sense can be conceptualized as a FIFO-based message-passing interface.

The QMU contains 512 queues that may be used as bins to organize PDU flows. The enqueuing and dequeueing of descriptors to the QMU queues is under software control, so software may implement any quality of service desired. This mechanism can be used to satisfy the traffic-management requirements of many applications. This method of traffic management is called *internal mode*.

For example, QMU queues may be allocated between the CPs at initialization time with a maximum of 128 queues per processor. In internal mode, the QMU notifies a CP when a descriptor is pending in its queue. The CP can then run an algorithm, such as a timer to support constant bit rate (CBR) transfers, specifying the order in which to dequeue descriptors from the various queues. Between timer expirations, the CP can check variable bit rate (VBR) or unspecified bit rate (UBR) queues.

For applications that require a much higher level of traffic-management support, the C-5e NP can be gluelessly coupled to an external traffic manager such as Motorola's Q-5 TMC. This method is termed *external mode*. The Q-5 TMC provides up to 256 K input queues and multiprotocol support, including IP, frame relay, ATM, Ethernet, and PoS. This enables QoS management functions to be applied to virtually any traffic type up to OC-48c bandwidths. With the Q-5 TMC, designers can implement very high-density per-flow and/or per-virtual channel (VC) queueing and fine-grained traffic shaping for a wide range of both packet-based and cell-based applications. Its flexible three-level scheduling hierarchy, with up to 4000 virtual channels, enables one to support a vast array of services, including deep channelization and integrated multicast elaboration.

14.2.5   Buffer Management Unit

The buffer management unit (BMU) is responsible for keeping track of packet payloads while a packet is inside the chip. When the CP receives a packet from the network, it sends both the packet and a "buffer tag" to the BMU. The BMU stores the packet in the location specified by the buffer tag. When a CP wants to transmit a packet, it sends a buffer tag to the BMU requesting that the payload at the location specified by the buffer tag be sent to the CP.

The data bus between the C-5e NP and the BMU is 128 bits wide and runs at 125 MHz. Thus, there are 16 Gbps of bandwidth between the BMU and the SDRAM. A total of 30 different-sized buffers can be set up in the BMU. The user selects the buffer type based on the traffic that is being received.

14.2.6   Fabric Processor

The on-chip fabric processor (FP) implements a high-speed interface that can connect to a switch fabric or to another C-Port network processor. The bus can be configured as Utopia 1, 2, or 3, from 8 bits to 32 bits wide, allowing connection to ATM devices. The FP is also designed to interoperate with third-party or industry-standard switch fabrics such as CSIX-L1.

The data bus is 32 bits wide in each direction and operates at up to 125 MHz. This allows for a total of 6.4 Gbps aggregate flow between the C-5e NP and the switch fabric. This is 1.4 Gbps over the maximum capacity of the C-5e NP, which is 5 Gbps. This extra bandwidth is often used for in-band signaling between the FP and the switch fabric or, alternatively, in-band signaling from the FP through the switch fabric to a different FP.

The interface to the switch fabric is cell based; however, it is suitable for sending both ATM cells and packets. The FP supports a cell size between 40B and 200B. When sending packets, the FP segments a packet into fixed-sized cells. Another important benefit of the extra 1.4 Gbps of FP bandwidth is to accommodate the bandwidth expansion that naturally results whenever variable-sized PDUs are segmented into fixed cell sizes. In the receive direction, the FP reassembles cells back into packets. The FP also supports link-level flow control to stop all transmission of cells. It can also respond to *per-flow* flow control messages so that it can stop transmitting a certain flow that is becoming congested in the switch fabric.

14.2.7 Internal Buses

The C-5e NP has three internal buses with a total bandwidth of approximately 60 Gbps: the payload bus, the ring bus, and the global bus. The payload bus has the highest bandwidth with a 35 Gbps capacity. It is used to transfer PDU descriptors and payload to and from the CPs, the FP, the XP, and the BMU. The QMU also sits on the payload bus. The ring bus connects the CPs and FP to the TLU. The ring bus enforces a controlled latency for classification and table lookups. This bounded latency is important because responses to TLU lookups must be returned in real time while PDUs are being received or transmitted. The global bus allows any processor or the external host to read any piece of memory in the chip or on the PCI bus. The global bus is primarily used by the XP to configure the chip-level subsystems at boot time. The XP can also use the global bus to harvest statistics that the CPs, for example, have stored in their local memories.

14.3 SOFTWARE ARCHITECTURE

The C-Port NP architecture was designed to support a simple programming model, which includes the ability to program C-Port NPs in standard C language using an API layer of abstraction. The C-Ware APIs define the most common networking activities, such as physical interface management, data forwarding, table lookups, buffer management, and queuing operations. In doing so, they hide the hardware complexity while exploiting its underlying power.

C-Ware API consists of services that address each of the chip functional blocks: protocol and protocol data unit (PDU) services, table services, buffer services, queue services, fabric services, kernel services, diagnostic services.

Motorola understands that equipment providers and OEMs have a tremendous investment in their software and that they need to leverage that investment over several product generations. That is where an API level of abstraction proves vital. Programming to the C-Ware APIs ensures software compatibility and scalability from generation to generation of the C-Port NP family and between CST releases. Customer applications that run on top of C-Ware APIs migrate from older C-Port NPs and CST to newer ones with a simple recompile and retest.

14.3.1   Reference Applications

The C-Ware Applications Library (CAL) provides a rich set of functional communications solutions that can be used as reference models or integrated into higher-level products or services. The applications are created from a robust set of well-known and proven communications software components (e.g., IP packet forwarding and SONET/SDH monitoring) that can be leveraged across multiple applications. These applications and components are written to the C-Ware APIs, thus ensuring software compatibility across generations of the C-Port NP family.

The CAL includes 10/100 Ethernet, Gigabit Ethernet, and FiberChannel switches and routers; a fibre channel gateway; packet-over-SONET for OC-3c/STM-1, OC-12, OC-12c/STM-4, OC-48 and OC-48c/STM-16; ATM SAR; AAL-2 and ATM cell switch; and voice-over-IP to voice-over-ATM media gateway. These applications are full featured and tested. For instance, an Ethernet application supports bridging, routing, VLAN, and priority queuing. Customers who license the C-Ware Software Toolset (CST) receive the entire source code of these applications and may use them in their products on a royalty-free basis under the terms of the CST license.

14.3.2   C-Ware Software Toolset (CST)

The CST provides a full suite of software tools for programming the C-Port NP family, including a standard GNU-based C compiler and debugger, a functional and performance-accurate simulation environment, GUI-based performance analysis tools, and traffic scripting tools. Code for the network processor RISC cores is compiled using the standard GNU C compiler. Code for the serial data processors is compiled with a proprietary compiler using a C-like programming syntax.

The simulation environment provides a cycle accurate model of the chip. All the registers, memory, RISC cores, buses, and other specialized hardware components are simulated. One can see everything that is executing in the chip on a per-cycle basis. The simulator shows where packets are in the chip, what is located in the various memories, and what line of code the RISC core is executing. Programs can first be debugged and tuned in this simulated environment with the benefit of maximum execution visibility. Unlike a Verilog model, which can take several hours to run, the CST simulates at about 2000 cycles per second.

After a program is written and loaded on the simulator, traffic can be fed into the simulator to verify the proper functioning of the application. The simulator expects traffic in a binary format that resembles what one would see with a logic analyzer on a bus between the C-Port NP and the PHY. The CST also provides tools that allow developers to easily create traffic in this format.

As the simulator receives traffic, a standard GNU debugger can monitor the program's behavior. The debugger allows the user to step through code, add watches, insert breakpoints, and so on.

The CST provides a graphical performance analyzer that can be used to find programming bottlenecks. With a product as powerful and flexible as the C-5e NP, there are always several ways to approach a given problem. The goal is to use all resources on the chip as efficiently as possible. If, for example, the TLU is being used to ~95% capacity but the RISC core is only used to ~20% capacity, a designer might offload some of the TLU's work to the CPRC, thus increasing total throughput. The performance analyzer reports the percent utilization of different parts of the chip. It also allows developers to insert tags in the code to measure how long it takes to go from one line of code to another. This is useful in fine-tuning an application once it is running.

14.3.3   C-Ware Development System (CDS)

Motorola offers a turnkey system that includes power supplies, network processor switch modules (SMs), and physical interface modules (PIMs) so that customers can "mix and match" interfaces to create a configuration that closely matches their final target system. This enables customers to prototype a complete system prior to final target system availability.

The SM contains the C-5e NP, its associated memories, and the other components needed to support it. It plugs into a CompactPCI midplane. The CompactPCI bus allows the SM to interface to the host module (an MCP750-based single board computer). Cards may be inserted into both the front and the back of the CDS chassis. The SM plugs into a slot on the front of the midplane. PIMs plug into the slots in the back. Motorola offers a variety of PIMs: 16 × OC-3, 4 × OC-12, 2 × GbE, and so on, as well as combination PIMS such as the Ethernet/OC-3 PIM that has 4 × 10/100, 4 × OC-3, and 1 × GbE.

Clock	266 MHz
Price	Suggested list price of $450 in volume
Technology	0.15 micron
Package	31 mm^2 840-pin HiTCE ceramic BGA with 1 mm ball pitch
Power	9.2 W typical, 13.0 W maximum

14.2

TABLE

Technology summary.

14.4　CONCLUSION

A technology summary of the C-5e network processor is shown in Table 14.2. It is designed to support applications requiring flexible implementation of protocols and interworking among those protocols, as well as bandwidths ranging from T1/E1 up to OC-48c. System designers wanting to minimize risk in their design and be able to scale their designs in next-generation systems will find the C-5e NP, and its programming environment, to provide the necessary programming flexibility and performance for a vast range of networking access and edge systems.

REFERENCES

[1]　　　*www.motorola.com/networkprocessors*

[2]　　　*www.motorola.com/smartnetworks*

PMC-Sierra, Inc.—ClassiPI

Vineet Dujari, Remby Taas, Ajit Shelat
PMC-Sierra, Inc.

The ClassiPI (classification by packet inspection) device assists network processors by offloading the complex and time-consuming task of complex packet classification. It is compatible with and interfaces without any glue logic to a variety of commercially available network processors. When used in conjunction with ClassiPI, the current generation of network processors can deliver OC-48 performance in feature-rich solutions as opposed to simple forwarding-type applications. Besides the glueless hardware interface, the ClassiPI architecture allows easy software interface to multicore NP architectures. It also allows efficient representation of access control list (ACL) type rules as compared to CAM devices, leading to smaller rule memory size, which in turn leads to lower power consumption. Finally, the ClassiPI device has special functionality that significantly speeds up applications that require payload (layer-7) processing.

15.1   TARGET APPLICATIONS

The target application primarily determines the classification requirements of the networking equipment. In simple switching and forwarding applications, exact match of L2 MAC address (or labels as in MPLS LSR) and longest prefix match of layer-3 address (for MPLS LER and forwarding) are required. More complex packet filtering applications such as firewall, VPN, and QoS-capable networking equipment require exact match, prefix, and range checks for layer-2, layer-3, and layer-4 addresses. Higher-layer applications such as server load balancing, Web caching, and intrusion detection require lookups in the payload (layer-7) portion of the packet.

As an example, consider a server load-balancing application. With the rapid increase in Internet traffic and the rising performance expectations of Internet users, it is imperative that OEM vendors deliver equipment to the infrastructure builders that makes possible the expected end user experience on the Web. Studies show that users do not visit Web sites if the requested Web pages fail to load within eight seconds. Similarly, with the gaining popularity of streaming audio and video on the Internet, satisfying user experience is vital to retain and gain users. Furthermore, Web-hosting infrastructure must support an architecture that guarantees high availability and is easy to maintain. In order to address these requirements, the Web-hosting infrastructure has evolved over the years from single-server Web-hosting sites to high-availability, multiserver clusters with intelligently distributed content per server.

Creating a high-performance Web-hosting infrastructure requires server load-balancing switches beyond the simple layer-3 or layer-4 switches; they need to be able to perform content-based switching. This deep content peering and classification ability is difficult to implement in conventional network processors given their limited instruction memory size and general inability to process data payload. A special challenge of content analysis lies in the fact that the content being searched, such as URLs, is variable in length and can occur at an arbitrary position within the packet. The ClassiPI device from PMC-Sierra addresses this limitation by performing deep packet classification. This device, designed for easy interface with a variety of network or custom ASIC processors, can offload the task of content-based packet classification from the processor. In addition to its layer-2, layer-3, and layer-4 lookup features, its unique layer-7 content search capability can find occurrences of a variety of variable length strings anywhere within the packet. Its on-chip rule memory and low power consumption allow the OEM vendor to build an optimized server load-balancing switch that implements layer-3 and layer-4 based firewall functions and layer-7 based intelligent server load balancing.

The general architecture of a ClassiPI-based system is shown in Figure 15.1. The network processor or customer ASIC sits in the data path and buffers the packets upon arrival. The ClassiPI device is attached to the generic search machine interface as a co-processor. The network processor or customer ASIC transfers the appropriate payload to the ClassiPI device depending on the type of lookup that

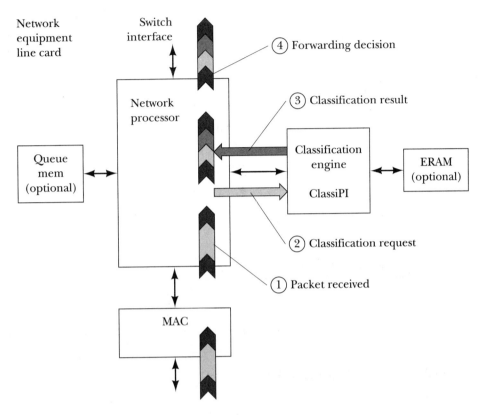

15.1   ClassiPI-based network equipment architecture.

FIGURE

needs to be performed. Based on the preprogrammed rule set in the ClassiPI device, the result of classification is returned to the processor that can further perform appropriate editing and forwarding of the packet.

The generic search machine interface for connecting the ClassiPI device to the network processor or customer ASIC is a standard synchronous SRAM bus. This allows easy glueless hookup to a variety of standard network processors available from companies such as Vitesse IQ2000 and Motorola C5.

The ClassiPI supports optional external SSRAMs connected using a separate private bus. Up to two external SSRAM devices can be connected per ClassiPI device. This external device can be used to implement more complex classification lookup sequences and to store packet parameters and user data associated with rules.

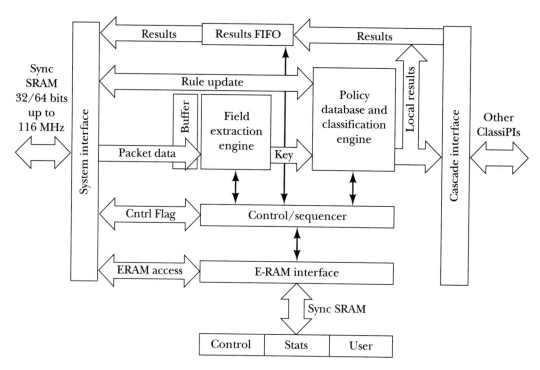

        ClassiPI device architecture.

15.2   CLASSIPI ARCHITECTURE

ClassiPI features an efficiently pipelined architecture, enabling a continuous
stream of packets to be fed into the device, while it continues to perform packet
parsing, key formation, and lookup operations. The internal architecture of the
ClassiPI device is shown in Figure 15.2. The classification engine block, assisted
by the control/sequencer block, implements the core classification function. The
other blocks provide the functionality required to interface ClassiPI to other
devices in the system, extract the payload, and present the desired commands and
parameters to the classification engine. More information about the important
blocks is provided in the following sections.

15.3   SYSTEM INTERFACE (SI)

The ClassiPI co-processor presents a general-purpose synchronous SRAM interface (configurable as 32 or 64 bits wide operating in SyncBurst or ZBT mode) for connecting to a processor, packet source, or DMA device. The system interface can run up to 116 MHz and is used to send packets or preextracted payload for classification. The interface contains an input packet buffer in which associated packet data is stored. The results of a classification operation are placed in the result FIFO that is accessed by the processor via this interface. The packet buffers and result FIFO have 88 Kb of embedded SRAM. This interface supports up to 32 independent channels, each of which appears to be an independent classification engine having a separate area in the input packet buffer and result FIFO. This mechanism greatly simplifies hardware- and software-level interfaces with external multicontext processors since each context of the external processor has an independent "virtual" classification engine available and no other hardware or software scheduling or arbitration mechanism is required. This interface is also used to access the control registers that are used to configure classification operations, key selections, and the rule database.

15.4   FIELD EXTRACTION ENGINE (FEE)

The main function of the field extraction engine is to form the key or field list that is required for a classification operation. The FEE can parse and extract Ethernet II, 802.3, and 802.1p/q headers, then determine where in the packet the layer-3 payload starts. It can extract key IP, TCP, and UDP header fields as well as payload data at any offset. The FEE can also extract some amount of TCP state information. The FEE is aware of and can handle the various idiosyncrasies of the IP and TCP headers. In addition to performing fixed header extraction, the FEE can also be programmed to extract data between a start and an end offset in the input data stream. It is also possible to bypass the FEE on a per-packet basis and send a preextracted key directly to ClassiPI.

15.5   CLASSIFICATION ENGINE (CE)

The classification engine implements a set of classification functions. Each classification function implements an operation and can be programmed to be associated with a rule set, a key, and a selection operator. The rule set is allocated space from a common pool of 16K rules. The classification engine contains 2.3 Mb of SRAM that makes up the 16K rule memory. Each rule is 136 bits wide, made up of a 108-bit-wide data field that can store values and masks related to the rule and a 24-bit control field that determines the classification function performed by this rule. Tightly embedded into this SRAM array are 256 sets of three 32-bit-wide and one 8-bit-wide ALUs and other processing logic. The rule memory is organized in 64 rows with 256 rules per row (64×256 equals 16K rules). When processing rules, the ClassiPI device fetches and operates upon one row per clock cycle, in other words, up to 768 (3×256) 32-bit and 256 8-bit operations can occur per clock cycle. The ALUs can be split (e.g., 16 bits per operation) and combined (e.g., 64 bits per operation) into more complex configurations also. This rule space can be extended to 128K rules using a cascade interface, as explained later.

15.5.1   Rule Capabilities

The ClassiPI architecture supports a wide range of rule formats. Besides supporting the equal to operation, the format allows specification of ranges using the less than and greater than operators as well as the mask operator. The architecture allows the classification engine to be configured to create multiple *classification functions,* each with varying numbers of rules, rules of varying complexity, and associated keys of varying widths. The rules are configurable in a variety of ways, from 108-bit layer-4 classifiers to wide-width classifiers of up to 192 bytes for layer-7 applications.

15.5.2   Search Operation

The fundamental operation performed by the classification engine is the search operation. The search operation selects a particular classification function and proceeds by performing a match operation for each specified rule in the classification function. The results depend on the selection operator specified in the search operation. The ClassiPI architecture supports two types of selection operators: highest priority match and multiple match. The highest priority match operator returns the rule that has the smallest index out of all the rules that match the packet data. In case of a multiple match, indexes of all the rules that match the packet data are reported. The results of a multiple match search operation are queued up in the results FIFO (see Figure 15.2).

    The highest priority match operation is used in applications such as layer-4 filtering and DiffServ. The multiple match search operation could be used to implement applications such as RMON, which maintains statistics (number of IP packets, TCP packets, IP fragments, etc.) and where more than one rule can match a packet.

15.6   EXTERNAL RAM (ERAM) INTERFACE

The co-processor has an interface to an external RAM that is used to store

1. The classification program in the command RAM (i.e., the C-RAM section)

2. The user programmable data associated with every rule in the *User* section

3. Packet count, byte count, and timestamp statistics maintained by the device on a per-rule basis in the *Stats* section

This external RAM interface runs at the system interface speed of up to 116 MHz. Since this is a private memory interface, it supports SyncBurst SSRAM devices only. This interface supports a variety of memory configurations depending on the application requirements. In simple applications, no external memory is required. In more complex applications, one or more external devices can be attached to this bus. In cascade applications, the command RAM section of the external memory has a one-to-many connectivity between memory and ClassiPI devices (i.e., one RAM connected to many ClassiPI devices), whereas the user and statistics memory has a one-to-one connectivity.

The ERAM interface has a shared address bus and two data buses—one for command and the other for statistics and user data; consequently, two types of cycles can run on this interface. When fetching the command word, the data read from the command section of the ERAM is delivered to all devices in the cascade; whereas accesses to the statistics and user section of the ERAM are targeted between the specific ClassiPI device and ERAM as determined by local on-chip ERAM configuration register ECR in each ClassiPI device. Programming of the ECR determines what statistics and user data are stored in the corresponding ERAM device.

15.7   CLASSIPI CONTROL AND SEQUENCER BLOCK

The ClassiPI control and sequencer block orchestrates the operation of the various blocks to perform packet classification. The classification sequence executed by the ClassiPI control and sequencer block can be either preprogrammed in an on-chip register, supplied along with each packet, supplied under program control by the processor, or programmed to be retrieved from the external RAM. The sequencer understands and creates the multiple sequences of classification operations, as well as the conditional and unconditional search operations in the classification program. It is responsible for feeding the extracted key from the FEE to the classification engine and selecting the matching rule set based on the selection operator. An embedded 4 Kb SRAM block is used to hold classification function specifications that are used to create the sequences of classification operation.

To ease debug, the ClassiPI supports a processor intervention mode. When this mode is enabled, the classification engine halts at every classification function boundary, allowing the processor to examine the state of the device before enabling the next step of the classification function sequence.

15.8   CASCADE INTERFACE

The cascade mechanism can be used to increase the number of rules in the rule database to a maximum of 128K. To minimize search time, a large filter database should be distributed among multiple devices to be of similar or equal-sized partitions and so they can be searched in parallel in approximately equal time. As explained later, results from multiple devices will be reported in the order of priority without any extra handshake required from the external processor.

The cascade interface is used to connect up to a maximum of eight ClassiPI devices. In the cascade configuration, each of the devices in the cascade receives the same key but operates on different rules in parallel. The cascade interface implements a handshake mechanism to make the cascade appear as a single large device to the network processor. On the processor interface, all devices in the cascade share the chip select signal (contrast this with an array of memory devices) besides the address, data, and other read/write control signals. The memory map of the device is split between global (common to all devices in the cascade) and local (assigned to individual devices) addresses. The cascade interface determines which write cycles will be accepted or ignored by each of the specific devices in the cascade; furthermore, this interface arbitrates reads from global addresses between various devices. For example, if two results need to be reported back to the processor and the results are from different devices, the first result read will be reported by the higher-priority device in the cascade, and the second result will be reported at the same read address by the lower-priority device.

15.9   CLASSIPI IMPLEMENTATION

ClassiPI is implemented using 0.18 micron technology and is available in a 352 pin BGA package. It consumes less than 4 W power under worst-case conditions. It uses two external voltage supplies: 3.3 V for (5 V tolerant) I/O interfaces and 1.5 V for core voltage. The device accepts an input clock at the interface frequency up to 116 MHz; it has two on-chip PLLs: one to generate clocks for the internal logic running at the interface frequency and the other to generate the classification engine core clock up to 232 MHz (2 × interface clock).

15.10   SOFTWARE ARCHITECTURE AND DEVELOPMENT KIT

The ClassiPI PM2329 Software Development Kit (SDK) is a development and debug tool for various networking applications that integrate the ClassiPI device. The ClassiPI SDK includes an API model and drivers, a framework model for various software applications, and a means for software development and debugging. Additionally, using the supplied sample applications, it demonstrates the features and functions of the ClassiPI device, and the operation and performance of the ClassiPI device on certain platforms and applications.

15.11   PLATFORMS

The ClassiPI SDK architecture is designed to be portable across a variety of platforms. There are generally two development modes for using the ClassiPI SDK:

+ In the software mode, useful before the target hardware platform is ready, the ClassiPI simulator (C-model) is used in a PC/workstation environment to simulate the device function.

+ In the hardware mode, when the real hardware platform is ready, the ClassiPI device is integrated into the system hardware.

The ClassiPI SDK has been ported to various platforms, which include Linux/WinNT PC environment and some existing network processor platforms. The ClassiPI SDK consists of add-on cards to the supported platforms, namely, PCI card (with ClassiPI device) that plugs to a PCI backplane (e.g., PC system), and daughter card (with ClassiPI device) that specifically attaches to available connectors in various NP platforms.

15.12   MODULES

The ClassiPI SDK consists of the following modules: software drivers, APIs, and various sample applications; functionally accurate simulator; and device debugger.

15.13   SOFTWARE DEVELOPMENT

The ClassiPI SDK architecture supports a layered software mechanism to provide a progressively higher-level view of the classification abstraction to the upper-layer software. Also, it supports data path coding to provide overall system functionality and performance.

The *control path* modules of the ClassiPI SDK embody the rule and associated resource management and configuration of the ClassiPI device for various networking applications. The core components comprised of drivers and different function routines that are developed by PMC-Sierra export a set of comprehensive application programming interfaces (APIs), which can be used to manage the ClassiPI by an application code.

Some sample applications highlighting the capabilities and usage of the ClassiPI device are supplied with the SDK core components. The sample software applications included in the ClassiPI SDK present a programming framework for the real implementation of the target network application function on a specific equipment platform utilizing the ClassiPI as a classification processor. The sample applications include packet payload string search for packet content processing, regular expression for high-level security applications, IP routing, and layer-3 through layer-7 filtering.

The *control path* modules have been written in C and have been compiled under Linux or VxWorks as appropriate to the platform.

The *data path* module is mainly composed of packet processing and packet forwarding. The code is dependent on the specific networking applications. It is also dependent on the network processor (CPU) used in a specific platform. The code for the sample applications in the ClassiPI SDK are written based on the microcode syntax of the network processor involved.

15.14   SIMULATOR

Before the target hardware with the ClassiPI device is ready, the SDK can function using the ClassiPI simulator. The ClassiPI simulator is a fully functional software implementation (C-model) of the ClassiPI device. It exports an interface rendering the defined register set of the chip, through which reads and writes can be issued by a software agent. The simulator is a stand-alone executable program that communicates via a socket interface.

The ClassiPI simulator is not a cycle accurate C model. However, a parameter option of the simulator can be set up to enable a controlled delay from request to result. A performance-modeling spreadsheet is available to allow the user to estimate (within 90% accuracy) the performance, latency, and delays when using ClassiPI under different scenarios. Using the spreadsheet results, the user can plug in the appropriate delay value as a simulator parameter.

15.15   DEBUGGER

The ClassiPI debugger is a stand-alone application that communicates with the ClassiPI simulator or device. The ClassiPI debugger provides a facility for debugging the ClassiPI device(s) on a given platform and networking application by providing various commands to view or access the device registers and network policy (rule) contents.

The ClassiPI debugger executes on the control path CPU of the platform. It provides a command line interface that is integrated locally into the platform's user interface shell or connected remotely by TCP/IP socket using a distant PC/workstation.

The user interacts with the ClassiPI debugger using a command line interface (CLI) or a graphical user interface (GUI). The user can issue commands to read and write registers and other pertinent resources of the ClassiPI devices on the platform. The debugger allows the following operations:

✦ Read or write of the ClassiPI local and global register set

✦ Read or write of the rule database in a variety of formats

✦ Read or write of the associated data—statistics and user defined

✦ Off-line write of input packet—data stream

✦ Off-line read of the classification result

Because the ClassiPI debugger provides visibility to the registers and other internal hardware resources of ClassiPI, a given application utilizing the ClassiPI device can be validated under different scenarios.

15.16   CLASSIPI APPLICATION EXAMPLE: A COMPLEX SECURITY-ENABLED ROUTER

A ClassiPI-based security-enabled router can be used for highly complex layer-2 through layer-7 packet classification in a high-security network. In this application, the ClassiPI's rule memory could be partitioned into four lookup tables to address the classification requirements at various layers, with sample table entries shown.

Layer-2 Table for Ethernet Bridging and Switching

```
Source or Destination MAC Address
00 00 00 00 5a
00 00 00 00 1b 7e
  :
  :
```

Layer-3 Table for Routing

```
Destination IP Address
123.45.67.89
123.45.67.x
123.x.x.x
  :
  :
```

Layer-4 Table for Access Control Filtering

Source IP Address	Destination IP Address	Source Port Number	Destination Port Number	Protocol
123.45.32.x	123.45.67.89	any	53(DNS)	UDP
123.45.111.x	111.11.x.x	21(Telnet)	any	any
:				
:				

Layer-7 Table for Payload Pattern Filtering

```
String patterns (case insensitive)
pmc-sierra.com
login
*.jpg
  :

  :
```

Assume, for example, one security policy enforced by this router is to block packets coming from hosts within the IP address range of 123.45.32.x that contain a DNS (domain name service) query for the site *pmc-sierra.com*. Now assume that a Web browser running on the host 123.45.32.176 attempts to access the *pmc-sierra.com* Web site. This will intiate a packet for a DNS query to look up the IP address of the *pmc-sierra.com* site. Given the security policy outlined earlier, this packet should be blocked by the router.

This DNS query packet will contain the following information:

```
Layer 2    Source MAC address = 00 00 00 00 3c f8 (host address)

           Destination MAC address = 00 00 00 00 00 5a (router address)
           Packet Type = x0800 (IP packet)

Layer 3    Protocol = 17 (UDP)

           Source IP address = 123.45.32.176 (host address)
           Destination IP address = 123.45.67.89 (DNS server address)

Layer 4    Source port number = 1075 (connection identifier)

           Destination port number = 53 (DNS query)

Layer 7    Payload contains the string pmc-sierra.com--offset arbitrary
```

When the packet is received by the router, it will be transferred to ClassiPI for packet classification. The ClassiPI will first perform source validation by extracting the source MAC address from the packet and performing a lookup using the layer-2 table. If a match is found, destination MAC lookup can proceed. If no match is found, the control plane processor of the equipment must update the layer-2 table. The ClassiPI will then extract the destination MAC address and perform a lookup using the same layer-2 table. In this example, entry 1 in the layer-2 table will match the extracted destination MAC address in the packet indicating that the packet must be further processed by the router. Had the destination MAC address not matched the router MAC address, the packet would have been switched to the appropriate interface (assuming another entry matched) or (in case of no match) dropped or sent to the control plane for further processing.

In this example, since the destination MAC address in the packet matched the router MAC address, local processing will continue. The ClassiPI will extract the destination IP address and perform a lookup using the layer-3 table. The ClassiPI will return the forwarding information base pointer associated with the matched destination address (entry 1 of the layer-3 table) that is assigned to the DNS server. The ClassiPI will also automatically extract the 5-tuple fields in the packet (source IP address, destination address, source port, destination port, protocol) and form a search key for the layer-4 table lookup. In the table example shown above, comparison on entry 1 in layer-4 table will generate a match condition. Using conditional sequencing, ClassiPI will select the layer-7 table partition associated with policy entry 1 in the layer-4 table. The ClassiPI will then perform a pattern scan on the payload of the packet. When the ClassiPI finds the string pmc-sierra.com within the payload, it will return a "block" tag to indicate that the packet must be dropped to enforce the required security policy.

15.17   PERFORMANCE

While currently available network processors can perform very simple switching functions at speeds approaching OC-48, any additional functionality commonly expected in today's equipment degrades the performance of a network processor–only design. The assist provided by the ClassiPI device makes possible true OC-48 class of networking equipment. The system interface provides a peak bandwidth of over 7.4 Gbps. Multichannel support allows multiple CPU cores in external processors to effectively eliminate any hardware or software arbitration overhead. Table 15.1 summarizes the implementation parameters of the ClassiPI.

15.18   CONCLUSION

In order to address the requirements of the network being deployed, network equipment is evolving to incorporate high functionality at a higher-performance level. For the network equipment designer, maintaining programming flexibility is key to offering a wide performance spectrum to address a variety of market segments and adapt to evolving standards while maintaining and enhancing the existing software base. The ClassiPI device offers a flexible and programmable assist to a variety of network processors to significantly enhance fast path performance of the equipment at lower-layer IP processing while the unique higher-layer processing capabilities of the ClassiPI make possible significant value-added features at higher IP layers.

Price	$200 in quantity
Technology	0.18 micron
Package	352-pin TEBGA
Required voltages	1.5–1.6 V core, 3.3.V I/O
Power	Under 4.0W worst-case maximum

15.1

TABLE

Technology summary.

REFERENCES

[1]   S. Iyer, R. R. Kompella, and A. Shelat, "ClassiPI: An Architecture for Fast and Flexible Packet Classification," *IEEE Network*, Vol. 15, Issue 2, Mar.–Apr. 2001, pp. 33–41.

[2]   V. Dujari, "Server Load Balancing," *Netronics*, October 2001, pp 24–28.

[3]   PMC-Sierra Web site, *www.pmc-sierra.com*.

16

TranSwitch—ASPEN: Flexible Network Processing for Access Solutions

Subhash C. Roy
TranSwitch Corporation

ASPEN [1, 2] combines network processor capabilities, processing either ATM cells or IP packets with a sustained throughput of 155 Mbps, along with the CellBus [3] data switching capabilities. ASPEN was introduced into the marketplace in 1998 and represents a first-generation network processor. It performs a host of communication functions utilizing multiple on-chip embedded processors, co-processors, and a shared bus/switch. The initial applications target data communications WAN (wide-area network) access segment, specifically DSL access multiplexers (DSLAM) and voice-over-IP switches. This paper will cover the basics of the target applications, architecture, and programming environment.

16.1   APPLICATIONS

The global telecommunications network is being transformed from its historical role as a provider of circuit-switched narrowband voice services to one that is primarily packet based, supporting a variety of data-oriented services. A new network architecture is emerging to address this transformation, and it is currently being deployed by new carriers and watched closely by incumbents. This architecture is ideally more elegant than its predecessor, requiring fewer layers of management,

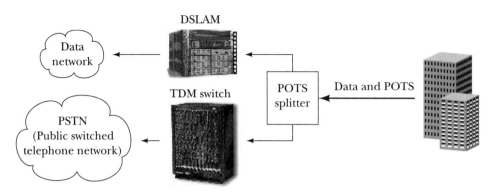

16.1   Overview of DSL network architecture with a POTS splitter.

FIGURE

protocol conversion, and multiplexing. The target application for the architecture has been the multiservice access concentrator and multiplexer, where the goal is high port count, with value-added functionality.

An important application example is DSLAMs. Digital subscriber line (DSL) is a short-haul, high-capacity transport technology that affords much higher bandwidth from POTS lines (twisted-pair copper facilities). DSL widens the bandwidth of a POTS line by using a larger spectrum than is used by voice, by packing more bits of data into each frequency band, and by minimizing crosstalk with echo cancellation or frequency division. An access line with DSL service is a nonloaded copper connection between the central office and customer premises that can provide simultaneous high-speed digital data access and POTS service. The most commonly deployed residential DSL technology is asymmetrical digital subscriber line (ADSL). ADSL is an asymmetrical service offering downstream transmission speeds of 1.54–6.14 Mbps and upstream speeds of 176–640 Kbps, depending on the distance from the customer's premises to the central office (CO). Figure 16.1 indicates where DSLAMs fit into an overall network architecture.

DSLAMs based on ADSL technology use ATM (asynchronous transfer mode) as their main transport mechanism. Standard ATM functions conforming to the ATM forum specifications are required, including cell processing, traffic management, OAM&P (operations and maintenance and performance), and switching.

DSLAM designs must implement various functions and provide for certain performance levels. One key required function is to provide a switching capability between input and output data streams. ASPEN is designed to operate with a shared bus called CellBus to provide this switching capability. CellBus can be

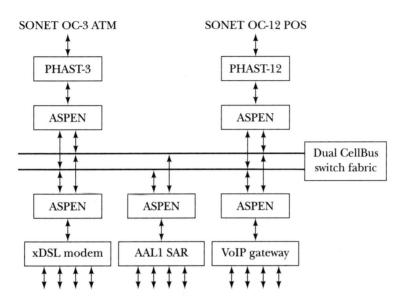

16.2

FIGURE

Typical CellBus multiservice access node architecture.

implemented either on a single circuit card or in a backplane configuration among multiple circuit cards. Since multiple ASPENs share the same bus, a central arbitration function is used to resolve bus access contention. The circuitry for two bus arbiters is included inside the ASPEN device. Any one ASPEN on a given bus in a system may be selected to perform the bus arbitration function for that bus. Any ASPEN that makes a request to the central bus arbiter for bus access to transmit a packet will be granted access based on a configurable priority and round robin treatment of the devices on the bus that have the same access priority.

Various packet switching or multiplexing structures can be formed by interconnecting several ASPEN devices over each of two 37-line parallel CellBus buses. Each CellBus has a 32-bit data path. Since the interconnect structure is a shared bus architecture, communication between any of the devices on the bus is possible. Each packet placed onto either CellBus by an ASPEN device can be routed either to one single CellBus device (unicast addressing) or to multiple CellBus devices (multicast addressing). Depending upon the needs of an application, up to 32 CellBus devices may be interconnected on either CellBus. Figure 16.2 shows a typical configuration employing two CellBuses, three ASPEN devices, and two PHAST devices. PHAST is an integrated SONET/SDH line termination device

[4, 5, 6] that performs ATM and point-to-point protocol (PPP) physical-layer processing. With a maximum bus frequency of up to 34 MHz, the raw bandwidth of each CellBus exceeds 1.024 Gbps using GTL+ technology.

While CellBus is targeted at the switching of fixed length packets such as ATM cells, variable length packets such as IP and Ethernet can also be switched and transported using the segmentation and reassembly capabilities inside ASPEN. By enabling the processing of different types of access rate traffic, ASPEN enables low-cost aggregation and concentration by subsuming all of the preceding functions into a single device.

16.2   ASPEN OPERATION AND ARCHITECTURE

In this section, the principal components of ASPEN and the flow of cells through these components are described.

16.2.1   Processors and Co-Processors

The ASPEN device architecture is based on three RISC processors, a set of co-processors, a bus/switch inteconnection system, and various supporting logic (see Figure 16.3). All of these are incorporated on a single chip. Each RISC processor is based on TranSwitch's ACE-RISC processor technology. The ACE processor is a single-issue, three-stage pipeline processor with an extended instruction set for communications applications. Each processor includes single-cycle context switching, 32 levels of interrupt-priority handling, extended bit-level data manipulation, and provision for up to six co-processors. The ACE is a 32-bit RISC consisting of 64 32-bit general-purpose registers (organized as two 32 register contexts), 1 Kb of data RAM, 128 Kb of instruction RAM, and a one-cycle ALU. ASPEN is fabricated with 0.25-micron technology and is implemented in a single 503-pin PBGA package with 332 signal I/Os. The entire device has a power dissipation of 2.38 W nominal and 2.9 W worst case, with a core voltage of 2.5 V.

Cells enter ASPEN from either the UTOPIA 2/2P interface or the CellBus switch fabric interface. UTOPIA 2 is a standard interface specified by the ATM Forum and used for the transfer of ATM cells. TranSwitch has extended the capabilities of this interface, called UTOPIA 2P, to allow the transfer of variable length packets. When the cells/packets enter the device from the CellBus (or UTOPIA interface), they are buffered in outlet (or inlet) queues to await scheduling toward the UTOPIA (or CellBus) interface. All control table storage and cell buffering is managed by ASPEN in shared external SSRAM. Host communication occurs over the dual port external RAM mailbox interface. The core architectural concept is based around the use of an internal on-chip bus/switch architecture to which all

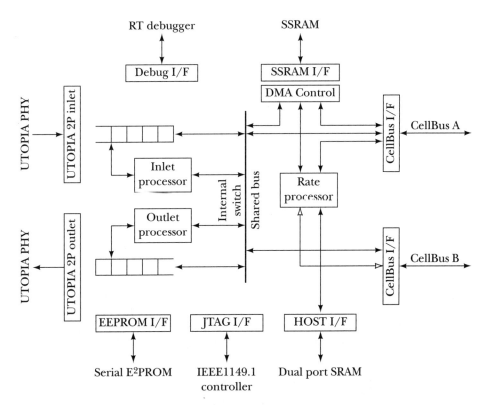

Overall ASPEN architecture (modules within box are on-chip).

internal resources (processors, hardware interfaces, etc.) are attached. The internal bus/switch is used for both data and control flow information passing, with arbitration for the bus/switch being handled within the interface logic associated with each connected resource (Figure 16.3).

Four on-chip hardware co-processors are available to the inlet ACE processor to enhance its functionality. These and other co-processors, though not shown explicitly in Figure 16.3, are associated with their corresponding processor modules and are replicated where necessary. The co-processors associated with the inlet ACE processor include a data controller, a timer, a configuration controller, and a bus interface controller.

✦ The data controller performs automated lookups based on either hashing or direct, multilevel search, packet header translation, byte-level data shifts/alignment, insertion of switch-routing information, and CRC-10/

CRC-32/BIP-16 verification for ATM OAM/AAL5 cells/flows. The data controller is capable of dealing with up to four distinct threads.

+ The ACE timer co-processor includes four programmable timers, and each timer may run at multiples of the system clock frequency (1, 1/4, 1/16, or 1/64).

+ The configuration co-processor enables the use of a number of other simpler co-processor functions such as processor watchdogs, real-time trace functions, reference checking all data structures used, and hardware configuration of the attached interface blocks.

+ The bus interface co-processor (BICOP) interfaces the terminal inlet, terminal outlet, and switch blocks to the internal bus interface. The BICOP handles the transfers of command words and data from the inlet processor (IP), outlet processor (OP), and Rate Processor (RP) to the direct memory access (DMA) controller for access to the external memory (SSRAM).

The outlet ACE processor has these four co-processors plus two more on-chip co-processors: a data router co-processor and a message compiler co-processor. The rate processor ACE uses the timer and configuration co-processors and an on-chip queue management co-processor (QMCOP).

16.2.2   Data Flow and Control

Cell movement through ASPEN can be described in terms of the following actions:

+ Incoming cells received from UTOPIA input (controlled by the inlet ACE processor)

+ Outgoing cells going to the UTOPIA output (controlled by the outlet ACE processor)

+ Movement of cells to and from the CellBus (controlled by the rate ACE processor)

An incoming cell is first received by the UTOPIA inlet block. The inlet ACE processor controls classification of the cell as either a user cell or OAM cell (see Figure 16.4). Using the ATM cell header and optional multi-PHY identifier, a lookup is performed to find if the cell belongs to a valid, active virtual connection. The header lookup hardware block in the data controller co-processor verifies if an incoming cell belongs to a valid connection and, if it does, returns the connection index of the incoming cell. Two types of header lookup are supported: direct lookup and direct/hashing. When a new cell/packet is received by the data controller co-processor (attached to the inlet ACE processor), a lookup is done

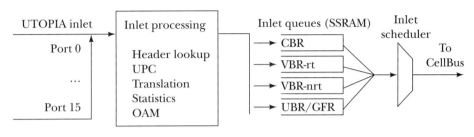

Inlet functional processing flow.

to the connection table, a per-connection data structure associated with received cells. A DMA message (up to two at any given time) to initiate the connection table lookup is generated by the header lookup hardware. For active connections, the connection table contains parameters needed by the inlet processor to perform the necessary value-added functions of usage parameter checking (UPC), buffering, OAM, and statistics gathering. Additionally, the VP/VC switching function is performed. Policing or usage parameter checking is performed on the cell loss priority (CLP) = 0 cell stream and the CLP = 0 + 1 cell stream. If the cell conforms to agreed-upon traffic contract parameters, the cell is translated as required and passed to the DMA controller for queuing. Four traffic queues are supported (Figure 16.4), supporting four levels of priority or class of service (CoS). Non-conforming cells are either CLP tagged or discarded, according to the traffic conformance definition in the ATM Forum specification.

If the received cell is an OAM cell, it is passed to the OAM processing unit, part of the data controller co-processor, to perform the OAM functions. F4/F5 OAM functions performed include alarm indication signal (AIS) cell generation and termination, remote defect indication (RDI) cell generation and termination, continuity check generation and termination, and loopback termination. After OAM is performed, the cells are passed to the DMA controller (DMAC) for queuing. The scheduling mechanism will be discussed after the reverse path is detailed.

The reverse path (from CellBus to UTOPIA outlet, Figure 16.5) is controlled by the outlet ACE processor. Here, incoming cells are received by a CellBus interface block and buffered directly into external queues (the SSRAM of Figure 16.3). There are four levels of CoS priority supported by the scheduler. The outlet ACE processor monitors the data buffers for cell space availability and, upon finding space available, requests a cell. In addition to the four co-processors described earlier, the outlet ACE processor has co-processors to perform the data router and message compiler functions.

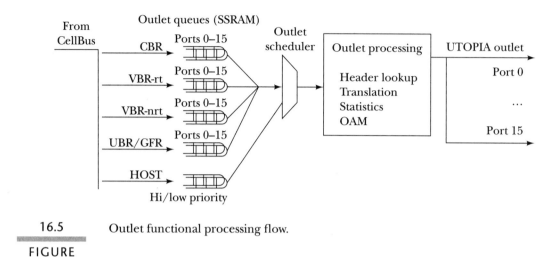

16.5   Outlet functional processing flow.

FIGURE

The data router and message compiler co-processors function as a unit for the retrieval of data and control information from the data/control store in external memory (see Figure 16.6). The BICOP receives cells from the DMAC upon request from the outlet ACE processor and the cells are queued up in an internal buffer. The data router then passes the header to the message compiler and the entire buffer to the data controller. If enabled, the message compiler then sends a header lookup message to the DMA and the lookup to the connection table is performed (cell-based VPI/VCI). Each connection table entry provides all parameters related to that connection (including the replacement cell header, statistics, OAM, etc.), enabling the outlet processor to perform its tasks and then transmit the cell/packet via the UTOPIA interface.

All cell queues, both for the inlet side and the outlet side, are contained in external SSRAM. Cells entering either from the UTOPIA inlet or from the CellBus are routed to queues in SSRAM. The queuing mechanisms for data going to or from the CellBus interfaces are handled by the third ACE processor, the rate processor (see Figure 16.7).

Traffic to and from the CellBus is controlled by the rate processor, associated on-chip co-processors (e.g., timer, configuration and queue management, QMCOP) and the CellBus interface logic (Figure 16.7). The QMCOP supports the rate processor by providing hardware assists and reading/writing to off-chip SSRAM. QMCOP has a special path for communication with the SSRAM and logic to obtain the shortest possible latencies for determining data buffer locations and updating pointer tables. It also handles CRC-32 generation for AAL5 flows.

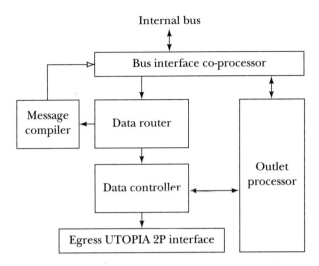

Outlet data flow.

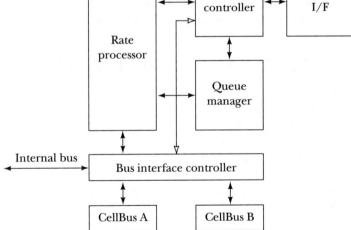

CellBus interface.

The data flow (CellBus frames) to or from the CellBus interface has four potential sources or destinations: the DMA controller, and the inlet, outlet, and rate ACE processors. In a typical data flow path, a CellBus frame is accepted into the ASPEN via a four-frame rate decoupling buffer. The data is initially screened based on the ASPEN's CellBus physical identity then forwarded. The data is then typically passed to the DMA controller to be queued externally in the SSRAM. The data can also be routed directly to each of the three ACE processors.

There are four inlet and outlet traffic queues (Figures 16.4 and 16.5) supporting four levels of priority (CoS). These queues are stored in buffers in external SSRAM. The priority levels, from highest to lowest, are CBR (constant bit rate), VBR-rt (variable bit rate real-time), VBR-nrt (variable bit rate non-real-time), and UBR/GFR (unspecified bit rate and guaranteed frame rate). For all priority levels, cells from the UTOPIA inlet are written into a single bulk queue (one for each priority level). For all priority levels, cells coming from the CellBus are written into per port queues (one for each priority, each with 16 port queues) where they are scheduled for the UTOPIA interface. Starvation prevention of the UBR/GFR outlet queue is achieved by defining a limit on VBR-nrt to allow UBR/GFR cells to the network after n VBR-nrt cells. On the outlet side, buffer overreservation is supported to allow sharing of VBR-nrt buffer space between all UTOPIA ports. This "fair sharing" scheme of the bulk queues permits much greater utilization of system hardware resources. On the outlet side, the UTOPIA port queues within a priority are serviced using a round robin discipline.

16.3   PROGRAMMING ENVIRONMENT

The programming environment itself is composed of a C compiler, application programming interface (API) function library, assembler, debugger, and simulator. The API serves as a function-based interface between the host processor and the ASPEN device in a customer environment (see Figure 16.8). It is a library of C language software utilities necessary for initializing, querying, and configuring the ASPEN device. The API is optimized around the "access methods" that will be required by the host for the ATM application. The device driver library provides a hardware abstraction layer between the host application software and ASPEN, thus hiding from the host the complexity of communicating with the ASPEN device. By enabling this level of abstraction, the API structure allows for hardware evolution of the ASPEN without forcing the customer to modify their system software to accommodate the new device. Extended functions, of course, would require new software. The C compiler is a standard ANSI C compiler for

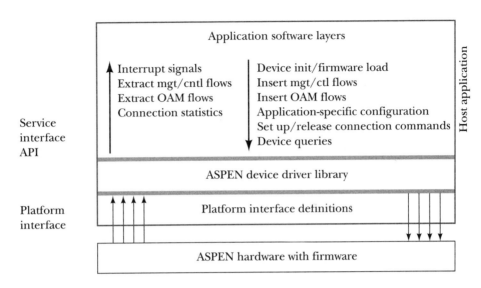

The figure contains the following labels:

Application software layers

Interrupt signals
Extract mgt/cntl flows
Extract OAM flows
Connection statistics

Device init/firmware load
Insert mgt/ctl flows
Insert OAM flows
Application-specific configuration
Set up/release connection commands
Device queries

Host application

Service
interface
API

ASPEN device driver library

Platform
interface

Platform interface definitions

ASPEN hardware with firmware

16.8

FIGURE

Software layers and interfaces available in an application environment.

the TranSwitch ACE processors, as is the assembler/debugger. The simulator is an instruction-level simulator geared toward giving accurate results in a very timely manner.

16.4   CONCLUSION

The ASPEN VLSI device is a member of a family of RISC-based cell/packet processors designed to support the requirements of next-generation multiservice and multiprotocol access systems. ASPEN device functionality is determined by upgradeable firmware that is downloaded into on-chip instruction RAM. The initial applications target the data communications WAN access segment, specifically, DSLAMs and voice-over-IP switches. The architectural approach of using an internal shared bus allowed for the fast development and modeling of the architecture. The ASPEN family has been extended recently to include applications for multitenant unit (MTU) and AAL2 for ATM voice by the addition of the ASPEN-PX. The first release of the ATM firmware implements the ATM layer processing functions of the ATM UNI/NNI and has been deployed in the field since 1998.

REFERENCES

[1]   *www.txc.com/products/prodc_aspen.shtml*

[2]   *www.transwitch.com/files/to/aedg2_o_.pdf*

[3]   *www.transwitch.com/files/tm/celp1_m1.pdf*

[4]   *www.txc.com/products/prodc_phast3p.shtml*

[5]   *www.txc.com/products/prodc_phast3n.shtml*

[6]   *www.txc.com/products/prodc_phast12e.shtml*

Index

numbers

3DES bulk encryption, 24
4GLs, 212

A

accelerators, 152
access segment, 159
accumulated curves, 72
advanced processor architectures, 5
Agere Scripting Language (ASL), 231
Agere System Interface (ASI), 219
    attributes, 223–224
    functions, 219–220
    state maintenance, 224
    See also PayloadPlus NP
AND operation, 97, 101
ANSI C compiler, 94–95
    bit packet insertion, 105
    implementation, 110–111
application development, 44–48
    classifier, 44–45
    conditioner, 45
    leverage third-party, 205
    scheduler, 45–48
application domain analysis, 146
application model, 168, 171–172, 176
application specific logic, 5
applications
    acceptable performance, 211

ASPEN, 307–310
    C-5e NP, 278–279
    Cisco Toaster2, 235–238
    ClassiPI, 291–293
    complexity, 4
    domains, 4
    Intel IXP2400 NP, 259–260
    Linux-based, 216–217
    off-the-shelf, 212–213
    PayloadPlus, 220
    PowerNP NP, 250
application-specific instruction processors
    (ASIPs), 91, 142
    classes, 92
    compilers for, 92
application-specific integrated circuits. *See*
    ASICs
application-system mapping, 173–174
arithmetic logic unit (M.ALU), 244
arrival curves, 58
    for all packet flows, 72
    approximated by combination of two line
        segments, 74
    definition, 59
    improved approximations, 76–79
    piecewise linear approximation,
        73–76
    remaining, 65, 66
    representation of, 59
    resulting, deriving, 69
    from service-level agreements, 59
    uses, 58

ASICs
   architecture limitations, 195
   design of, 193
   design process, 203
   distributed packet buffer, 239
   hardwired, 200
   layer-2 switch based on, 193, 194
   layer-3 packet classification
      implementation in, 194
   off-the-shelf CPU in tandem with, 200
   performance challenges and, 199–200
   redesign of, 195
   routers, 199
   switches, 199
   system design/build time, 203
   Toaster, 235
ASPEN, 307–317
   ACE processor, 313
   application programming interface (API),
      316
   applications, 307–310
   arbitration function, 309
   architecture illustration, 311
   assembler, 316
   bus interface co-processor (BICOP), 312,
      314
   C compiler, 316
   cell movement through, 312
   CellBus, 308–309
   CellBus interface, 315
   conclusion, 317
   configuration co-processor, 312
   co-processors, 310–312
   data controller, 311–312
   data flow and control, 312–316
   data router co-processor, 312
   debugger, 316
   defined, 307
   device functionality, 317
   devices, interconnecting, 309
   external SSRAM, 314
   "fair sharing" scheme, 316
   function library, 316
   inlet functional processing flow, 313
   inlet/outlet traffic queues, 316
   message compiler co-processor, 312
   operation and architecture, 310–316
   outlet data flow, 315
   outlet functional processing flow, 314
   priority levels, 316
   processors, 310–312
   programming environment, 316–317

   queue management co-processor
      (QMCOP), 312, 314
   simulator, 316
   software layers and interfaces, 317
asymmetrical digital subscriber line (ADSL),
   308
ATM, 207
   DSLAMs and, 308
   Forum specification, 313

▬▬ B

Backus-Naur grammar specification, 99
bandwidth, 195–196
   increase, 195
   latent demand for, 196
   renewed demand for, 196
behavioral aggregate (BA) classifier, 44
benchmark suite, 158–160
benchmarking, 11–24
   approach summary, 145
   compiler backend optimizations, 112
   complication factors, 12
   framework overview, 12
   goals, 141–142
   hierarchy, 12–13
   template, 155
benchmarking methodologies, 146–157
   comparable, 146
   environment specification, 149–154
   example specification, 155–157
   functional specification, 148
   future work, 163
   indicative, 147
   measurement specification, 154–155
   for NPUs, 148–155
   precisely defined, 147–148
   principles, 146–157
   representative, 146
   summary, 163
benchmarking reference platform, 13–15
   definition of, 14–15
   illustrated, 14
   internals, 14
benchmarks
   architecture-specific, 15
   choosing, 158–159
   CommBench, 126–128
   comparative result, 146
   defined, 146
   environment, 142

environment specification, 147
four-layer approach, 11, 12
functional specification, 13–14, 147
functionality, 142
function-level, 12–13, 21–23
goals, 11
granularity, 147, 158
from GSM-kernel source code, 112
hardware-level, 13, 15–18
header processing, 23
indicative result, 147
Intel IXP1200, 13
measurement specification, 147
microlevel, 13, 18–21
microprocessor, 13
need for, 11
NPU, 141–142
payload processing, 23
precisely defined result, 147–148
representative of real-world applications,
    142
representative result, 146
routing, 23
selecting, 142
standards bodies, 24
system-level, 12
bit packets, 93
    arrays, 108
    concatenation of, 104
    detection, 104–106
    insertion, 105–106
    insertion benefits, 112
    isolation, 97, 105
    parameters, 104
bit-level data flow
    exact analysis, 96
    illustrated, 95
bitstream-oriented protocols, 93
broadcast packets, 156
buffer management unit (BMU), 280, 286

C

C-5e NP, 277–290
    block diagram, 281
    buffer management unit (BMU), 280, 286
    channel processor RISC core (CPRC),
        280, 282
    channel processors, 281–284
    CMTS using, 279
    control plane access, 280

C-Ware APIs, 287–288
C-Ware Applications Library (CAL), 288
C-Ware Development System (CDS), 289
C-Ware Software Toolset (CST), 288–289
defined, 277
executive processor (XP), 284
external devices support, 277
external traffic management, 285–286
fabric processor (FP), 280, 286–287
hardware architecture, 280–287
internal buses, 280, 287
line interfaces support, 280
with M-5 channel adapter, 277
queue management unit (QMU), 280,
    285–286
reference applications, 288
serial data processor internals, 283
serial data processors (SDPs), 280, 281,
    282
software architecture, 287–290
switch modules (SMs), 289
table lookup unit (TLU), 280, 284–285
target applications, 278–279
technology summary, 282, 290
    See also Motorola
cable modem termination system (CMTS),
    279
cache
    aggregate performance, 129
    area, 135–137
    configuration impact, 137
    configuration performance, 135, 136
    effective size, 129
    effective usage, 124–125
    miss rates, 122, 124, 128
    on-chip, 124–125, 133
    optimal number of threads, 135
    performance trends, 133–135
    pollution, 124, 133
    sizes, 130–131
    small, performance, 135
    write-back, 128
C/C++ language, 212
CellBus, 308–309
    defined, 308
    interface, 315
    interface, data flow to/from, 316
    multiservice access node architecture,
        309
    switching target, 310
    traffic to/from, 314
    See also ASPEN

chip area, 121
    distribution, 137
    equation, 121
    processing power per, 120
    usage, 135–137
Cisco express forwarding (CEF), 238
Cisco Toaster2 NP, 7, 27–28, 32–35, 235–248
    centralized configuration example, 236
    centralized system packet flow, 238–239
    clock, 35
    components, 37–40
    conclusion, 248
    context map, 40
    contexts entering, 33
    contexts leaving, 34
    control point, 35
    cycle map, 38–40
    defined, 32
    development methodology and
        environment, 246–247
    distributed configuration example, 237
    distributed system packet flow, 239–240
    with DMA device, 32–33
    external column memory controller
        (XMC), 240, 241
    family, 248
    generic buffer, 37
    hardware architecture, 240
    illustrated, 33
    input header buffer (IHB), 240, 241
    internal column memory (ICM), 240, 241
    lock controller, 245
    multiple configuration support, 236
    organization, 28
    output header buffer (OHB), 240,
        241–242
    packet interfaces, 240
    performance claims, 247
    PEs, 32, 33, 34
    pipelining, 237
    queue performance metrics, 49–51
    route processor interface (RPI), 240, 245
    software architecture, 246
    systems, 235
    tag buffer, 245
    target applications, 235–238
    Toaster, 38
    Toaster column, 38
    Toaster core, 37–38
    Toaster memory hierarchy, 40–41
    Toaster microcontroller (TMC), 240,
        242–244

classification, 202
    deep packet, 202, 292
    defined, 207
    packet lookup and (PALAC), 29
classification engine (CE), 295–297
    defined, 295–296
    rule capabilities, 296
    search operation, 296–297
    See also ClassiPI
classifier, 44–45
    behavioral aggregate (BA), 44
    multifield (MF), 44, 45
    See also application development
ClassiPI, 291–305
    application example, 302–304
    architecture, 294
    architecture illustration, 294
    cascade interface, 298
    classification engine (CE), 295–297
    control and sequencer block, 297–298
    control path modules, 300
    data path module, 300
    debugger, 301–302
    deep packet classification, 292
    defined, 291
    device connections, 298
    external RAM (ERAM) interface, 297
    external SSRAMs support, 293
    field extraction engine (FEE), 295
    generic search machine interface, 293
    implementation, 299
    layer-7 content search capability, 292
    lookup features, 292
    network equipment architecture, 293
    performance, 304
    platforms, 299–300
    rule capabilities, 296
    rule processing, 296
    sample applications, 300
    SDK, 299
    SDK modules, 300
    search operation, 296–297
    security-enabled router, 302–304
    simulator, 301
    software architecture, 299
    software development, 300
    system interface (SI), 295
    target applications, 291–293
    technology summary, 305
Click
    C++ API, 169
    code, 171

distribution, 169
packet delivery mechanism, 179
packet-flow description, 174
polling with, 177
shared memory multiprocessor support,
171
simulator, 157, 160
system running in kernel mode, 174
VPN encryption configuration, 185
worklist, 171
Click configurations, 169
as application specifications, 171
defined, 169
example, 169
illustrated, 170
IP router, 184
mapping, 187
profiling, 171, 172
Click Modular Router, 169–171
clock rates
FPP performance and, 223
higher, 137
performance depending on, 134
CommBench, 23–24, 126–128, 143
analysis, 143
application computational complexity,
128
applications, 126–127
benchmark comparison, 145
cache miss rates, 128
header processing, 23
NP benchmarks, 143
SPEC CPU benchmark comparison,
128
workloads, 128–129
communication tasks, 61
compiler backend optimizations, 91–112
benchmarking, 112
bit-level data flow analysis, 95–99
code selection, 99–106
dead code elimination, 109–110
implementation, 110–111
location, in Infineon NP C compiler,
111
register allocation, 106–108
results, 112
compilers, 212
ANSI C, 94–95
ASIP, 92
GNU C, 91
hand-tailored, 93
Infineon NP C, 110, 111

component network simulator
(ComNetSim), 27–28, 30–32
application development and, 44–48
configuration, 48
context map, 40
cycle map, 38–40
detailed architectural framework, 27
DiffServ components, 44
direct memory access (DMA) component,
30, 32, 36–37
experiments and results, 48–52
generic buffer, 37
illustrated, 30
implementation of, 35–44
input interface, 35–36
Input Parser, 31
modeling, 27
network processing component (NPC),
30, 32
network processor, 37–44
organization, 48
output interface, 32, 44
program template, 28
purpose, 29–30
queue performance metrics, 49–51
self-similar traffic generator (SSTG), 31
Toaster, 38
Toaster column, 38
Toaster core, 37–38
trace generator, 31
traffic-modeling component, 27
weighted round robin (WRR) algorithm,
28
compression, 208
conditional task graph, 60
conditioner, 45
content addressable memories (CAMs), 207,
219
context map, 40
context pipeline, 268–269
advantage, 268
defined, 268
illustrated, 269
undesirable cases, 269
See also Intel IXP2400 NP
control plane
functions, 208–209
integration, 216
Linux operating system, 216
software, 216
co-processors, 138, 152
core segment, 159

cost
  measure, 80
  NP, 214
  total system, 214
C-Port NP family, 278
CPUs
  ASIC tradeoff, 195
  centralized router architecture, 192
  distributed router architecture, 193
  general-purpose, 203
  multiple general-purpose, 198
  performance, 196–197
  processing inability, 197
CRC calculation, 23
critical sections, 271–272
crossover operator, 83
C-Ware APIs, 287–288
C-Ware Applications Library (CAL), 288
C-Ware Development System (CDS), 289
C-Ware Software Toolset (CST), 288–289
  defined, 288
  graphical performance analyzer, 289
  simulation environment, 288
  See also C-5e NP
cycle map, 38–40

D

data flow analysis, 97
  bit-true, 109
  integer-based, 109
data flow graph (DFG), 95
  assembly code, 103
  defined, 95
  edges, 97
  example, 99, 100
  loop-free, 97
  representation, 99
data flow trees, 101
data plane
  functions, 208
  integration, 216
  software, 216
De Morgan's theorem, 101
dead code
  elimination, 109–110
  identification, 109
  location, 109, 110
deadlines, 60
decomposed forest, 101
deep packet classification, 202, 292

definition-use (DEF-USE)
  analysis of virtual registers, 107
  chains, 95
  dependencies, 95
delays
  bounds on, 73
  end-to-end, 64, 70
  maximum, 73
denial-of-service attacks, 199
design space exploration, 55–87
  case study, 81–86
  concept illustration, 81
  final population of, 84
  framework for, 56–57
  as multiobjective optimization problem,
    56
  outer loop performance of, 80
  population of, 83
  possibilities, 79
  speeding up, 57
  system-level, 57
  usage scenarios, 57
design techniques, 4–7
  advanced processor architectures, 5
  application specific logic, 5
  macroparallelism, 5, 6
device under test (DUT), 153
Dhrystone, 143
DiffServ, 200, 254
  applications development, 52
  code point (DSCP), 44
digital signal processors (DSPs), 91–92
DMA
  buffers, 178
  controller (DMAC), 313
  descriptor, 178
  transactions, 179
DMA component, 30, 32, 36–37
  defined, 36
  external packet memory (XPM), 36–37
  fabric output queue (FOQ), 37
  internal packet memory (IPM), 36
  link input queue (LIQ), 36
  to toaster context (TTC) buffer, 36
  See also component network simulator
    (ComNetSim)
DRAM
  access time, 123
  bandwidth efficiency, 17
  latency curve, 17
  loaded latencies, 17, 18
  in LPM microlevel benchmark, 20

DSL
  access line with, 308
  bandwidth limitation, 92
  network architecture overview, 308
DSL access multiplexers (DSLAM),
    307
  based on ADSL technology, 308
  designs, 308
dynamic cost functions, 102–103
  defined, 103
  example, 104

E

edge segment, 159
EEMBC, 24, 143–144
  benchmark comparison, 145
  defined, 143
  networking benchmarks, 144
effective operand address (EOA), 244
elasticity buffers, 271
Embedded Microprocessor Benchmark
    Consortium. See EEMBC
embedded processor complex (EPC),
    252
encryption, 208
end-to-end deadlines, 60
end-to-end delays, 64, 70
environment specification, 147, 149–154
  defined, 147
  example, 156–157
  packet sources/sinks, 153
  See also specifications
Ertl's tree pattern matching, 100–103
Ethernet, 207
  bridges, 192
  de facto standardization, 200
  framers-on-die, 204
  interfaces, 151
  IP router Click configuration, 170
  MAC framers, 214
  packet sizes, 153
  switches, 192
evolutionary optimizer, 83
external column memory (XCM), 34, 41
  as column-level structure, 41
  defined, 41
  read latency, 46
external column memory controller (XMC),
    240, 241
  arbitration, 241

defined, 241
  See also Cisco Toaster2 NP
external packet memory (XPM), 36–37

F

fabric output queue (FOQ), 37
fabric processor (FP), 280, 286–287
  cell size support, 287
  data bus, 286
  defined, 286
  interoperation, 286
  switch fabric interface, 287
  See also C-5e NP
fast path processing, 191–193
  emergence of, 192–193
  functionality assignment, 192
  time-sensitive functions, 192
  See also packet processing
Fast Pattern Processor (FPP), 219, 225–228
  arithmetic logic unit (ALU), 228
  block buffers and context memory, 227
  checksum/CRC engine, 227–228
  classification conclusions, 226
  configuration bus interface, 228
  data buffer controller, 227
  defined, 225
  external memories, 228
  FPL, 226, 230–231
  functional blocks, 227–228
  functional bus interface, 228
  functions, 219
  input framer, 227
  interfaces, 221
  internal architecture, 226
  key attributes, 222–223
  memory use, 223
  output interface, 227
  passes, 227
  pattern processing engine (PPE), 226,
      227
  pattern-matching behavior, 226
  performance at lower clock speeds, 223
  programmability, 222–223
  SAR, 223
  searches, 223
  See also PayloadPlus NP
fiber-optic access, 196
field extraction engine (FEE), 295
file_agent function, 35
firewall filtering, 199

fixed priority scheduling, 66–68
  example, 68
  representation of, 68
  resources in, 66
  See also scheduling
forwarding
  Cisco express (CEF), 238
  IP, 24, 85
  IPv4, 21–23, 155, 157, 159
  latency, 174
  maximum loss-free, rate (MLFFR), 175
forwarding rate, 174
  SMP-based router, 182
  uniprocessor-based router, 179
  VPN router, 186
framing
  defined, 206–207
  SONET, 207
functional pipeline, 169–171
  advantages, 270
  defined, 269
  designing, 270
  disadvantages, 271
  illustrated, 270
  parallel execution benefits, 269–270
  See also Intel IXP2400 NP
functional specification, 13–14, 147, 148
  defined, 147
  example, 156
  role, 148
  See also specifications
function-level benchmarks, 21–23
  in benchmark hierarchy, 21
  defined, 12–13
  IPv4 forwarding, 21–23
  uses, 21
  See also benchmarks

G

gateways
  defined, 151–152
  deployment scenario, 152, 154, 163
  environment model, 153
generalized processor sharing (GPS), 66,
  68–70
get_packet function, 35
GNU C compiler, 91
granularity, benchmark, 147, 158
graphical editor, 83
GSM bandwidth limitation, 92

H

hardware-level benchmarks, 15–18
  as architecture-specific benchmarks, 15
  in benchmark hierarchy, 15
  defined, 13
  Intel IXP1200 NP, 15–18
  latencies, 16–17
  microlevel benchmarks and, 19
  performance comparisons and, 15
  throughput, 16
  uses, 15
  See also benchmarks
header-processing applications (HPAs), 126
header-processing benchmarks, 23
headroom, 155
high-level languages (HLLs), 91
  platform independence, 91
  software development, 93
host processing, 206

I

IBM. *See* PowerNP NP
IETF, 24
  Benchmarking Methodology Workgroup,
    153, 161
  network connected devices data set, 153
improved approximations, 76–79
Infineon NP C compiler, 110, 111
Infineon NPU architecture, 94
input header buffer (IHB), 240, 241
input interface, 35–36
  aggregate rate, 35
  configured rate, 35
  defined, 35
  See also component network simulator
    (ComNetSim)
Input Parser, 31
instruction level parallelism (ILP), 6
instruction set architecture (ISA), 5
Intel benchmarking, 144–145
  characteristics, 145
  focus, 144
Intel Internet Exchange Architecture (IXA)
  NPUs, 272, 273
  portability framework, 272–273
  SDK, 266–267
Intel IXP1200 NP, 11
  benchmarks, 13
  Developers Workbench tools, 160

hardware-level benchmarks, 15–18
IPv4 forwarding function-level
   benchmark, 21–23, 161
IPv4 packet forwarding profile, 159
loaded latencies, 18
LPM microlevel benchmark, 20
MPLS on, 162
NAPT on, 162
performance, 13
performance measurement, 160
unloaded latencies, 16
Intel IXP2400 NP, 259–275
   context pipeline, 268–269
   critical sections, 271–272
   CSIX flow control bus, 262
   DDR DRAM, 2
   defined, 259
   development tools, 267–268
   elasticity buffers, 271
   external interfaces supported by, 260–262
   functional pipeline, 269–271
   hardware architecture, 260–266
   internal architecture illustration, 263
   line card solution, 261
   microengine development environment
     (MDE), 267
   microengines (MEs), 264–265
   PCI bus, 266
   performance summary, 273
   portability framework, 272–273
   programming model, 268–272
   QDR SRAM, 262, 265–266
   scratchpad unit, 266
   software development environment,
     266–273
   summary, 274–275
   target applications, 259–260
   target markets, 260
   technology summary, 275
   XPI, 266
   XScale core, 263–264
Intel XScale core, 263–264
interfaces
   architectural, 150
   control, 156
   Ethernet, 151
   input, 174
   integration, 150–151
   modeling, 157
   output, 174
   packet trace, 160
   parameters, 151

system-level, 150
interference graph
   defined, 106–107
   super (SIG), 107, 108
internal column memory (ICM), 34, 40, 240,
   241
   as column-level structure, 40
   defined, 40, 241
   lookup, 45
   organization, 241
   read latency, 46
internal packet memory (IPM), 36
intrusion detection, 199
I/O bus, 175
I/O channel, 124–125
   bandwidth, 125, 126
   load, 126
   uses, 125
   width, 131–132
IP
   evolution of, 200
   forwarding, 24, 85
   packet format, 200
   security. *See* IPSec
   See also IPv4 forwarding
IPS/area, 131, 132
IPSec, 168
   encapsulation/tunneling, 200
   VPNs, 169, 184–186
IPv4 forwarding, 21–23, 155
   Click diagram, 157
   IXP1200 profile, 159
   latency, 23
   loss rate, 22
   throughput, 22

J

jitter
   average, 49–50
   characteristics, 50
JPEG coding, 127

L

L2TP tunneling, 200
LAN layer-2 protocols, 200–201
LANCE compiler system, 110
latencies, 16–17
   estimates, 175

latencies *(cont.)*
    forwarding, 174
    IPv4 forwarding, 23
    loaded, 17, 18
    measured, 17
    read, 46
    unloaded, 16
    See also hardware-level benchmarks
lattice
    by Budiu and Goldstein, 96
    extended, 97
    grid, 97–98
layer-2 protocols, 200–201
    ATM, 201
    LAN, 200–201
    specification evolution within, 201
    WAN, 201
layer-3 switching, 194
line card configurations, 151
    common, 152
    low-end, 151
link input queue (LIQ), 36
Linux-based applications, 216–217
loaded latencies
    defined, 17
    IXP1200, illustrated, 18
    measuring, 17
    See also latencies
loading microengines, 17, 18
longest prefix matches (LPMs), 19
    for IXP1200 microengine, 20
    lookups, 20
    performance, 20, 21
    routing lookup, 158
    routing tables, 156
loss rate, IPv4 forwarding, 22

M

MAC frame tags, 200
macroparallelism, 5
    employing, 6
    illustrated, 7
maximum loss-free forwarding rate
    (MLFFR), 175
    reduction, 186
    SMP PC example, 183
    uniprocessor PC example, 178
MD5 signature generation, 23, 24
M/D/I model, 123

measurement
    means, 142
    of throughput, 154
measurement specification, 147, 154–155
    defined, 147
    example, 157
    units, 154
    See also specifications
MediaBench, 96, 143
memory
    access time, 124
    bandwidth, 125
    cache, 133–135
    consumption, 86
    context, 227
    DRAM, 17, 18, 20, 123, 308
    external column (XCM), 34, 41, 46
    external packet (XPM), 36–37
    internal column (ICM), 34, 40, 45–46,
        240, 241
    internal packet (IPM), 36
    management, 138
    maximum shared, backlog, 73
    misses, 122
    queue length comparison, 124
    request handling, 41–44
    requirements, 73, 118
    scheduling, 246–247
    SRAM, 17, 18, 20, 133, 262, 265–266
memory channel, 125–126, 131
    load, fixing, 125
    load, performance depending on, 133
    performance trends, 132
    width, limiting, 131
    width, performance depending on, 134
memory requests
    handling, 41–44
    states, 42–43
    transactions, 42
memory system, 121, 122–125
    off-chip memory access, 122–124
    on-chip cache, 124–125
microengine development environment
    (MDE), 267
microengines (MEs), 264–265
    contexts, 264
    control store, 264
    data path registers, 264–265
    defined, 264
    exclusive modification privileges between,
        271–272

exclusive modification privileges between
threads in, 272
partition for IPv4 forwarding + DiffServ
application, 274
special hardware blocks, 265
See also Intel IXP2400 NP
microlevel benchmarks, 18–21
application, 19
defined, 13
examples, 19
hardware-level benchmarks and, 19
LPM, 19, 20
uses, 19
See also benchmarks
modeling framework, 167–187
alpha release, 187
application model, 171–172
application-system mapping, 173–174
Click Modular Router, 169–171
code declaring traffic, application, and
system models, 176
description, 168–177
emphasis, 168
implementation, 176–177
metrics and performance estimates,
174–175
operation, 175–176
questions answered by, 167
system model, 172–173
traffic model, 173
users, 168
modification, 207
Moore's law, 1, 196
Motorola
M-5 channel adapter, 277
Q-5 traffic management co-processor, 277,
286
See also C-5e NP
MPEG coding, 127
multiobjective design space exploration,
55–87
case study, 81–86
concept illustration, 81
final population of, 84
framework for, 56–57
as optimization problem, 56
outer loop performance of, 80
population of, 83
possibilities, 79
speeding up, 57
system-level, 57
usage scenario, 57

multivendor integration, 215
mutation operator, 83

N

NetBench, 23, 144
benchmark comparison, 145
defined, 144
Network Address Port Translation (NAPT),
161
network address translation (NAT) routers,
169
network intelligence, 197–199
network interface cards (NICs), 152–153,
191
network processing component (NPC), 30,
32
defined, 32
functioning of, 32
See also component network simulator
(ComNetSim)
Network Processing Forum, 11, 24
network processor (ComNetSim), 37–44
memory request handling, 41–44
Toaster components, 37–40
Toaster memory hierarchy, 40–41
network processor (NP) solutions
choice of programming language,
211–212
cost, 214
degree of programmability/applicability,
210–211
differentiating, 209–210
ease of programmability, 211
evaluating, 209–215
multivendor integration, 215
off-the-shelf applications and, 212–213
on performance-programmability
continuum, 209
performance, 213
platform-oriented, 209
total system cost, 214
vendors, 214–215
network processor units (NPUs), 92
benchmarking methodology for, 148–155
benchmarking template, 155
benchmarks, 141–142
Infineon, 94
Intel IXA, 272, 273
interfaces, 150
vendors, 141

network processors (NPs)
   ASPEN, 307–317
   benchmarking, 11–24
   benchmarking methodology, 141–163
   C-5e, 277–290
   Cisco Toaster2, 7, 27–28, 32–35
   ClassiPI, 291–305
   compiler backend optimizations, 91–112
   cost, 214
   defined, 1
   design challenges, 3–4
   design considerations, 117
   design elements, 2
   design guidelines, 137
   design techniques, 4–7
   development factors, 1
   as disruptive technology, 204
   flexibility, 27
   functionality changes and, 8
   industry analyst's perspective, 191–218
   Intel IXP1200, 11, 13, 15–18, 21–23,
      160–161
   Intel IXP2400, 259–275
   market, 210
   modifications, 203–205
   multiple chips, 13
   optimization, 11, 82
   overall architecture, 118
   parallel processors, 117
   parallelism, 204
   PayloadPlus NP, 219–233
   pipelining, 204
   PowerNP, 249–258
   processing units, 55
   real-time processing demands, 1, 2
   in router application, 2
   scalability, 213
   system parameters, 129–130
   task graph, 82
   workload, 128–129
network simulator (NS), 29
NPF Benchmarking Working Group
      (NPF-BWG), 144
   benchmark comparison, 145
   defined, 144
   headroom, 155

O

off-chip memory access, 122–124
Olive tree parser generator, 99, 100
   dynamic cost functions and, 103–104

output, 99
on-chip area equation, 121
on-chip cache, 124–125
on-the-fly application-layer processing,
      217–218
optimal configuration, 130–132
optimization(s)
   compiler backend, 91–112
   performance model, 126
   system parameters for, 130
OR operation, 97, 98, 101
output interface, 32, 44
   defined, 44
   statistics, 44
   See also component network simulator
      (ComNetSim)

P

packet flows
   description, 64
   fixed priority scheduling of, 68
   input, 70
   interleaves, 58
   maximum delay, 73
   scenarios, 60
   transformation block diagram, 67
   workload generated by, 58–60
packet lookup and classification (PALAC),
      29
packet processing
   architecture illustration, 208
   bandwidth and, 195–196
   characteristics, 56
   complexity, 202
   CPU vs. ASIC tradeoff, 195
   CPUs and, 196–197
   defined, 206
   fast path, 191–193
   history of, 191–199
   network intelligence and, 197–199
   slow path, 191–193
packets
   bit, 93, 97
   broadcast, 156
   different length, 93
   IP, 194
   minimum-sized, 186
   processing, 174
   pushing, 182
   queue sizes, 156
   scheduling, 118

size distributions, 186–187
sizes, 153–154
variable-sized, 154
Parallel eXpress Forwarding (PXF), 235
parallel processors, 117
parallelism, 204
    instruction level (ILP), 6
    macroparallelism, 5, 6, 7
pareto-optimal
    definition of, 80
    design points, 85
    objective vectors, 80
    resource allocations, 85
    system architecture, 83
parsing, 202
    defined, 207
    tree, grammar, 102
pattern matching
    defined, 99
    tree, 99–103
payload processing benchmarks, 23
PayloadPlus NP, 219–233
    3G/Media gateway application example,
        225
    Agere System Interface (ASI), 219–220,
        223–224
    architecture, 220–225
    DSP solution combination, 225
    Fast Pattern Processor (FPP), 219,
        222–223, 225–228
    line card configuration, 221
    OC48c, 222
    pattern-matching optimization, 220
    performance, 221
    performance benefits, 232–233
    pipeline breakdown, 221
    programming, 230
    Routing Switch Processor (RSP), 219, 223,
        228–230
    software architecture, 230–232
    target applications, 220
    task processing domains, 222
    technology summary, 233
    third-party engagements, 232
    Voice Packet Processor (VPP), 224
PayloadPlus software development
        environment (SDE), 231–232
    components, 231
    defined, 231
    illustrated, 232
payload-processing applications (PPAs), 126

performance, 213
    acceptable, 211
    bottlenecks, 147, 158
    Cisco Toaster2 NP, 247
    ClassiPI, 304
    Intel IXP2400 NP, 273
    measure, 80
    PayloadPlus NP, 221, 232–233
    PowerNP NP, 257–258
    processing, 120
    scalability, 213
performance model, 119–126
    cache, 120
    chip area, 121
    conclusions, 138
    extensions, 138
    goal, 120
    memory and I/O channels, 125–126
    memory system, 122–125
    optimization, 126
    overview, 117
    processing performance, 120
    results summary, 137
    system clusters, 119
    system parameters, 119, 129–130
performance trends, 132–137
    cache memory, 133–135
    chip area usage, 135–137
    memory channel, 132
    processor, 132–133
phase length, 237–238
PHAST devices, 309–310
physical MAC multiplexer (PMM), 253
physical-layer processing, 206
piecewise linear approximation, 73–75
    of arrival/service curves, 73–74
    example, 74–75
pipelines
    context, 268–269
    functional, 269–271
    IXP2400 NP, 268–271
    PayloadPlus NP, breakdown, 221
pipelining, 204
    optimal software, 237
    Toasters, 237
PMC-Sierra. See ClassiPI
ports
    number of, 151
    push/pull processing, 171
    speed of, 151
    type of, 151

PowerNP NP, 249–258
    aggregate processing capability, 257
    applications, 250
    architecture illustration, 251
    completion unit, 253
    conclusion, 258
    control memory arbiter, 253
    CP options, 253
    cycle budgets per packet, 257
    data plane protocols, 255
    dispatch unit, 252
    DPPU co-processor, 252
    egress DF interfaces, 254
    embedded processor complex (EPC), 252
    example application, 250
    fabrication technology, 251
    features, 249
    hardware architecture, 251–254
    headroom over IP forwarding, 257–258
    ingress data flow (DF) interfaces, 254
    PCI interface, 250
    performance, 257–258
    physical MAC multiplexer (PMM), 253
    "run-to-completion" programming
        model, 255
    scheduler, 254
    software, 255–257
    software architecture, 255–256
    software development toolkit, 256–257
    switch interface (SWI), 253–254
    tree search engine (TSE), 252–253
PREFETCH request, 41
processing
    performance, 120
    pull, 171
    push, 171
    units, 55
programmability
    degree of, 210–211
    ease of, 211
    Fast Pattern Processor (FPP), 222–223
    need for, 199–203
    of parsing and classification elements, 202
    time-to-market pressures and, 202–203
programmable state machines (PSMs), 207
programming languages, 211–212
    4GLs, 212
    C/C++, 212
pull processing, 171
push processing, 171
Python programming language, 176

Q

Q-5 traffic management co-processor, 277,
    286
QoS, 254
    algorithms, 197
    gradations, 197
    greater implementation of, 196
    guarantees, 3
    parameters, 57
queue management unit (QMU), 280,
    285–286
    defined, 285
    queues, 285
    See also C-5e NP
queue metrics
    high-rate, 50
    low-rate, 51
    on simulated Toaster models, 49
queuing, 208

R

READ request, 41
real-time calculus, 64
real-time language translation service, 218
reference code libraries, 212–213
register allocation, 106–108
    constraints, 107
    for supernodes, 108
register arrays
    allocation constraints, 107
    defined, 106
registers
    concatenation of two bit-packets, 104
    physical, 107
    pointer, 106
    virtual, 106, 107
repair operator, 83
requests
    computing, 65
    deadlines and, 60
    handling, 41–44
    memory, 41–44
    PREFETCH, 41, 42
    READ, 41
    states, 42–43
    transactions, 42
    types, 41
    WRITE, 41, 42

resource allocations, 70
    pareto-optimal, 85
    performance, 86
resource nodes, 71
resources
    ARM, 86
    definition of, 62–63
    in fixed priority scheduling, 66
    general-purpose, 82
    instances, 62–63
    mapping tasks to, 63, 83
    set of, 83
    types, 82, 83
    utilization of, 175
RISC instruction sets, 203
RISC processors, 3
    instruction set architecture (ISA), 5
    miss probability, 124
round robin (RR) approach, 36
route processor interface (RPI), 240, 245
    defined, 245
    lock mechanism, 245
"route-once, switch-many" architecture, 193
routers
    architecture, 149
    ASIC-accelerated, 199
    centralized CPU architecture, 192
    classic, 191–192
    distributed CPU architecture, 193
    hybridization of, 193–194
    line card configurations, 151, 152
    NAT, 169
    SMP-based, 182
    software-based, 191
    system organization for, 173
    uniprocessor-based, 179
    VPN, 186
routing
    benchmarks, 23
    IP experiments, 182
Routing Switch Processor (RSP), 219,
        228–230
    architecture, 228
    functions, 219, 221
    input interface, 229
    internal architecture illustration, 229
    internal scheduler, 230
    key attributes, 223
    output interface, 230
    PDU assembler, 229
    programmable traffic management
        options, 225

stream editor compute engine, 229, 230
traffic management compute engine, 228
traffic shaper compute engine, 229
transmit command, 222
transmit queue logic, 230
See also PayloadPlus NP

S

scalability, 213
scheduler, 45–48, 118
    defined, 45
    WRR, 45
    See also application development
scheduling
    fixed priority, 66–68
    GPS, 66, 68–70
    internal, nodes, 87
    memory, 246–247
    nonpreemptive, 69
    packet, 118
    policies, 63, 65–70
scheduling networks, 63–79
    analysis using, 63–79
    building blocks of, 64–65
    construction, 70–72
    of one flow, 87
security-related services, 217
self-similar traffic generator (SSTG), 31
serial data processors (SDPs), 280, 281, 282
service curves, 82
    accumulated, 73
    approximated by combination of two line
        segments, 74
    corresponding to resource, 69
    defined, 61
    definition of, 62
    improved approximations, 76–79
    piecewise linear approximation of, 73–76
    remaining, 65, 66
    representation of, 62
    upper, 62
service-level agreements. See SLAs
service-level management (SLM), 198–199
    probes, 199
    solutions, 198
shared memory multiprocessor (SMP)
        systems, 171
SimpleScalar simulator, 144, 169–171,
        177
single rate two-color marker (SRTCM), 45

SLAs, 217
    layer-2 basis, 198
    parameters, 198
slow path processing, 191–193
    emergence of, 192–193
    functionality assignment, 192
    time-insensitive functions, 192
    See also packet processing
SMP PC, 180–183
    accuracy, 183
    Click operation, 180
    defined, 180
    forwarding rate vs. input rate for, 182
    MLFFR, 183
    system organization, 180
    See also system modeling
software functions, 208
source operand fetch (SOF), 244
SPEA2 evolutionary multiobjective optimizer,
    81
SPEC, 24, 143
    CPU benchmark, 128
    SPEC95, 24
    SpecINT95, 96
specifications
    English description, 147–148
    environment, 147, 149–154, 156–157
    example, 155–157
    executable description, 148
    functional, 13–14, 147, 148, 156
    measurement, 147, 154–155, 157
SRAM
    loaded latencies, 17, 18
    in LPM microlevel benchmark, 20
    on-chip, 133
    QDR, 262, 265–266
subset equality relation, 109, 110
super-interference graph (SIG), 107
    construction of, 108
    interference graph transformation into,
        107
switches
    ASIC-based, 199
    Ethernet, 192–193
    hybridization of, 193–194
    layer-2, 193, 194
    layer-3, 194
switching function, 206
system architecture, 60–63
    allocated resources, 83
    definition of, 70
    description of, 70–71

pareto-optimal, 83
properties, 72–73
system model, 168, 172–173
    declaration code, 176
    elements, 172
    illustrated, 173
    objects, 172
    uniprocessor PC example, 177
system modeling, 167, 177–183
    SMP PC, 180–183
    uniprocessor PC, 177–179
system parameters, 129–130
    list of, 119, 130
    optimal configuration, 130–132
    performance trends, 132–137
system properties, 72–73
system-level benchmarks, 12
system-on-a-chip (SoC)
    communication architectures, 58
    design, 55

T

table lookup unit (TLU), 280, 284–285
    defined, 284
    design, 284
    subtables, 285
    See also C-5e NP
tag buffer, 40
tags, 47
    defined, 46
    structure, 48
task graph, 82
tasks
    communication, 61
    conditional graph, 60
    execution, 60
    processing, 63
    to resource mapping, 63, 83
    structure, 59
TCPDump, 160
threads
    number of, memory channel width and,
        134
    number of, performance impact, 133
    number of, processor clock rate and,
        134
    optimal hardware contexts, 137
    optimal number of, 130
    optimal number of, for cache
        configuration, 135

throughputs, 16, 55
  aggregate packet-forwarding, 157
  defined, 154
  estimates, 175
  IPv4 forwarding, 22
  measurement of, 154
tightly coupled state machine (TCSM), 244
time in market (TIM), 204–205
time to market (TTM), 204
  as critical factor, 202
  pressures, 202–203
Toaster microcontroller (TMC), 240,
    242–245
  branch unit, 243–244
  defined, 242
  high-performance memory subsystem,
    242
  instruction fetch and decode unit (IFID),
    243
  modifications, 242
  M-unit, 244
  performance-monitoring mechanism, 243
  prefetch interface, 243
  in processor complex, 243
  S-unit, 244
  X-unit, 244
  See also Cisco Toaster2 NP
trace-driven simulation, 138
traffic generator, 31
traffic model, 169, 173
  declaration code, 176
  defined, 173
TranSwitch. *See* ASPEN
tree pattern matching
  algorithm, 99–100
  Ertl's grammar composition, 100–103
  grammar to detect bit packet operations,
    105
  optimal, 99
  with standard grammar, 103
tree search engine (TSE), 252–253
tree-parsing grammar
  with Ertl's extensions, 102
  short-form, 102
trends, 215–218
  control plane/data plane integration, 216
  Linux-based applications, 216–217
  on-the-fly application-layer processing,
    217–218
  operational at OC-192, 215–216
  performance, 132–137
two-rate three-color marker (TRTCM), 45

U

uniprocessor PC modeling, 177–179
  base system parameters, 178
  defined, 177
  forwarding rate vs. input rate, 179
  MLFFR, 178
  per-phase details for Click IP routing,
    180
  system model, 177
  See also system modeling
usage message checking (UPC), 313
usage scenarios, 57

V

value-added services, 217
vendors
  NPU, 141
  off-the-shelf packet processing
    applications, 205
  solutions, 214–215
  solutions differentiation, 209–210
  value propositions, 204–205
very long instruction word (VLIW), 34
virtual private networks. *See* VPNs
virtual registers, 106
  DEF-USE analysis of, 107
  internal, number of, 107–108
  sets of, 106
  See also registers
VLSI design, 3–4
Voice Packet Processor (VPP), 224
VPNs, 254
  decryption configuration, 184
  encryption configuration, 185
  encryption/decryption, 84–86,
    168
  forwarding rate vs. input rate, 186
  IPSec, 169
  outsourced, 218

W

WANs
  ASPEN and, 307
  layer-2 protocols, 201
WDM (wavelength division multiplexing), 4
weighted random early detection (WRED),
    268

weighted round robin (WRR) algorithm, 28, 36
    data structures, 47
    implementation requirements, 46
    scheduler, 39, 45–46
    weight counter, 46
workloads, 128–129
    aggregate cache performance of, 129
    computational complexity, 129
    data cache miss rates, 129
    load and store frequencies, 129
    optimal configuration, 130–132

processing distribution, 128
processing power, 132
types, 128
WRITE request, 41

 X

XScale
    core, 263–264
    technology peripherals interface (XPI), 266

About the Editors

Patrick Crowley is currently a Ph.D. candidate in the Department of Computer Science and Engineering at the University of Washington. Before arriving in Seattle, he earned a B.A. degree, summa cum laude, from Illinois Wesleyan University, where he studied mathematics, physics, and computer science. Patrick's research interests are in the area of computer systems architecture, with a present focus on the design and analysis of programmable packet processing systems. He is an active participant in the architecture research community and a reviewer for several conferences (ASPLOS, ISCA) and journals (IEEE TOCS). He was an organizer and member of the program committee of the HPCA8 Workshop on Network Processors (2002). Upon completing his Ph.D., Patrick intends to pursue a university research and teaching career.

Mark A. Franklin received his B.A., B.S.E.E., and M.S.E.E. from Columbia University, and his Ph.D. in EE from Carnegie-Mellon University. He is currently at Washington University in St. Louis where he has a joint appointment in the Departments of Electrical Engineering and Computer Science and holds the Urbauer Chair in Engineering. He founded and is director of the Computer and Communications Research Center and until recently was the director of the Undergraduate Program in Computer Engineering. Dr. Franklin is engaged in research, teaching, and consulting in the areas of computer and communications architectures, ASIC and embedded processor design, parallel and distributed systems, and systems performance evaluation. He is a fellow of the IEEE, a member of the ACM, and has been an organizer and reviewer for numerous professional conferences, including the HPCA8 Workshop on Network Processors (2002). He has been chair of the IEEE TCCA (Technical Committee on Computer Architecture) and vice-chairman of the ACM SIGARCH (Special Interest Group on Computer Architecture).

Haldun Hadimioglu received his B.S. and M.S. degrees in Electrical Engineering at Middle East Technical University, Ankara, Turkey and his Ph.D. in Computer Science from Polytechnic University in New York. He is currently an Industry Associate Professor in the Computer Science Department and a member of the Computer Engineering faculty at the Polytechnic University. From 1980 to 1982, he worked as a research engineer at PETAS, Ankara, Turkey. Dr. Hadimioglu's research and teaching interests include computer architecture, parallel and distributed systems, networking, and VLSI design. He was a guest editor of the special issue on "Advances in High Performance Memory Systems," *IEEE Transactions on Computers* (Nov. 2001) and has reviewed papers for leading journals. Dr. Hadimioglu is a member of the IEEE, the ACM, and Sigma Xi. He has been an organizer of various workshops, including the ISCA Memory Wall (2000), ISCA Memory Performance Issues (2002, 2001), and HPCA8 Workshop on Network Processors (2002). He received Dedicated Faculty and Outstanding Faculty awards from Polytechnic students in 1995 and 1993, respectively.

Peter Z. Onufryk received his B.S.E.E. from Rutgers University, M.S.E.E. from Purdue University, and Ph.D. in Electrical and Computer Engineering from Rutgers University. He is currently a director in the Internetworking Products Division at Integrated Device Technology, Inc., where he is responsible for architecture definition and validation of communications products. Before joining IDT, Peter was a researcher for thirteen years at AT&T Labs-Research (formally AT&T Bell Labs), where he worked on communications systems and parallel computer architectures. These included a number of parallel, cache-coherent multiprocessor and dataflow based machines that were targeted toward high performance military systems. Other work there focused on packet telephony and early network processors. Peter is a member of the IEEE and was an organizer and program committee member of the HPCA8 Workshop on Network Processors (2002). Peter is the architect of four communications processors as well as numerous ASICs, boards, and systems.